A LONG WAY
FROM WYANDRA

A LONG WAY FROM WYANDRA

My story—from the bush to Black Caviar

PETER MOODY

with Trevor Marshallsea

ALLEN&UNWIN
SYDNEY • MELBOURNE • AUCKLAND • LONDON

First published in 2017

Copyright © Peter Moody 2017

Allen & Unwin
83 Alexander Street
Crows Nest NSW 2065
Australia
Phone: (61 2) 8425 0100
Email: info@allenandunwin.com
Web: www.allenandunwin.com

Cataloguing-in-Publication details are available
from the National Library of Australia
www.trove.nla.gov.au

ISBN 978 1 76029 520 2

Set in 12.5/17.5 pt Garamond Premier Pro by Bookhouse, Sydney
Printed and bound in Australia by Griffin Press

10 9 8 7 6 5 4 3 2 1

MIX
Paper from
responsible sources
FSC® C009448

The paper in this book is FSC® certified. FSC® promotes environmentally responsible, socially beneficial and economically viable management of the world's forests.

Contents

Prologue

On the morning of Sunday, 24 June 2012, Australians were waking up to the news that the racing phenomenon Black Caviar had done it.

Despite an exhausting list of problems that would undoubtedly have stopped a mortal horse, the great mare had conquered Royal Ascot, keeping her perfect record intact by winning the Diamond Jubilee Stakes. As everyone knows, she fell in by a head. But to overcome what she'd been through to win, at start 22 of her unbeaten 25, was comfortably her most incredible effort, among many, on a racetrack. To this day, only a handful of people know the full story of what had happened to the big girl in a week that was one of the most stressful of my life.

Had it not been for her enormous heart, we would have made the long trip home defeated, with our tail between our legs. And while I had built a reputation as a decent horse trainer, I would have felt like the biggest idiot in the world, with the disappointment of a nation on my shoulders.

Had the Ascot vets had a look at her on the morning of the race, they probably would have scratched her. In fact, had this been any other horse, I'd have scratched it myself. Thankfully, we don't have anything to regret now. Nelly, as we knew her, got the job done. If there is one lingering disappointment, it's that so much post-race talk focused on my great mate, the superb jockey Luke Nolen, and how he had stopped riding out the mare 20 metres short of the line. No one would have worried about Luke's ride had they known of the ordeals the horse had been through just to get to the race.

In fact, seeing what the run had done to her, from the time she got a post-race pat from the queen to when I saw her the next morning, I made up my mind she should be retired. I flew home thinking the Black Caviar story, which had gripped Australia in such an unbelievable way for three years, was over. I'd always said that seeing such a big horse run so fast made me scared that bits would start flying off her, like some cartoon runaway train. And by then her injury toll—the tendon strains, the torn muscles, the problem feet, the bone chips—seemed like they had finally rung the bell on her career.

If all that wasn't enough, a few days after the race, while standing in a typically lovely English paddock, she suffered a very un-lovely attack by a swarm of bees. Forget about racing again—she came perilously close to losing her life. I'd thought the comparisons to Phar Lap that had been made throughout her career were a bit silly and irrelevant. But echoing his story by dying in a paddock after winning overseas? That would have been ridiculous.

It was an incredible saga, and I'm extremely lucky to have played a role in it. Black Caviar indeed was the Phar Lap of her time. I'm not talking ability—you really can't compare horses from such radically different eras. Apart from anything else, the thoroughbred is a vastly different animal now from what it was then. I'm talking about the phenomenon she was, the hype she created. At the height of it, it was pure and simple crazy: Beatlemania.

For this boy from the bush, the pressure was sometimes almost too much. Everyone wanted a piece of this mare who had become the nation's horse—and not just in Australia. I had *Vogue* and *Time* magazine calling from New York. People were always dropping by for a look. At one stage it even looked like the queen was going to pop in! I had to pinch myself.

After her wins, far from going out to celebrate, I usually went home and collapsed on the couch, just thinking, 'Thank God that's over'. Sometimes I even wished she would just go and get beaten—then she would have been just another horse. Thankfully, it was never long before I'd smack myself in the head and tell myself to stop being an idiot.

I used to fall into bed, sleep like the dead, then the phone would start ringing at six the next morning and the circus would start again, building up until her next start. Repeat all over again. A lot of people might have forgotten I had a hundred other horses in my stable to think about!

But at Royal Ascot, I didn't have the option of my usual routine. Where do you go to celebrate a big win there? The Dorchester? The Ritz? Buckingham Palace?

Not quite. As Australia was taking in what Black Caviar had accomplished on the other side of the world, several hours after the race I was still stuck in the Ascot car park!

I had tried to leave. There was a plan to meet the horse's wonderful owners in London, or grab a feed at our base in Newmarket. But as our driver edged us out of the car park, progress was so slow that we stopped to take a leak. Suitably relieved, we hopped back in to resume the trip.

But there was trouble. The car wouldn't start.

We got out to take a look, but let's just say that as a mechanic I made a very good horse trainer. I had two mates with me and they were just as useless. Since my wife Sarah—my 'rock' and a huge part of Moody Racing—had stayed with our three daughters in Melbourne, I had travelled with Michael Bryant and Brett Cavanough on something of a boys' own adventure to Royal Ascot. Mick is a magician as a horse chiropractor but he's not as good with cars. Brett is a trainer and horse breaker who can teach any young thoroughbred good manners, but again, a duffer with an engine.

So as the sun set over Royal Ascot, and the triumph—and the enormous relief—of that day sank in, the car park was where we stayed.

Other racegoers came to lend a hand. As we got chatting they figured out who we were. We'd got sick of our Ascot uniform of top hat and tails by then, so we changed into some civvies we had brought. But this being an English summer, it was starting to get pretty cold. Fortunately, some of our new chums helped us out with an odd array of jackets, hats and whatever. Better still, they also helped us out with beer and food from their eskies as we were passed around, looking like dress-up day from *Play School*, from one car boot party to the next.

In the end it was a super evening. I was too knackered to have enjoyed a nice restaurant anyway. Plus, I'm probably more at home in a laid-back environment with a couple of mates, even if there wasn't any XXXX beer around.

As the evening went on, occasionally Brett and I would look at each other, smile and shake our heads. As a couple of blokes from country Queensland, we don't really have too many sentimental discussions. But the moment wasn't lost on us.

It was Brett who, one Saturday afternoon in 1986, came and found me in Charleville and said he could get me a job in Sydney, at the stables of the great Tommy Smith.

Nearly thirty years later and ten thousand miles away, here were Brett and me, raising our warm beers in the car park of Royal Ascot, toasting one of the greatest racehorses the world had seen, my luck at having trained her, and the journey I'd had from tiny Wyandra to becoming a four-time premiership-winning trainer in the mecca of Australian racing, Melbourne. Accidental though it was, I couldn't have wished for a sweeter celebration.

It's been some ride, blessed with many wonderful moments, horses and people. There have also been times—many of them—when I've longed for the bush life I left behind, envying mates who opted for a less pressurised world of shearing sheep, mending fences, or working on the railways. It can be a lonely life, too, training horses, though people wouldn't realise. Perversely, it seemed to get lonelier, the bigger and more successful I became.

And then, less than three years after that Ascot triumph, I watched as the last horse left my stable, finalising an unscheduled—and fairly traumatic—end to my training career.

Despite that unexpected last chapter, I can reflect on an incredible journey, and a richly rewarding one. I'm immensely grateful for the life racing has given me: the people, the stories and the horses. Gallopers such as Typhoon Tracy, Dissident, Magnus, and all the way back to General Nediym and my first Group 1 winner Amalfi.

And of course, I'm extremely grateful for one horse in particular.

1

Wyandra

There were always horses.

Growing up on a farm in the mid-1970s, you learnt to ride about the same time you learnt to walk.

As the youngest of four, with three older sisters, I got hand-me-down horses like other kids got hand-me-down bikes or clothes. My first was Boy Lucas, a taffy-coloured pony who came to me, suitably worn out and sedate, when he was about 30. The first thoroughbred I had anything to do with came soon after—another old gelding, but a big monster of a thing, by the name of Doubtful.

Boy Lucas was old but he could still get over a hurdle, and I'm told I won a showjumping event on him when I was five. Someone probably just tied me on, whacked him on the arse and I hung on for dear life, but it seems I got the job done.

We were always into something horse-related—pony club, local shows, gymkhanas, whatever was going. My sisters all rode, and I tagged along behind. We had horses like other people have cats and dogs, and, while they might be a bit daunting for some, I know I felt an affinity with them from very early on.

It is tempting to describe these as all wonderful times and happy days, but that would be only half of it. They all *start*ed well—excitement, expectation, getting yourself and your horse ready and piling into the car. But they all ended in the same depressingly familiar way. We had to leave early. Or we had stayed too late. There was yelling, abuse, trouble. I learnt early on that was what happens with alcoholism.

My dad, Garth Moody, was by all reports a very good horseman. He was also a chronic alcoholic. For one reason or another, the drink took control of his life, from before I was born.

My mum, Jan, was left to do most of the work around our farm while Dad spent most of each day at the pub. I can remember him coming home drunk and violent and yelling and screaming, as drunks did, and everyone staying well out of his way. While I can't remember him hitting Mum, I have no doubt he probably did. Was I too young to notice or appreciate what was going on? Or do you not want to remember your father being a violent drunk? Do you suppress it? I'm still not sure.

I'd rather it hadn't been this way but, while alcoholism was the dominant factor of my early years, it ended up playing a major role in how my life and career have played out.

While my dad had his defining weakness, I've been fortunate all my life to be surrounded by strong, capable women. My mother is the prime example. When I was eight, she decided she had had enough of that shitty life with Dad. With my three sisters away at boarding school, she packed me up and we moved to the nearest big town, Charleville. That took courage. She really had nothing to go to, but decided whatever lay ahead it was better than the alternative.

Under my father's unsteady watch, the family farm went to rack and ruin and ended up being sold off. It's sad to think but, in his forties, Dad had to go and live with his parents, in Brisbane. Had he not been a hopeless alcoholic, had life on the farm been more doable, there's a good chance I could have stayed there till now, doing the same as a lot of my old mates have been doing. I'd rather it had evolved in a different way, of course, but if Dad hadn't drunk the farm away, I probably wouldn't have had the opportunities that were presented to me.

I wouldn't for a minute give thanks that Dad was an alcoholic. What I do say is you've got to find a positive out of every negative.

....

I guess it really was a long way from where I grew up to Royal Ascot. But where I grew up is a long way from anywhere.

If you drive west from Brisbane for about nine hours you'll get to Charleville. Head south of there for another hour, alongside the Warrego River, and you'll reach Wyandra. It's a little town with eight streets, where the base population is a few dozen but rises and falls with the movements of the shearers and railway workers.

Seven miles east was Alpha, the cattle and sheep farm, covered in greenish scrub, where I spent my first few years. After acquiring a neighbouring property the family had about 100,000 acres that stretched back to the edge of town.

My ancestors got to the area in a roundabout way. And though it might surprise anyone who's heard me drop my aitches or the odd bit of colourful language, or seen me sink the odd stubby of XXXX at the Birdsville races, there's some blue blood in my pedigree.

My great-great-great-grandfather on Mum's side was a decorated seaman called Captain Edward Biddulph, from Staffordshire. I'm not too well versed in family details, but you can find him on the internet.

And since I've been away from racing, I've become a keen student of war history, and my ancestor's story is fascinating.

I have no idea, of course, whether I'm anything like he was, but he did seem to like having a go. When he was all of thirteen, in 1803, he joined Lord Nelson's British navy, and was off to see the world and win many medals in action. Eventually, in 1831, the by-then Captain Biddulph moved to New South Wales. And he made headlines doing it, since he sailed the very first steamer to ever come to the country, the *Sophia Jane*.

According to one article, the steam ship, which must have seemed like the space shuttle back then, 'created quite a stir' for the people of the colony when it arrived in Sydney Harbour. It transported passengers and mail between Newcastle, Sydney and Wollongong, before coming to grief on a reef in 1844. I still have a couple of gold spoons from the ship. At about $15,000 each, they are probably worth more than the most expensive racing trophy I've got!

Captain Biddulph started the family's involvement in horses, after being granted some land near Maitland, in the Hunter Valley, which he turned into a stud. Records show he had a starter at the first race meeting held at Maitland, in July 1833, while an advertisement in the *Sydney Morning Herald* of 20 May 1844 offers 'superior brood mares just arrived from Captain Biddulph's station on the Hunter'. He died in Newcastle in 1851, but the family had been established as people of the land. Around 1885 they found their way to western Queensland.

The blue blood actually means we've got a real-live baronet in the family, though I only found that out during the research for this book. In the 1950s, my great-grandfather Frank Biddulph was standing around minding his own business in Queensland when he became the ninth Baronet of London and Westmouth Manor. Someone in England had died, and the baronetcy, created in 1665 for one Sir

Theophilus Biddulph, fell to him. I now have a distant cousin in Brisbane who is the eleventh baronet. I should look him up and crack a XXXX with him.

Unfortunately, since I'm a Moody and not a Biddulph, there's no chance of the title passing to me, so there goes that retirement plan.

....

Mum's father Mike (real name Malcolm) was a manager for Vesteys, the big land-holders and cattle operators. When he was based in the Kimberley in northern Western Australia, Mum and her two brothers would fly for two days on the mail plane to get to boarding school at Alice Springs. Mike was into racing, mostly with stockhorses, and one year won the Negri River Cup, about 500 miles south-west of Darwin, which is not quite a racing byword but was a big deal out there. Mum remembers the big trip to the race weekend, camping out at the 'track' for four or five days as a young girl.

Mike and family finally ended up on a cattle station called Mount Playfair, near Tambo, to the north of Charleville. Mum eventually became a secretary at the big wool-broking firm Winchcombe Carson in Charleville, and through socialising in Charleville met my dad.

On his side of the family, the Moodys were always a presence around Wyandra after it was established in the late 1800s. John (also from the Hunter Valley) and Charlotte settled the family grazing property, Alpha, where I ended up growing up. They had no fewer than twelve kids—though some in the family believe as many as fifteen were born—which helps explain how Wyandra became like Moodyville. My first school, the Wyandra State School, was on Moody Street, and of the 25 or so kids, probably ten of them were Moodys.

My father was Lionel Moody, but went by his middle name of Garth. His father, the youngest of those twelve children, was Vincent

Moody, but went by his middle name of Gordon, which is why I came to be Peter Gordon Moody.

As well as being graziers, Gordon's father and some relatives were stonemasons, who were probably responsible for the town's tombstones and pubs—of which, for such a small town, there were a fairly plentiful six. Aside from taking over Alpha, Grandpa Gordon ran one of those pubs. Perhaps the view from his side of the bar stopped him becoming a heavy drinker, like his son.

Gordon, who I called Fa-Fa (Father's Father) always had the form guide out, and as a kid I always wondered why. Later in life I found out: he had been a pretty big SP bookmaker, operating from his pub. You can imagine the scene, probably echoed in thousands of pubs across the country back then: a big crowd, the races crackling on the radio, and blokes having bets with the SP, my granddad.

Eventually, Gordon and my grandmother Elspeth semi-retired to Brisbane and Alpha was left to my dad to manage, with predictable results.

....

I came along in the winter of 1969. With no hospital in Wyandra, Mum had to go to Charleville for a week, staying with friends until I was ready to come out. She was lucky the weather was favourable because, when it rained heavily, the dirt road turned to mud and made the trip impossible. I timed my run a little late and Mum ended up being there for two weeks, but I eventually emerged on 31 July. As fate would have it, that is a big day in racing as it is the last day of the season. Mind you, being born a few hours later, on 1 August, when all horses have their designated birthday, might have been more auspicious.

I was pretty much raised as an only child, since my sisters Fiona, Tanya and Alison are from six to ten years older than me, and were at boarding school in Brisbane most of the time. When my sisters were home, I remember spending a lot of time being something of a dress-up doll for them (I'm not sure I was too happy about it!). My mother says the fact I was usually surrounded by adults meant I learnt to get along well with older people as I grew up, which would come in handy during my early years in racing.

We did have a nanny, a local girl called Sharon Roberts, to help with me while Mum was doing her best with the farm and Dad was doing what he did, but I'd say Sharon had enough to do in the house and I was left to my own devices outside. I'd go out after breakfast and get about outside until I heard the dinner bell. I could get down to the stables, the pigsties, the machinery sheds. For a big adventure I might go all the way down to the cattle yards. As a kid I thought they were nearly five miles from the house. I went back a few years ago and it turns out they were about 200 yards away!

We didn't go without but we didn't have any luxuries. My kids today might be horrified, but my favourite 'toy' was an empty Milo tin, which had a wire attached to it and which I'd drag around doing various things with all day, chiefly making noise. One sign of farm life was that my other favourite toy was a .303 rifle. It had the bolt taken out, so I could only pretend to shoot it, but it would probably look fairly unusual to see a five-year-old lugging one around today.

I had a dog, a blue heeler–dingo cross, that was very fond of snakes, as in it used to catch and kill them and drag their dead bodies up to the house, which was no doubt a thrill for my mum.

We didn't have TV, and we weren't on the grid, our electricity coming instead from diesel generators. The phone was a bit of a shambles. A bunch of properties shared the same number, and it was up to the operator to dial with a different ring pattern depending on who the call was for. Two shorts and a long meant it was for us. People could still listen in if they wanted, so if you heard a 'click' you knew someone was eavesdropping. Not surprisingly, most people knew each other's business.

We also weren't connected to any town water. Our water came from an artesian bore, and there were some big and exciting days when the bore drains, like shallow little creeks, would have to be freshly delved, or cleaned out. We kids would get behind this tractor, driven by Mum, which dragged the wooden delver behind it, and as it churned up the bottom we followed along picking up yabbies, turtles and whatever else got turned up, and of course getting covered in mud in the process.

Some mornings you'd wake up and there was no water in the house, which usually only meant one thing—a clash of boars and bores. The wild pigs around the property had got into a bore drain and smashed the banks, meaning the water spilt out all over the place instead of being channelled to the house. So we all went to 'fix' it, though apparently I just used it as an excuse to splash about in the mud, much like the pigs.

There was a more serious bit of mischief involving water. The story goes that one day when I was three, I decided to have a swim in our dam. The only logistical problem with this was that I couldn't swim an inch. Apparently that didn't deter me, and I wandered in, cowboy boots and all.

There were always a few workers on the farm and thankfully one of them, a ringer named Eddie Hornberg, saw me as I walked in, toppled over and went under. He ran over, dragged me off the bottom and pumped the water out of me. It's a bit scary to think, but if he hadn't have spotted me nobody would have.

After I retired in 2016 I went to Toowoomba to see some old friends at the Weetwood Handicap meeting. I told that story to a woman I was having a beer with and it turned out she knew this man who had saved my life. I asked her how and she said: 'I was married to the filthy rotten bastard!' At least Eddie did something right, or I wouldn't be around to tell the story. There would be no trainer P.G. Moody, nor this book that you're reading now!

....

As a kid you had rugby league in winter, cricket in the summer, and there was racing in the cooler months. The Charleville Cup was on Melbourne Cup day, then the Roma Cup was usually the Saturday week after that, and that ended western racing until it kicked off again in autumn.

Country racing's a huge part of country life. That's partly why I've always been keen to run my horses in the bush throughout my career. In fact, horses—races, gymkhanas, shows, pony clubs, stockhorses— were largely what kept a lot of those rural communities going. Every property had stockhorses, and most had a thoroughbred stallion to breed their stockhorses. They also bred their own racehorses, which fed and funded a lot of the country racing.

I was probably growing up at the end of an era where horses were still prominent. Motorbikes, helicopters and four-wheel drives then took away a lot of the horse element, which ultimately took away a lot of those horse events, and that impacted on racing too.

But up until then all the kids in the bush rode a horse and everyone went to pony club. We went out in the morning and caught our horses in the paddock, and then we were always heading off somewhere with the truck loaded up with horses.

The local hub was the Niemenmulla Pony Club, on the banks of the Warrego. My godfather Cyril Pollard ran it on his property, and I rode down there on old Boy Lucas or big Doubtful. Cyril belted all of us kids around the bush, and I guess he was my first teacher in horsemanship.

I'm told that around the pony club they used to call me Georgie Moore, after the famous jockey, because apparently I was all arms and legs flapping about everywhere. He was also a Queenslander who worked with Tommy Smith, but that's where the similarities between us end. In any case, it was pretty evident early on that I was going to be far too big for a life in the saddle. As a fair indication, I ended up playing as a prop forward in rugby league. I was far more Artie Beetson than Billy Slater, the current league star—a fellow Melbourne-based Queenslander and a mate of mine—who actually rode trackwork for Gai Waterhouse before his footy career kicked off.

I used to ride pretty well, though I wasn't a great rider. My skills were probably in other departments. Some of the best footy coaches aren't necessarily the best players. They have an ability to read people and read the sport. I was the same with horses. I think from early on I had an affinity with them, but was better at directing than riding.

The biggest race meeting for us was of course the Wyandra Cup, in the autumn. It was on this mongrel little dirt track—with a circumference only about seven furlongs, or 1400 metres, and an old wooden running rail. Most people know there aren't many tracks I wouldn't take my horses to as a trainer, but this one would have tested my limits.

And while I was also known for taking my horses all over Victoria, out in western Queensland there were some real distances to comprehend, besides some evocative place names. Horses would come from Bourke, Quilpie, Charleville, Cunnamulla, Augathella, Surat, Tambo, Blackall, Morven, Mitchell, Roma—even Barcaldine and Longreach, which were nearly 400 miles away. We also went to several of those places for their race meetings. In the spring we headed west for the Diamantina races, now known as the Simpson Desert Racing Carnival, with races at Bedourie, Betoota and the famous Birdsville Cup.

These were, and still are, dirt or sand tracks, so you can imagine the dust, the heat and the noise of these days.

Mum and Dad owned a few racehorses, and one big highlight was them winning the Wyandra Cup one year in the '70s with a horse called Sad Sack. I have that cup in my house somewhere. Eventually, though, they stopped racing at Wyandra, which was sad. Like a lot of race clubs in country Australia, insurance premiums killed them, and the lack of funding.

So these were my earliest racing memories but, though it might surprise a few people, I was never really much into the racing. I can remember seeing the horses going round but I can't say it really gripped me from day one or anything. We kids were probably mostly down the creek making mud pies, trying to smoke cigarettes, or commit some other mischief.

All the same, racing was never far away, partly due to the influence of my cousins, Brett and Alan 'Alf' Moody. They lived in town, across the road from the pub, so because of Dad I had many opportunities to hang out with them, and we grew up like brothers.

Brett's two years older than Alfie and me, which counted for a lot in our favourite game. The three of us would sit on their couch, Brett in the middle and Alf and me on the arms. Brett would call races, using old racebooks for the fields, and Alf and I would ride the arms of the couch, scrubbing the 'ears' off it like mad, and then, in the closing stages, going berserk with the 'whip'—a rolled-up newspaper or a wooden spoon.

It was great fun, and sounds like innocent fun, except Brett would also run a little book on it. Before each race he'd announce the field and the market, and the three of us would each have a little bet. Alf and I, who were about seven, couldn't work out why the horses Brett picked seemed to win all the time, while we seemed very unlucky. Ours would win the occasional one, but his would win four out of five, and usually at better odds than ours! We didn't know it then but those early days shaped Brett's adult life. He went on to be a full-time thief. No, just kidding—he became a racecaller, calling mostly around Queensland's Darling Downs, which he still does today.

We didn't give our parents too much strife. Probably the worst of it was a habit that still gets me in trouble a bit today: Mum occasionally had to wash my mouth out with soap due to the odd bit of expressive language. To this day Alf says he can't believe I can get through a sentence when speaking to the media without at least one or two swearwords dropping out. I guess I've learnt how to conduct myself in public at least!

As the years went on, we three Moodys did get into racing a bit more. The TAB finally came to Wyandra. There was still no PubTAB, but this being a small town we kind of had ButcherTAB. The tote shared a roof with Itzstein's Butchery, and was also run by a Moody—Alf and Brett's mum, Wendy. Blokes would walk around from the pub to have their bets, since my Fa-Fa's little side business had long since gone.

Brett, Alf and I would be in the TAB listening to races, probably getting under Wendy's feet and having 50-cent doubles or trebles. I still wasn't any racing tragic. Probably the first horse I remember was Sir Dapper, and he didn't race till I was thirteen. It was only a few years after that I was actually down there and working among such horses at Randwick.

They were the memories, the good times—growing up with Brett and Alf, doing what kids do, making a mess, running a rort, jumping off the roof thinking we were Superman, and flogging the hell out of the couch thinking we were jockeys.

....

My Dad used to ride a lot as a young fella. I remember seeing photos of him playing polocrosse, riding in rodeos or the odd race meeting. I presume he broke horses in, but I didn't see that. Unfortunately when I was a kid Dad was too far down the alcoholism path, so I didn't get to witness his horsemanship. It's a bit sad for me to this day—that I didn't get to learn horse skills from my father. I probably inherited some, but I didn't get to learn from him.

Why did he become an alcoholic? Was it an illness? Or just a weakness? Was it the harsh life on the land? The pressure of running a station? Boredom? He was from a big drinking family, but I doubt the uncles and great-uncles I have heard stories about drank as much as Dad. In the end, I've grown up thinking the theories are just excuses. Some people, like some horses, want to take the soft option and not try. These days they treat alcoholism, but out there back then, it would have just been locked away in the closet and not talked about.

It wasn't most days. It was *every* day. After school I'd walk up and wait outside the pub until Dad was ready to leave. Wherever we went—pony club, local show, race meeting, a tennis or golf day—he always ended up hitting the piss and things would get ugly. Time after time. Day after day.

When his parents moved to Brisbane and he was left to run the show, it just all got too much for him and he probably got worse. He only had one sister, and she'd married the bloke two doors up and they had his property. It was a great shame really—this big and grand property, Alpha, that had been started a hundred years earlier by his grandfather, who I would assume had a lot of go in him, left in the hands of a chronic alcoholic.

I think the banks ended up owning most of it, and it was eventually sold. I went back there many years later with my sisters to spread Dad's ashes and unfortunately, the homestead had burnt down. It all seemed a bit sad really. A waste.

So how do I feel about it now?

I loved my dad and had a good relationship with him. You wouldn't have called it warm and fuzzy, but he looked after me. He was never nasty to me. Obviously, though, family life was very rugged early on.

When I was a teenager I went to see Dad in Brisbane now and again. I have some good memories from that. He took me to the Brisbane Commonwealth Games in 1982, and to the last gallops meeting on the sand track at Albion Park. One thing that stuck in my mind—though I've got a memory like a sieve—is that a horse called Lire News won the last race. I saw jockeys like Mick Dittman and Mike Pelling and got real excited. Fancy that I was legging them up on horses not too long after that! (Stretching things probably past an acceptable limit, I have even ended up with a framed and autographed picture on my man-cave wall of Pelling in the nude! Before you jump to conclusions, the jockey who became my mate is riding a horse in a particularly bizarre photo shoot. Thank Christ it's from side-on.)

As the years went by, Dad and I had the odd phone chat or visit, but I think he realised that, while he wasn't estranged, he wasn't there for me, or my sisters, as a father.

When I moved to Brisbane in my early twenties, Dad's parents had died and he was pretty stuffed. He was on his way out himself. I'm not sure what kind of cancer he had, but I don't think there were many kinds he didn't have: he'd lived and played so hard. He came and lived with Sarah and me for six months—the longest time I had spent with him since I was about seven—but, with a new baby on the ground and a stable to run, we just weren't able to provide the care he needed. He went to stay with my sister Alison and died in 1995, in his mid-fifties.

I didn't blame Dad for anything. It was what it was, and I don't think there's much use wallowing or dwelling too much on the past.

In fact, it was probably a mark of respect that I ended up naming a horse after him. Garth was a gelding by the horse who put me on

the map, General Nediym, and was owned by Sarah. He won four of
seven starts—one at Moonee Valley—then we sold him for a good
price to Hong Kong. So you might say I ended up doing OK out of
one Garth.

But while I loved my dad, clearly he didn't have a big influence
on me. As an alcoholic that's probably a good thing. I do love a beer
but, because of Dad, I've always been very careful of how much I
drink and everything I do, because I never wanted to end up the same.

....

Dad's drinking of course put a lot of pressure on my mother, Jan.
She had to try to keep things together, and worked her backside off
to make ends meet. With three daughters at boarding school, that
must have been tough. Alison had finished high school by the time
my parents split up, but Mum had to have paid for the tail end of
Tanya and Fiona's schooling herself. I went through the state school
system. I might have even done Mum a favour by dropping out after
Year 10, not that there was ever much doubt there.

Mum is the one constant who has been there throughout for me.
And she's a beautiful woman. I know most people like their mum,
but you'd struggle to hear anyone say a bad word about her.

But the poor woman missed out all round, really. She was the
eldest in her family, but, since she moved away, her brothers inherited
the family property. She married the heir to another property but he
became an alcoholic, the property was lost and she got nothing out
of that either. I don't think my dad's side of the family helped her
out at all.

Mum was fairly no-nonsense when I was a kid, but very soft, gentle
and caring, although she was probably at her wits' end. She was one
of those country women who was always busy. She became a local
councillor, and was even sounded out by the National Party to run

for parliament. I don't think she could have coped with all the bullshit politicians speak to give that a go. To this day she's one of these people who does everything for everyone except herself.

She moved from Dalby to Brisbane and helped Sarah and me greatly when I started training on my own and we had three little kids. That's why it was so special that when I travelled to Melbourne in 2001 and won my first Group 1—the Victoria Derby with Amalfi—Mum came with me.

As big as we grew, Mum painstakingly kept a scrapbook on my career. It has been nice, since we had some success, to be able to treat her to the odd overseas holiday as a bit of a 'thank you'. But really, there's no way I can ever thank her enough.

2

A Course Is Set

Finally, thankfully, Mum pulled the pin on that awful marriage and she and I moved to Charleville when I was eight.

Like a lot of desperate women, she went to the CWA. It was a big old house in the middle of town, with a flat upstairs and a hostel area below. Mum was given the job of running the hostel, and she and I lived upstairs. She ran the shelter, but she was sheltering herself. Dad stayed on the farm; I saw him occasionally but then he moved to Brisbane.

There aren't many times I've felt intimidated, but going to a big new school was one of them. I went from a two-room school with about 25 kids to this huge school. And I had gone from Wyandra, where I knew everyone and was related to half of them, to Charleville where I didn't know any bastard. It didn't help that I stuck out a bit too, like a farm kid. I took this old leather satchel that I loved, but everyone took the piss out of me for it, so I ditched that pretty quick.

Things changed and I settled in. In fact, in a rare example of achievement in the education system, I ended up school captain in

Year 7. I'm not sure if my name's on a plaque there somewhere. No doubt you'll find it on the back of a shithouse door, though.

I tried to get along with most people, as I do to this day, which is something I get from Mum. She could sit in the gutter with someone down on their luck, or have afternoon tea with the governor-general and be just as comfortable in both situations. My ability to handle people later in life—whether they are business people who own horses, Arab sheikhs or brickies' labourers—is a trait I learnt from my mother, and I think it has helped me a lot.

After about a year Mum teamed up with a new partner, Tony Facey, and we moved in with him. He had a house on a dirt road with some stables behind, so life with horses continued.

Tony was well known in horse circles in country Queensland and, like Dad, was a very good horseman. He had moved to Queensland at fifteen from where he grew up near Cranbourne, south-east of Melbourne—coincidentally close to where we live now. He had married a Wyandra girl and had kids, but was estranged from that family.

Tony was a bit of everything—contract musterer, drover, rodeo rider, jockey and racehorse trainer. He was a national rodeo champion and has even got a mention in the Australian Stockman's Hall of Fame in Longreach.

He was a big, hard bastard who did things bush-style. If he wanted to put a horse on a truck, he often just backed the truck up to a mound or a ridge, rode the horse up from behind and jumped it on. He caught wild brumbies using spear traps around waterholes. They worked like a crab pot. Horses would walk in but couldn't walk out again, with these sharp spears pointing at them. Tony roped them and sold them.

And tough? Cousin Alf later moved in with us in Charleville and worked as a strapper for Tony. One day they were leaving the races at Surat and, as Tony was driving his old Bedford truck out of the car park, he stopped to have a bet and told Alf to wait in the truck.

An hour later, Alf couldn't resist going to look for him. He couldn't find him and came back to the truck, but it was gone. Tony had returned and taken off, to teach him a lesson. Here was Alf, all of thirteen, being left to find his own way home. And home was more than 200 miles away! Eventually he got a lift, and they caught up to Tony and flagged him down. All Tony said was: 'Told ya to wait in the truck'.

Mum had started work at the old Commonwealth Employment Service (CES), where she would work for many years, and she was soon the breadwinner. By contrast, Tony lived day by day, and was a bit hopeless. He always had some money-making scheme—selling brumbies, goats, watermelons, anything. There was always a rort on somewhere. But he ended up giving away more than he earned. At least it showed his kind side.

Tony ended up dying aged only 51, from a blood disorder. He had been quite influential for me from when I was about nine till when I was fourteen. He would give me a smack in the ear or a boot up the arse like a father would to a son, but it wasn't a violent relationship. At the same time, we were never that close. He had plenty of faults, chief among them his lack of respect for money. But again, maybe as with Dad, I learnt what not to be. Tony probably never warmed to me too much. I was always Garth's son, not his. But at least I was smart enough to learn from him some of the dos and don'ts around horses.

Through primary school and into high school, I was still messing around with pony clubs, but then other things took over, like playing league and cricket.

I played league all my life, until my knees gave it up in my mid-twenties, and it remains my biggest sporting passion outside racing. I try to go to at least one State of Origin game a year, and watch us stuff those Cockroaches from New South Wales. I played most things I could have a go at, like the odd spot of lawn bowls and a fair bit of tennis; Mum remembers I could switch the racquet from my right hand to my left if it was needed. Maybe these ambidextrous tendencies helped me rotate four or five stopwatches at trackwork in later life!

Away from sport I did some 'roo shooting and pig chasing. Feral pigs were a problem. You'd go out with some dogs and they'd go into the bush and chase the pigs out. You'd be waiting there to run after them and tackle them, and stab them up under the foreleg in the heart. They'd get turned into dog meat. It was probably more fun than it sounds now, and I guess it was one way of building your typical big boys from the bush.

School ticked by, more of a way to hang out with my mates than anything else. I was a fair student—I wasn't a dope. I could read, write and count, and didn't think I needed much more.

But then, finally, my big interest did come along.

....

Racing had been there in the background but, aged about eleven, I started taking it more seriously. As with my catapulting into Sydney a few years later, I have Brett Cavanough to thank.

Tony had a young fella doing some work for him, and that's how I met the bloke I call one of my best mates almost four decades later. Brett, seven years my senior, also helped his grandfather, another trainer named Frank Cavanough. Since Brett was about to leave Charleville, he asked if I'd like to help Frank. I thought I'd see what it was like.

Before and after school, I helped out at Frank's stables. With me was another kid called Neville Gorrie, who Brett also lined up. Neville was a good bloke and a mate of mine. We went to school together, played footy together and hung out a bit, though later we lost contact.

Other things took Neville's fancy after a while, but I stayed on with old Frank and I guess you'd say he tried to make a man—and a horseman—out of me.

Where do I start with Frank? He was a rough old bastard who, if you looked at him the wrong way, would knock you on your arse to pull you into line pretty quick. After putting up with him, I'd go home and cop the odd smack in the ear from Tony too. So I was getting it from both sides!

Mind you, without a father to influence me, it was probably what I needed. Tony was my stepfather without really being a stepfather, and Frank—without him I probably would have ended up a drug-fucked alcoholic or something. Maybe that sounds dramatic but there's a fair chance something could have gone wrong in a place like that. I could have at least become uncontrollable.

Frank, who was about 70, certainly had an old-school way of keeping me under control, and some novel ideas on the use of gear that's really meant for horses. If you backchatted him, you'd cop a smack in the ear if you were in arm's reach. If you weren't, he'd think nothing of throwing a shoeing hammer at you or swinging a bridle round to hook you in the side of the head or up the guts.

Once, I gave him some lip and thought I had got away with it as I went into the feed room. But then I heard the door shut behind me. Old Frank had followed me in and, I don't need to tell you, he gave me a decent belting, and not for the last time. I came to quite dislike that feed room.

'That boy of Garth's—you can't tell him anything,' was a comment from him that came back to me. But my mum did say that I was apparently very dear to him. Talk about tough love!

Come to think of it, Frank was maybe even going a bit senile. His wife long departed, he was alone—living in an old caravan with two blue heeler dogs—and was probably a bit long in the tooth to be doing some of the things he was doing, which led to frustration and crankiness. He came to treat me more as an adult, though I was only around thirteen. I guess in his world that was when you became a man. Apart from the horses, he taught me how to act with people. It was a life-building exercise.

Frank picked me up about 5 a.m. every day and Mum made sure I was up so he wouldn't honk his horn and wake the neighbours. I did the usual stable stuff—picked up shit, rode work, tended to the horses—then went to school, then went back in the afternoons. I learnt how to feed them, groom them, and I would even shoe them.

Frank had horses at Charleville racecourse, conveniently located across the road from the high school, and a few on the property of local bookie David Power, who he trained for. I'm proud to say I'm still close mates with 'Crockett' to this day. I have trained for him and still race horses with him.

The education with Frank was sink-or-swim stuff. We had some decent bush horses but some mongrels as well. I'll never forget one bolting old bastard called Hamarchris. Crockett had a 600-metre sand track and Frank would make me take him out there most days. Every single time the old bastard would take off with me on his back and go around at a million mile an hour. You couldn't pull him up till he pulled himself up.

We'd take horses up into the sandhills. Frank would chase me on a pony with a big stick, whack my horse on the arse and try to teach it to go. It was like something out of the *Phar Lap* movie, only with a somewhat lower quality of horse. I might have worn a helmet, but I doubt it. I wasn't the bravest rider around but at least there was sand underneath you.

It was from the early days with Frank that I started a habit that helped me a lot in my development with racehorses—and throughout my career. I started keeping what became my pretty well-known notebook. I took a school exercise book and a pen to the stables, and wrote down anything I thought might be important. When I got home, I added in anything else I had seen that day. It didn't matter how inconsequential it seemed, I'd write it down. 'This horse doesn't like the whip', or 'This horse gets fed this and that', or 'Owner Mr Smith came to town today to look at his horse'. Frank told my mum: 'Every time I tell him something, he writes it in this bloody book!'

Later, at Tommy Smith's, I'd keep notes about the horses and their owners, their races, how they travelled, finishing positions, anything. People have said from early on that they only needed to tell me something once, whereas with a lot of other young blokes stuff would go in one ear and out the other. While I never went back and read any of it, writing stuff down—and sometimes it was extremely mundane—helped me make sure things would stick in my mind, and always has done.

....

Old Frank and I soon became a well-known duo taking horses around the bush. While it wasn't unusual for a trainer to have a young bloke working for him, what made us different was that I used to do the driving—from when I was twelve!

Frank wasn't keen on those long drives at his age. Since I was a big kid and could reach the pedals, he just got me to do it. I would later get into some mischief as a teenager driving in the bush, banging the odd car up here and there. (At this point I would like to apologise to my sister Fiona for what I did to her Morris Minor. On more than one occasion.)

Despite these later misadventures, I was always pretty careful driving Frank's old ute, especially as a twelve-year-old towing a two-horse float. I could drive through any town except Charleville. It was a police training centre, so there were always lots of coppers around.

Frank would drive us out of town about a mile or so, then he'd pull over and we would swap seats. He would drop straight off to sleep and I would drive the 120 miles to Cunnamulla or the 180 miles to Roma or wherever and wake him up at the track.

The cops sometimes drove past and saw us both—old Frank asleep and this kid driving—and just shook their heads. Often they had been at the races too, having a punt and several beers, so they couldn't really pull me up and nick me.

When I eventually went to Charleville police station to get my learner's permit, the old inspector looked at me and said: 'You're bloody kidding!' He told me to go away and come back a week later. On principle, they weren't going to give it to me first time round because they knew I'd been driving around western Queensland for years!

....

Frank would give me 30 or 40 bucks a week. The races we won were normally worth $600 or $700, and I got a little sling from that, too. So I was never short of a dollar.

My favourite horse was an old gelding called Scenic Rock, who I had a share in owning with Frank, though I was still only thirteen and it probably wasn't all that legal. Scenic Rock won a lot of races, highlighted by the Tambo and Cunnamulla cups.

Crockett always had some handy ones with Frank, including Coming Country, who won about seven or eight races for us. There is a great photo I love, taken after she won at Roma in 1984. There are the horse and jockey, Tom Johnstone. There's me holding her, about fifteen years old, with a mop of hair under my Akubra and, of course, a pen in my top pocket. And there's Frank standing to the side, looking cranky.

That was my world and my routine for those few years. Frank was obviously smart with a horse, because he and Crockett would set one up and back it, and it would usually win. I was probably kept shielded from that side of it, especially as there might have been a bit of ducks and drakes going on.

They were great formative years that helped me build life experience. Frank especially, and Tony Facey, taught me a lot of things about being a horseman in general, and I guess helped steer me towards becoming a man. I appreciate those sides of it, but in reality I probably learnt nothing too specific or technical from them that I ended up applying to top-level big-city thoroughbreds.

It was a different world. The racehorse is so much different now, especially in Australia. They have been bred a lot finer, mostly due to the influx of European stallions, who evolved in softer environments. The typical city horse has cannon bones like your finger and hoofs like teacups. Out in the bush, it was more like tree trunks and dinner plates. It didn't matter what you did with them—you couldn't hurt them. They were built like Sherman tanks. Now, they're like a finely tuned Formula One car, and one tiny thing being wrong can upset the whole machine.

We used to gallop the fuck out of them—two or three times a week—and then travel 150 miles to race, and repeat this week after week. Once, we drove one more than 350 miles east to run it twice in one day! We were only a hundred miles from the ocean, for God's sake. Frank declined that trip, but sent Brett and me instead. The horse, Scarlet Beau, got beaten a lip in his first race, but won his second.

There was a skill I wouldn't need all that much in Melbourne: how to race a horse twice in one day. (The secret, which I'm happy to pass on now, is to keep it walking between its races so it doesn't cool down and get stiff. You're welcome.)

I was still lucky, as a kid with horses as his passion. I studied them, learnt their habits and their ways—ways to pacify them and keep 'em quiet. Mind you, it probably wasn't a great place for that, since Frank and Tony were a bit volatile.

There wasn't a lot of science to it in the bush. It was basically trot, canter or gallop. But it was good for my familiarisation with horses. My love of the horse, and of the racehorse in particular, was growing.

....

Old Frank died of a heart attack when I was living in Sydney and about eighteen. I remember taking the phone call, and being very upset. I was probably as close to him as anyone could have been. I then had to go tell Brett's mother her dad had died. That probably ended up a bit of a mess, but I guess I got through it.

Brett and I went back home and cleared out Frank's caravan. Then, since it was pretty dilapidated, we decided to burn it. We made this ceremonial bonfire of it on someone's big front yard—which you could do out there—and then went to Brisbane, to see him buried next to his wife in Mount Gravatt cemetery.

To this day it's a bit sad for me that the three blokes who were probably my biggest influences—Frank, Tony and Dad—didn't live long enough to see me be successful. Dad lived the longest, but died in 1995.

For all the backhanders and the boots in the arse, I'd have liked to think at least one of them might have been there to say 'Well done on winning your first Group 1', or 'Well done on winning that premiership at Ipswich' when I first started.

I could have said: 'Well, you thought I was a useless bastard. Here you are, wrong!' They might not have thought that—I don't know—but I never had an opportunity to show them I was going to be successful.

I guess, though, it is one of the things that has made me quite driven from an early age: knowing I would have to tackle things pretty much by myself without someone watching over me.

3

A Soldier for the Little General

The moment that changed my life and set me on course to become a horse trainer came like a bolt from the blue, turning a typically mundane Saturday afternoon in Charleville into a barely believable whirlwind.

In 1986 I was a pretty average, nondescript big lump from the bush who'd just left school at the first exit ramp. I did sit a scholarship test to go to the esteemed Toowoomba Grammar School (TGS) for Years 11 and 12, but I don't remember being too keen on it. I guess if they had accepted me we would have thought about it.

Working at the CES, Mum knew what jobs were around, and she had this habit of asking me what I was going to do with my life. I applied for apprenticeships—mine worker, diesel mechanic, and some others—but had no real interest, and probably just did it to appease Mum.

I was like a lot of bush louts at sixteen. I was still with Frank but was a bit directionless. I probably assumed I'd stay out there and make a living like most blokes—in the railways, shearing sheds, or as a ringer on a station perhaps. Cousin Alf was much the same. We were happy to be country kids and root around in the bush.

One thing we could do, which they don't teach you in school, was play pool, which we did at Chif's Billiard Hall. Chif himself was a lovely old bloke called Rodney Kinivan, known for taking his wireless outside and sitting under a tree to listen to the races. He still does it today, and I know he was one of my biggest supporters throughout my career.

Alf and I were just two average kids in the pool hall, playing games for money, practising drinking beer and smoking cigarettes, and the odd joint to ease the boredom. In general, we weren't doing a terrible bloody lot with ourselves really.

We were in Chif's on one of these long Saturday afternoons when Brett Cavanough walked in. I hadn't had much to do with him since he'd moved to Sydney, but now he had lobbed back in town for some reason. We spoke about what he'd been doing in Sydney, but I'd say it didn't interest us much and we kept playing pool. Then, after finally ascertaining what Alf and I were doing with our lives—bugger all—he said something from outer space.

'I can get you a job at Tommy Smith's if you want.'

The comment hung in the air for a bit.

'Yeah, right,' said Alf.

'I bloody can!' said Brett.

Alf and I largely dismissed him (to put it politely) but after a while he was still insisting he wasn't geeing us up.

'I'll bloody show you!' he said. He walked out and across the road to the post office. Alf and I watched him put some coins into the payphone, and gave each other a couple of glances, then no doubt resumed looking nonchalant and not bothered as Brett made his way back.

'Here!' he said, as he gave me a piece of paper. 'You get to Tulloch Lodge at Randwick and you ask for that bloke.'

It still took a while to sink in. For a couple of teenagers in a pool hall in western Queensland, it was a bit hard to fathom that we could, just like that, go and be gainfully employed with the biggest racehorse trainer in the country—one of the biggest in the world. Smith had trained horses we had heard of, almost like in fairytales. He had trained Kingston Town, for God's sake, and here we were supposed to believe we could be plucked from a game of pool in the bush to go work for him?

Finally, we realised the story really was feasible. Brett had been in Sydney with his mum and stepfather, John Drennan, who broke in horses for Smith. Tommy's brother and right-hand man, Ernie, had liked what he'd seen of Brett. The brothers were from the bush themselves, and Ernie asked Brett if he knew of any other good country lads, as he was tired of the lazy city kids who kept turning up.

So here I was, with a piece of paper in my hand that said little more than 'Terry Catip, Tulloch Lodge, Randwick'.

Once the penny had dropped, everything was a blur. I'd never really thought about leaving Charleville, but now this opportunity was in front of me, I was like 'When's the next bus?!'

I had to tell Mum. I had my reservations about leaving her, especially since Tony had died not long before. At the same time Mum knew this was a big opportunity for her son. I also knew she was very popular and busy, so she wouldn't be lonely. She admitted years later she wasn't too relaxed about it all. Sydney was a huge place, so far away, with notorious places like Kings Cross, and I was a sixteen-year-old from Charleville. But Mum also felt that, despite appearances, I was fairly mature for my age, and she knew I wasn't scared of hard work. So she gave me her blessing and, better still, two bus tickets, and instead of going to T.G.S. I was off to T.J.S.

Alf and I threw a few things into our bags. I had $80 and Alf had $75. And before we knew it—I think the very next day—the two of us were sat up the back of a bus, pulling out of Charleville to make our way to Sydney.

There was no great seizing of a moment. No vows, resolutions or declarations. I didn't stick my head out the window and yell 'YOU BASTARDS WILL NEVER SEE ME AGAIN!' To be honest, we were probably a bit numb, a bit excited, but no doubt scared as well.

I know one thing—I was glad Alfie was there. He hadn't had as much to do with horses as me, but he thought it would be a good idea to come along. Maybe the idea was for him to go to watch over me. In any case, I was eternally grateful he came. I probably wouldn't have had the balls to do it alone.

The bus drove out of my home town and headed east to Toowoomba, where it did a right turn for Sydney. The trip was the best part of two days, and I remember we were very sore in the hindquarters when we got there. I wasn't hatching plans or setting goals or anything like that. I was basically going along to give it a go. We slept and talked rot the whole trip.

....

We weren't two shrinking violets but we weren't at all worldly—perhaps especially me. I had no special possessions in my bag, but I had packed something I thought might be handy—a little bag of dope. We used to have the odd choof, though I'd soon give that away, since it was all heads down and bums up working.

I slept most of the way on the bus but, at one point deep into the journey, I felt Alfie shaking me. I woke up, looked around and saw the stone pylons of the famous Sydney Harbour Bridge. The strange thing was we weren't moving.

'What's going on?' I asked.

Alf fixed me with a look and said in a deadpan voice: 'This is where the police get on and check to make sure nobody's carrying anything illegal'.

My heart jumped, my face dropped and I started shitting myself. What a bloody idiot! We'd come all this way, with this great chance to make something of ourselves, and I was gonna stuff it up before we even got across the—

The bus started moving again, through the first set of toll gates I'd ever seen in my life. Alf started grinning. I know he thought it was very funny.

Right in line with Mum's misgivings about the whole venture, the bus dropped us off under the big Coca-Cola sign in Kings Cross. It was pouring with rain as we tried to flag down a cab.

....

For two louts from western Queensland, the scene greeting us at the famous Tulloch Lodge was from Alice in Wonderland.

There was straw! I'd never seen the stuff before. The horses were housed in these magnificent stables, with about three foot of straw in each box. In the bush they were on sawdust, or just dirt. Some of them were just outside the whole time, snoozing under a tree.

Tommy's horses all had two or three rugs on. They were bandaged on all four legs, to stop them hurting themselves. The bush horses I was used to probably would have seen them and called 'em soft. I quickly saw it was a million miles from the bush. I got the feeling this was going to be an unbelievable experience.

While the horses were pampered, we strappers got a room in the house by the stables where the staff lived. We were basically given a job and a bed. But boy did we come to love those beds.

The work was intense. In fact, we were pretty overawed by it, not to mention knackered. We had to get up at 2.30 in the morning. I was used to getting up early for old Frank, but those 5.00 a.m. starts were lazy sleep-ins compared to this. Alfie and I were like 'Christ, what's going on here?'

We were up at 2.30 and worked till 8.30, then have a shower and go to bed. We got up again at midday and worked through till 3.00 p.m., had a feed and a shower and went back to bed. This was every day, seven mornings a week. We did get two afternoons off. Luxury!

I relished the experience, but all we did was work and sleep, work and sleep. We were just rooted the whole time.

As for the work, you learnt there was a whole different way of doing things in the way you cared for your horses. You'd be given three horses to look after and they were *your* horses. You groomed them, mucked their stalls out, bedded them, took them to the track and brought them home. You tended their feet twice a day. You brushed them twice a day. You took pride in what you did. This was the great T.J. Smith's. It was a well-oiled machine and you wanted to be a worthy part of it.

They used to really instil that work ethic, which is something that's lost in the industry now. The strappers really competed to have their horse looking the best, and tended to the best. Everyone wanted to look after the best horses, and there were some good ones going around.

That rain that first greeted us set in for a couple of weeks, and with trackwork not possible we just did endless hours of walking our horses everywhere, like in the Randwick betting ring under the grandstand. Eventually we settled in to more normal stable life. Well, I did. Alfie wasn't doing so well. I was probably a bit more passionate about it than he was, which made the 2.30 starts slightly easier to reconcile for me. And he wasn't getting any lucky breaks.

One of his first horses was a smart one called Able Star. It won a barrier trial by four lengths one day and Alf was getting excited. Then the horse went sore and had to spell. Then the horse was found in its paddock, deceased. It might have been a snake bite or a heart attack. The cause of death wasn't the important bit for Alf.

His next horse was one called Burrabogie Boy, owned by Tommy's bright and bubbly daughter Gai, who of course became champion trainer Gai Waterhouse. She was an interesting, effusive woman even back then and was often around the stables—but, noticeably, only after her Uncle Ernie had left for the day.

'Now Alan,' she said, on presenting him with Burrabogie Boy, 'this horse is a very, very good horse. You look after this horse, Alan!' Alf was over the moon at being entrusted with its care.

At its first start, Burrabogie Boy ran seventeenth of seventeen in a Warwick Farm mid-week maiden. Alf said, 'Thanks very much, Gai', and went home soon afterwards, starting a long career with Queensland Railways.

At first I panicked a bit, but we both realised he wasn't really coping. I was just grateful, as I am to this day, that he came at all.

....

At T.J. Smith's there were three stabling areas and I was in the main one—Tulloch Lodge—which was in turn divided into a top yard and a bottom yard. The top yard was run by Errol Wilson, known by the flattering nickname of 'The Black Rat', while John Brady, or 'Crewie', ran the bottom yard. Terry Catip was the stable foreman overseeing both yards. Ernie Smith was the racing manager for the whole empire, and at the very top, of course, was Tommy, who everyone just called Boss.

I didn't have much to do with the 'The Little General' one on one, because of our respective positions in the food chain, but you always knew when he was about. You heard his famous squeaky little voice. And you saw his big Rolls Royce out the front.

The first time I met him was a Sunday afternoon when he came to look at one of my horses. Perhaps because of my junior status, my boxes were a bit hard to get to. From the entrance you had to go through about four or five stable doors and gates, which we usually left open for convenience. He asked my name and where I was from, and I probably just gibbered something back, because I was in awe of the man. Then he left and, perhaps to show a professional front or perhaps just because he'd had a few wines with his Sunday lunch, he closed and bolted every door and gate behind him! It took me an hour to get out of the joint.

While I couldn't call Smith a mentor, just to be in his presence was an inspiration. To see him out in the middle at trackwork of a morning—barking out orders in his little voice, directing the traffic, horses going every which way—was a sight to behold. The only minor shame was that he was probably a little past his prime when I was there. In fact, I arrived the season his 33-year reign as Sydney's premier came to an end. I hope that was a coincidence! Mind you, we still had horses like Bounding Away, who was fantastic. And while Brian Mayfield-Smith won for three years in a row, Tommy won one last premiership after that, by eighteen wins.

My mentor was really Terry Catip, who had got his job as a mate of Mick Dittman, who had moved from Queensland to be stable rider. Terry used to struggle with people a bit but he was a gifted horseman. He never rode them but he was unbelievable at detecting problems with a horse before anyone else. He worked closely with the vets and was like the lead mechanic in an F1 team.

Terry showed that tough love again. Early on he told me to 'Go and get your bloody hair cut'. It's hard to imagine now, but I had hair all over the place, looking like the first foal by Ciaron Maher out of Krusty the Clown. Terry also sent me to St Vinnie's to buy a suit to wear to the races. We had the odd run-in, usually involving me ducking out the back gate to get to the local pie shop (I've always been a good doer with the nosebag on). Terry insists there was a time when

I got the sooks and wanted to go home. I can't remember it but, if it happened, it was probably during one such blue about the pie shop.

Terry also said years later that he always felt I was a bit different. For one thing, I was six foot one-and-a-half and fairly hefty, in a stable full of little blokes who were often ex-jockeys. Other than that, he was maybe just happy to have a head-down-arse-up bloke from the bush, who was thrilled to be there.

I used to jump in, work hard and never be late. When I had a spare moment I followed the vets and farriers around, taking it all in, and of course writing everything in my book: pedigrees; owners' details; horses' racing programs; ailments and treatments, old remedies and new ones; how to use bran mashes and Epsom salts; how to make poultices to put on horses' feet—things you didn't need in the bush because not much went wrong with those horses. Crewie would teach you how to bandage a horse—*properly*. Compared to what we'd been doing in Charleville—galloping them and racing them—this was like doing a PhD in equine science.

You just learnt so much from blokes like Terry: the attention to detail with a horse that might help you pick up a problem very early or prevent something really bad from happening.

....

Tulloch Lodge was a little community unto itself, and was an eye opener. The place obviously ran pretty successfully but no doubt there were a few practices that might raise eyebrows today.

The staff house was home to about ten blokes, and there were a couple of dozen other workers who lived off-site. The staff were a bit of a rough-and-ready line-up of various characters from various walks of life, and of varying degrees of capability or hopelessness.

There were blokes like the Black Rat, who was a bandy-legged old bastard—in a good way, but still an old bastard. Crewie was a great and loyal man who had only ever worked at Smith's, and still does now, aged 80.

I learnt a lot from Charlie Cloos, a real character and Tommy's favourite trackwork rider. There was big Lofty, who left the police force because he loved horses. There was Lizard, who was always on the bong but also loved his horses. In fact, lots of blokes were on the bong, probably ten times a day. I'm sure Tommy knew what was going on but it was only dope. Some blokes were drug-addled or alcoholics, but they all had this real love of the horse, and a desire to look after them.

While our digs were basic, we were looked after. One morning a week a Chinese bloke called Hoppy would do all our washing and ironing. He picked it up on payday and, if you didn't pay him, you'd have no clothes for a week.

Also on paydays, three or four cars would pull up with all this gear in the boot—jeans, shirts, jumpers, coats, hats, watches, you could even line up a TV or stereo. One of these blokes even turned my Queensland driver's licence into a New South Wales one for $20. You didn't ask where the gear came from, and if you missed something you could get it down the pub later on.

I seemed to get on with everyone, even though I wasn't into the dope or the drinking. In fact, with a few of the more hopeless blokes living from payday to payday—or getting paid on Friday and being broke on Monday—I started to do all right for myself as a bit of a loan shark. It even got to the stage where on payday I'd collect my wage, and the wages of two or three other blokes who owed me.

The wages were only $112 a week, but if you strapped a Wednesday winner you'd get an extra $150, and it was $250 for a Saturday winner. Winning owners would usually give you a cash 'sling' for a job well done, which Tommy encouraged. Plus, every time the stable had a

Group 1 winner, everyone got $50! For a kid from the bush it was bloody amazing.

With these incentives, people took pride in what they did, and were proud to represent the Smith stable, like you'd represent a football team. The rivalry with other stables was fierce, especially at this time. When you'd see a strapper from the Mayfield-Smith stable you'd just about feel like thumping them or spitting at them. There was also a rivalry between T.J. and Bart Cummings. Though he wasn't such a premiership threat, there wasn't a lot of love between the two men.

There was also trouble within our competitive stable, with arguments or punch-ups always breaking out—over girls, horses, missing gear, whatever. Crewie and the Black Rat had a simple version of what human resources people might today call 'conflict resolution'. The blokes in the fight would be sent into the sand yard to sort it out, with the rest of us stopping to watch. I got thrown in a few times, which helps explain my misshapen nose (along with my league career and the odd head-butt from a horse).

Another way of dealing with wayward strappers that you also couldn't get away with today—I'm still amazed we did then—involved the part of the stable salubriously known as 'the shit pits'. They were big pits holding the soiled straw and manure. Anyone who was an arse of a kid or gave cheek would be thrown in there and the lid would be closed. You'd have to let them out after a little while, or the ammonia or the steam would kill 'em!

In the name of nearly harmless fun, the boys would get up to some fairly outrageous stuff. Once, they stripped one bloke off, put him in a chaff bag, put him on the back of a public bus and sent him down to Maroubra. Other times they'd tar and feather blokes.

Some of the older strappers would belt the younger ones if they didn't look after their horses. It certainly wasn't a place for the faint-hearted, and was vastly different from how stables function today—or any workplace really!

....

Things were clearly going well for me because after only a couple of months I was getting some plum jobs, probably due to Terry. He probably saw something in me that I couldn't see myself. Maybe it was just the fact I wasn't running to my room every half-hour to hit the bong.

I got to go to the races and do the saddling up, which was a well-oiled machine in itself. Tommy famously liked his horses to be in the first four or five during a race—a sound philosophy that reduces bad luck and that Gai and I carried into our training days. But Tommy also demanded his horses should be first in the mounting yard, making the stable look professional and ready for battle. So you'd be flat out saddling up soon after each race and getting them out. And, like Chris Waller today, he often had three or four in a race.

At trackwork, I used to ride work but I was getting too big. The most common job was to be in the stripping stalls, with all of its mayhem and horses going everywhere, but before long I was sent out to the middle to help jockeys on and off horses. So here I was, a few years after staring at him over the fence at Albion Park, legging Mick Dittman onto some of the best horses in the land! Or Mark de Montfort, Noel Barker and others. Everyone who wanted to be anyone was there to ride work for Tommy.

And there were several other trainers you could observe, like Cummings, Mayfield-Smith, and Neville Begg, who was great with fillies and mares. I'd watch how they'd go at trackwork, then, after getting matey with some of their staff, I could pop into their stables later in the day and get a closer look. I had all this knowledge around me, and I was like a sponge.

If you stood out as a good worker you generally got good horses, which brought you good slings. The stable star Bounding Away was already taken, although I couldn't have hoped to get her that early anyway, though I did saddle her up a couple of times. But soon after arriving I got a very good one in Lygon Arms.

The Bletchingly gelding, who won a Doncaster after I'd left, was one of the best horses I've had anything to do with. I nearly hit the jackpot with him early on, when he was beaten a lip in the 1987 Golden Slipper. Just to aggravate things further, he was collared by Marauding, trained by Mayfield-Smith. I bumped into that horse's jockey, Ronny Quinton, who's now a trainer, at a function recently and reminded him how he'd cost me the Slipper—and a big win on the punt—that day, and knocked about five horses out of the way to do so!

Having come so close at this first attempt, I probably felt these big races looked easy, but the Slipper would end up eluding me forever, though I was with some worthy contenders like General Nediym, Reward For Effort and Headway.

....

Living in Tulloch Lodge was great, but in my second year I moved into a flat with a couple of Queensland mates who also worked at Smith's—Donald 'Ducky' Baker, and Mark 'Boof' Currie (because every Australian should have at least one mate called Boof).

This felt quite grown up, since I was still only seventeen, though Ducky and Boof sometimes used that to their advantage, the rotten bastards. They'd sometimes sneak into my room when I was asleep and change my alarm. It'd go off, I'd jump out of bed and race down the stables and I'd find everyone was still asleep because it was still only about midnight. I'd have to bludge a spot on someone's floor to get a couple more hours' sleep.

Or during the winter when it got dark early, they'd set my alarm for about 6 p.m. I'd wake up thinking it was 2.30 a.m. and charge out, get halfway down Anzac Parade and think, 'Geez there's a lot of traffic around', before the penny dropped.

We usually worked with quality horses, but there were some rogues too. Ironically, it was one of the latter that earned me my first ever mention in a city newspaper, which, helpfully for telling this story, Mum still has in a scrapbook.

In January 1988, I had gone to Canterbury with Lygon Arms and this filly engaged in an earlier race, called Tjarra, who was handy but had some bad manners. I was bent down taping her hind legs, and the next thing I remember was waking up in hospital. I found out the horse had kicked me on the top of the head and knocked me straight out.

The next day, under a headline of 'Injured Strapper's Tip Wins', the *Daily Mirror* reported that, as I was being carried away on a stretcher, by way of gratitude I kept saying to the ambulance blokes: 'Make sure you back Lygon Arms!'

Thankfully, when I woke up I found out Lygon Arms had indeed got up. In another sign of how workplace practices and concussion management has changed, they let me out of hospital that evening and I went to work at 2.30 the next morning.

There were some other horses people had to keep an eye on as well. Randwick being where it is, you'd hear stories of horses getting loose and heading down Anzac Parade for a trip into the city. Imagine seeing your expensive thoroughbred do that! The police called us one Sunday and I had to go fetch one from the Sydney Cricket Ground, though it turned out to be one from the Betty Lane stable. She gave me $20 for dropping it back.

I didn't see a Smith horse get away, on land at least.

As late as the late eighties, there was no pool for horses at Randwick. That staggers me, since I value swimming so highly in training. We used to swim our horses in Botany Bay, beside the Sydney Airport runway. Some would be towed behind a rowboat, but I'd volunteer to swim in the water with the horses (thanks to that pie shop, I had a good layer of protection from the cold in winter). You swam out in front of the horse holding its lead and then, as it came to you, you got under its neck and wrapped your legs around its neck from below, holding onto the reins so you could steer it. It's certainly one way of getting intimate with your horse. The main trick was when you were getting back to the beach you had to swim away in time, or they'd walk out straight over the top of you.

One day a horse got away from a colleague, swam about 300 metres away, and went into someone's backyard. The owner shut his back gate and kept the horse there. It made the TV news: that someone had found this racehorse in his backyard. We got him back, thankfully, since he showed some promise. This sort of thing never happens to the slow ones.

Things were going well enough for me that, at eighteen, I was also asked to take two horses—the favourite Wolseley Road, and long-shot Unforeseen—to the Gold Coast for the second Magic Millions colts and geldings race in 1988. It must have gone well, since I don't remember much about it, other than we didn't win.

Soon after this, Lygon Arms earned me another feather in my cap: the strappers' award for best-presented horse at Randwick on George Main Stakes day. Mum's kept a photo of me making what I assume was my first-ever acceptance speech. (I must have gone after the winning jockey, because I'm stooped down to speak into the microphone.) I remember being pretty proud about it. I was proud to get anything back then! I didn't know, of course, that I'd go on to judge similar awards in later life.

I learnt a massive amount at Smith's, but again, though I worshipped Tommy, you couldn't train today's finer horses as hard as he did. They all had the famous T.J. Smith 'muscle and bone' look. Bart Cummings' horses, by contrast, had that Cummings look—big and round and gross and massive.

Bart would set a horse for one race, like the Melbourne Cup. Tommy would too, but he'd want to win every lead-up race as well. While Smith's was a massive factory with a high rotation of horses, I particularly admired Neville Begg for his patience with horses, especially the fillies and mares. That was something I'd need a lot of with Black Caviar.

After about two years at Tommy's, I thought I'd try learning from a different school. With a mate from Begg's stable, I got to work with the great Colin Hayes at Lindsay Park in South Australia. He'd revolutionised things with that training and breeding complex. Horses worked in laneways, up and down hills. It was good to see there was an alternative to just belting them round a track every day, like at Tommy's. There was an accent on variety, which would be one of the keys to my training approach.

But with respect to Hayes, I didn't learn a lot there. For starters, there was only one trainer to watch. Plus, as newbies, we weren't involved in anything much. I did get to meet my future adversaries in David Hayes and Tony McEvoy, who was Colin's foreman, but after three months we pulled the pin.

I went back to Smith's, but after a couple of months I decided I wanted to go home to Charleville. I was about to turn nineteen and wanted to be a young bloke in the bush again—play a bit of footy, drink a bit of grog. Mum was still there and she had a couple of horses I would train, besides getting some others.

Most importantly, I think I'd decided by then that I knew everything!

4

Teenage Trainer

Tommy Smith had Bragger. Colin Hayes had Surefoot. Bart Cummings had Wells. They say trainers always remember their first winner.

Not me.

To be kind to myself, I guess it might say something about my business-like approach, my habit, conscious or otherwise, of flicking out of my brain stuff that isn't important anymore. In turn, that's possibly connected to my clear No. 1 credo as a trainer—keep it simple.

For the purposes of this book, I narrowed it down to two horses, Solo Sailor or Laurentilla. Further research—some calls to Mum—confirmed it was Solo Sailor, winning a 1400-metre maiden at Charleville, on 23 July 1988, eight days before I turned nineteen.

I can't recall the race, whether I was jumping up and down in a head-bobbing finish or sucking on a fag as the thing pissed in by ten lengths. I'm not sure what instructions this teenaged trainer gave to the jockey, though I do at least remember that was Ken Pope. (He'd go a long way from those humble settings too, winning an Oakleigh Plate at Caulfield in 2009 on Swiss Ace.)

But I'm sure it would have been a thrill. In this period back in Charleville anything resembling a solid achievement was no doubt a thrill.

You might call this my 'gap' half-year—before I got my act together. To put it less kindly, I didn't really have an act.

I was ambitious, yes, but also keen to be a young lout in the bush again. But I at least felt I was going to be a horse trainer. Well, sort of. Training was a strong passion, but I wasn't sure I could make a living out of it. I was probably too young to know definitely what I wanted to do, but training was something I could have a dab at.

First, I had to source my stock—my horses—and this happened in typical bush fashion. There were no yearling sales, no auctions of tried stock. Instead, one day a truck pulled up at Charleville racecourse and out hopped Barry Miller.

Waljo, as we call him, was a mate of Dad's from Cunnamulla who had set up in Brisbane and would have great success there, training one of Queensland's best horses, Show A Heart. But at this stage Miller was a bloke doing his best. He was taking a trip somewhere, with a truckload of horses to sell on the way. I got Solo Sailor and Laurentilla from him. I then had to do what trainers always have to do, whether it's Solo Sailor or Black Caviar—convince some owners to pay for them. The need was acute. Despite my years at Smith's and my hobby of loan sharking, I didn't have a pot to piss in.

Bill and Dot Goodman lived across the road from Mum, and I'd known them since I was a kid. All these years later, I convinced them to part with five or six hundred bucks for the thrill of owning a racehorse in Solo Sailor. And thus they became the first owners I ever trained for. They probably just felt they could help keep me off the streets.

Then Vaughan Johnson, a family friend and state MP for Longreach, bought old Laurentilla for me.

I was away, I thought. What actually unfolded was a very tough grind.

Solo Sailor eventually won two or three races, though it was a drastic change from those heady days in Sydney. Here's a contrast: I'd gone from leading in a horse who ran second in a Golden Slipper to having a horse that ran second twice in a day. At least it wasn't by design.

I'd taken Solo Sailor to Morven, 60 miles east of Charleville, and he ran second in an early race, which had attracted a bumper entry of three horses. But the stewards decided that since one of the barriers hadn't opened, thus inconveniencing a third of the field, they'd run it again after the last. Solo Sailor got nutted again there. The shame was that one of the original three horses had already left, so he was second of two.

Old Laurentilla had been through the mill. I'm not sure I ever won a race with him, but I did take him to one big meeting—the Enngonia Cup, in northern New South Wales, where the prizemoney was better. We made that six-hour round trip to get beaten a lip again. I felt I was a long way from Royal Randwick.

I picked up another horse when old Scarlet Beau came back into my hands. Raced by local identity Ted 'Fruity' Bruton, he was the horse we had raced twice in a day (intentionally) at Wondai for old Frank four years earlier. He was old enough to vote by the time I convinced Fruity to give him to me, but we had some fun with him.

By that, I don't mean punting. Racing's never been about that for me. I've seen too many people grabbed by it and it's like alcoholism—it can become a disease. Instead, I got my adrenaline fix out of training horses, and trying to win a dollar that way. As time went on I'd have to say to some clients: 'Look, we're not a punting stable. I can tell you how your horse is going, but I'm not going to set it up for any big punting sting'.

In any case, my attempts to make a living out of training horses back then were such that I couldn't afford to bet. Still, I was having a bit of fun. I'd drive long distances to take to the races on a Saturday, then on Sundays take another long drive to play footy. I was enjoying that, playing in a tough bush league with blokes good enough to make it in the city had they tried. However, I blew out my knee in one game and it finished me for the season.

I'd finally get both knees operated on about eight years later, by doctors who were stunned I'd put up with them for so long. But when I blew the knee out the first time I couldn't afford to do anything about it. As a trainer, I wasn't exactly setting the world on fire. In fact, I had to take other jobs to get a quid. With Mum working at the CES, I had the inside running on several positions, none of them any good.

I worked at a mechanic's, bringing no mechanical ability whatsoever. I did some unskilled labouring. I worked with a refrigeration mechanic. I put the air-conditioning ducts in the ceiling of Charleville racecourse's new grandstand. (Now that was a prick of a job, getting in there amongst all the prickly fibreglass insulation. It made you as itchy as hell, but I did it.) It was tough going, and my career path still wasn't totally clear. I knew I had an affinity with horses, but I couldn't honestly say I was good with them yet. Horses like Solo Sailor and Laurentilla—did I get the most out of them? Probably not. I'd taken plenty of knowledge in but I probably still hadn't learnt.

Laurentilla used to run second a lot. I've no doubt now I'd know how to cure him of that and make him win, but back then I probably wasn't applying too much science to it. I vividly recall one such second place at Blackall one day, because I smashed my ute up on the drive home by hitting a roo. Or a pig. Or both. The ute sat in the panel beater's for a month because I couldn't afford to fix it. Finally, Laurentilla's owner, Vaughan Johnson, paid to get it fixed.

These were the less than auspicious early days of my training career. While I had a bit of fun, I eventually realised it was going to be very hard to make a living being a racehorse trainer out there. And I was just too young, and didn't have the right mentality.

Thankfully, after about six months, I was thrown a lifeline from someone I call a huge influence on my life. This time it wasn't a mate, or even my mum. It was someone I'd never heard of.

5

Foreman Material

A friend rang from Sydney late in 1988 and said the trainer she worked for, Bill Mitchell, was looking for a stable foreman. I responded without hesitation.

'Who?'

I'd knocked around in Sydney but I'd never heard the name before. It turned out he was a young trainer himself. And the name was a pretty good one.

He was the son of a man universally known as 'J.D.', though his full name, best said in a posh accent, was Major James David Mitchell. The family had come from England in the 1960s with their three royally named sons, Arthur, William and Harold. They were a little bit the opposite of myself (though had I known then that I was related to a baronet I might have bandied that about a bit). The boys had been educated at a highbrow Sydney school, where Kerry and James Packer had also gone. I'd not heard of that either, but I'd come to remember it by a little piss-taking phrase I heard: If you can't have a little girl, have a Cranbrook boy instead.

Most importantly, J.D. and his sons were running Yarraman Park stud at Scone, which they had bought in 1968 from jockey George Moore. I was still pretty naive to the breeding scene but I came to know that Yarraman Park was one of the most successful privately owned stud farms in the country. While J.D. passed away in 2011, Arthur and Harry still run the place.

Middle brother Bill, or Francis William, ran the stud's racing arm. He had got his trainer's licence when only 24 in 1983, and when he contacted me he had just moved from Warwick Farm to prestigious Randwick. It seemed he was a young trainer going places.

The opportunity to go back to Sydney in the prime role of stable foreman, aged only nineteen, was a golden one. I didn't know anything about Bill. To be fair, he didn't know anything about me. But he later said that, being young himself, he had been keen to have younger people working under him.

I jumped at the chance, setting out for Sydney again in my freshly repaired ute. It was the longest of all the drives I'd done, and this one really sent me on my way.

....

I was on a one-month trial period at Bill's stable, which was actually a set of fourteen temporary Porta-Stalls on the hill by Randwick's 1600-metre start (they were still there in 2016!). We'd see if I fitted the bill—being Bill's No. 2 and managing the handful of older blokes he had there. It obviously worked because we were together for ten years.

I found Bill a great fella. He could have a bit of a brusque manner that could rub some people up the wrong way, but he was fantastic to me and I found him a very interesting trainer to work for. He was 28 then, so a couple of generations removed from the likes of Tommy Smith and Bart Cummings. That brought a fresh approach. He had also worked with Neville Begg, who I admired, and had had his mind opened by working overseas. He had worked in England with the also regal-sounding Fulke Johnson Houghton and—unusually for an Australian racing person—he had worked in the US, with Hall of Fame trainer Neil Drysdale.

Most wouldn't think of Bill in the same breath as a Tommy Smith or a Chris Waller, but he was a very good trainer—one of the best I worked for. With his worldly experience came unbelievable knowledge, and I learnt loads from him.

Bill would work out his horses' strengths and weaknesses. He'd be patient. He was meticulous at placing horses in the right company to win. I like to think that was one of my strengths later on, and I learnt a lot of that from Bill.

Placement was particularly important for us. It was a pretty small stable at first and Bill, a young bloke expecting his first baby, used to live by his wits a bit. He joined forces with Rod Quinn, who was a very good 'money' rider, and Bill would pick out a race, at Kembla Grange or Newcastle or some such, have a bet and usually win. That strategy was vital, because, while we were at Randwick, we only had a small team of mostly provincial-level horses.

It was great to observe Bill's patience, after the hustle of the T.J. Smith factory. Bill was also prepared to try new things: new techniques and new science. He teamed up with a very good young vet called Michael Robinson, who was ahead of his time in getting horses right. He was very advanced at intra-articular medicine, in which they used to inject a horse's knees and fetlocks and get them pain-free and able to perform at their optimum. That wasn't around much at the time, even at Smith's. But Bill had seen it in America.

Bill and Michael were new school. Modern. They explored all legal avenues to get horses as pain-free and healthy as they could. That was particularly helpful with our best two horses, From The Planet and Livistona Lane, who had soundness issues.

I've always been fortunate to have clever people around me who are great at diagnosing problems with horses. Terry Catip was unbelievable. Then, in the next era, watching Billy get the horses right, and Michael get them medically right, took it to another level. And years later I'd meet probably the smartest bloke I've ever worked with—chiropractor Michael Bryant, who worked with Black Caviar and many others of mine.

Picking stuff up early and treating it is crucial for a trainer. You have to be an amateur vet yourself, trying to identify minor problems before they lead to a horse breaking down completely. Of course the great complicating factor is I've never had one come up and tell me what's wrong!

....

Bill was more relaxed than most older-school trainers. He was diligent but he enjoyed the odd game of golf too. Maybe he just had a better work–life balance than I was later able to achieve when I got big.

He said to me once: 'Play golf? Of course I play golf! You've got to switch the phone off. Some owner might ring you, you don't know who it is, you don't know who his horse is, dunno where it is or what it's doing. You've gotta have a break.' He was also fond of a quote from Lee Freedman: 'You don't want to come into this game with depression. You'll get it soon enough.'

The result was Bill would leave a lot of the running of the stable to me, which suited me fine. Bill would in fact say years later that I was 'on a mission'—eager to be involved in all parts of the business: races, sales, vets, farriers, dentists. He was pretty right. He also marvelled that I powered along on the healthy staples of cigarettes and Coke, without the need for coffee, which I've never acquired the taste for despite the early starts.

The responsibility was great for me, though at times the older blokes working under me weren't that pleased about it. Some were excellent horsemen, but probably not as reliable as you'd need in a fair-dinkum stable. One was Charlie Cloos, the trackwork rider I'd learnt a lot from at Smith's. Another was Alan Unwin from the big Unwin racing family of Rockhampton. They were a fair bit older than me but probably didn't want the responsibility of running a stable.

It was a little hard. There were blokes you'd admired and who had helped you grow up, and now you're their boss. I had to tell them to pull their heads in, on occasion. I was maybe a bit forthright, but you'd see things that weren't being done right and you'd have to say something, and they wouldn't be happy about it.

Again, the conflict resolution systems in use back then were pretty rudimentary, which is a nice way of saying that maybe they told me to pull my head in and I probably told them to get fucked. I was a big boy, not with any raps on myself as a pugilist—I've always been more of a pacifist, really—but no one messed around with me. Still, there was a bit of resentment from the older blokes. So much so that one day, after I'd been there a couple of months, they staged a full-blown mutiny.

I must have been working them too hard, or we'd probably exchanged a few choice words, because these four blokes one day marched up to Bill and said: 'Either he goes, or we go!'

Bill sized up the revolt and said: 'Oh. That's a bit sad.' He gave them their wages and they left.

That showed some backbone from Bill, and made me feel ten foot tall. The downside, of course, was that there was now me, Bill and one young kid to run the stable. We were working our arses off for a while there until we built the staff up again.

....

With all this care, patience, attention to detail and the odd betting coup, the stable soon expanded—from fourteen boxes when I started, to 24, then to 34.

While we had mostly provincial horses at first, we also had From The Planet and Livistona Lane. They were pretty unexposed at first, but they became Group 1 horses and our flag-bearers. From The Planet won one of the big Randwick 'miles' that started just beside our stables—the Epsom Handicap in 1989. Livistona Lane came close to winning two in one year, running second to Super Impose in the Doncaster and Epsom of 1991.

We also got to have the wonderful Queensland colt Stylish Century, though we didn't get to enjoy him too much. He was a fabulous horse who won three Group 1s, but he could have had greater success if better managed. Here was an early lesson in dealing with owners, in this case, the enigmatic Dick Monaghan.

Stylish Century was first trained on the Gold Coast by Noel Doyle, who stabled with us when the horse finished mid-field in the 1989 Golden Slipper. Dick then switched to Bart Cummings, who won the Group 1 Spring Champion Stakes with him at Randwick. The unknown owner and the legendary trainer were in disagreement, however, over Dick's desire for the horse to lead. After he finished tenth in the Caulfield Stakes in his next race—when a blundered start cost him any chance of leading anyway—he was taken off Bart and given to Bill.

Dick wanted Stylish to run in the Cox Plate, just like he pretty much wanted him to run in everything. Bill only got him ten days before that race, but our instant stable star came agonisingly close to winning, nutted on the line by Colin Hayes' Almaraad.

A week later, Stylish Century led throughout to impressively win the Victoria Derby, giving Bill his second Group 1 after From The Planet's Epsom a few weeks before. In a major surprise for Bill,

Dick then paid a late acceptance fee to have the horse start in the Melbourne Cup. Under a postage-stamp weight of 47.5 kilograms, he led, of course, but was gone by the 600 metres and ran a distant last.

We had him for another year, for two more wins and four seconds. We sent him into the 1990 Japan Cup, but that went horribly. His jockey Kevin Moses hopped off to fix something on the way to the gates, and Stylish bolted, galloping 1000 metres full tilt. Controversially, he was declared fit to run, but finished tenth, to Australia's Better Loosen Up.

That, sadly, was the end of us and Stylish Century. After Japan, Dick decided he'd take out his own licence and train the horse himself. All up, I'm told the horse had almost as many trainers as wins, with seven conditioners and eleven victories.

Stylish Century was a lovely, nuggety little colt with a great nature, and unbelievable ability, winning three Group 1s and coming second in three others. But no one saw the best of the horse because of the owner's pressure to run him and run him and run him. He could have been better if handled better—less racing and more patience. When so much can go wrong with a thoroughbred anyway, throwing a headstrong owner into the equation can be a trainer's worst nightmare.

....

While Stylish Century was in Japan I had my first overseas trip by taking Livistona Lane to the Hong Kong Cup. I think I went there and not Japan because Livistona Lane needed a lot of maintenance, which I guess was a vote of confidence in me.

It was an unbelievable, eye-opening experience for this 21-year-old from the bush. It wasn't quite my first time on a plane—but I did have to get a passport organised. The trip was memorable for a few reasons. The horses were basically just in the back half of a passenger plane, rather than the special treatment or separate planes they have now.

The other boys and I—there were a few of us going from different stables—could sit and watch a movie, then step through the back door and go have a look at our horses.

This trip was also about the only time I slept in! My alarm didn't go off one morning at the quarters where we stayed at Sha Tin race-course. Thankfully, I felt a thump and woke up with jockey Jimmy Cassidy standing over me saying, 'Are we gonna work this bloody horse today or what?' We had to scramble to the track for our allotted time and only just got there, otherwise Livistona Lane would have missed a vital work-out.

And unfortunately the horse was second again! It shot to the front on straightening but the 1800 metres just found him out and he was caught by another Sydney horse, Kessem.

These being the early days of international horse travel, we then came home to do quarantine—not at the well-appointed Werribee complex they have now, but in a little yard under Melbourne's Westgate Bridge.

It was a great trip, a good learning experience for a young bloke. And for a small stable like ours to have two horses going to places like those was just phenomenal. It showed Bill was on the right path, and I was learning from him all the time.

....

It was during these five years with Bill in Sydney that it really solidified for me: I wanted to be a horse trainer.

Bill would leave me to my own devices a bit, since he was often away at carnivals, and I was part of the decision-making process, rather than just following orders like at Smith's.

I learnt how to train with Bill's horses, how to do different things. I probably had too much of the T.J. Smith 'bull at a gate' mentality about me, whereas with Bill I learnt more patience. We got a lot of satisfaction in teasing results out of these unsound horses, especially our stars From The Planet and Livistona Lane. And Bill showed me the importance of placing your horses well. Coupled with my background of travelling around the Queensland bush, this would help shape my whole training approach. It was just really satisfying to see horses win. Even a Kembla Grange maiden if that's their level—it's still satisfying.

So in Melbourne, years later, I'd have no qualms taking a moderate horse to somewhere like Donald or Bairnsdale to get a win out of them. When I first moved down there other trainers would take the piss out of me for going to these places. It wasn't the done thing, I suppose, if you wanted to be considered a big-time city trainer.

'Where are you going today, Pete?' they'd say at trackwork. 'Swan Hill? Stony Creek?'

From under my trademark white floppy towelling hat, which they also took the piss out of, I'd chirp back: 'Traralgon!' 'Murtoa!' 'Warracknabeal!'

I didn't give a stuff. I'd come from a place where we drove vast distances for a race, like the 375 miles to Wondai. It was nothing for me to drive to somewhere like Donald, 175 miles from Melbourne. In the bush you'd drive that far for a feed of Kentucky Fried Chicken.

I did like to go to these tracks myself, rather than send a stable representative. I always said that, if I didn't go, it'd be like a footy coach not turning up to watch his team in a match. This did get harder later on, when our team got big. Sometimes I'd still be at Caulfield working horses when the float would have to leave to get to the bush track in question on time.

And you'd get a thrill for the owners. I read a stat that said of all the thousands of yearlings sold every year, only 3 per cent of them go on to actually win a race. They're tough odds.

This approach in Melbourne helped me develop a very good strike rate, and to win the Victorian country trainers' premiership in only my second full season down south, 2003–04. (I might have thought I'd get a few more but Darren Weir came along. I finished second to him no fewer than ten times! I did pick up three overall state premierships though, for city and country combined, from 2009 through 2012.)

Perhaps the best thing about travelling, though, was the psychological effect it had on the horses. It taught them to be winners.

There is nothing more frustrating than a horse who's got loads of ability but won't apply itself. We've all met people who had the ability to make loads more of their lives than they did. Horses are exactly the same.

You'd get horses who, I guess, take the soft option. They're a herd animal. Their instinct is to run at the front of the herd. But then some decide to just run with the pack. You'd keep checking if there was some health issue, but you wouldn't find one.

Or you'd see horses just get sick of it all. The harder they're ridden, the less they'd try. They'd be like: 'Bugger that'. The horse just needed some encouragement to stretch its neck out and hit the line.

Taking horses to the bush and getting them to win an easy race would have a profound impact on their heads. They don't know if they're in a Cox Plate or a Moe maiden. You made them feel ten foot tall and bulletproof. Winning or losing can become a habit for horses, as with people. They can get into a rut, or things don't fall into place, and the easy option is to not put in. I'd hate to see my kids do it, and I hated seeing my horses do it. Encouraging them to find the line and win—that's a big plus.

And they do know they've won. They must know, and they like it. It's a different feeling from when they haven't. They know they get lauded and patted and people make a fuss. They know they can run past other horses. I'm sure they learn to become winners, or to try harder at least. You'd see them back at the stable with a bit more spunk about them, strutting about with a bit more presence.

When we moved to Melbourne I brought with me this nondescript unraced four-year-old called Lecerbrac. We went bush and he won at Bairnsdale and Echuca, then Ballarat and Wangaratta. Deep down I didn't think he was city class, but he then won a mid-week race at Sandown. I then got an offer and sold him to Singapore for $100,000, and I just thought: 'Shit—that was just a very moderate horse, but he went bush and learnt how to win'.

Lecerbrac was no Black Caviar but had a special place in my heart. The name is Carbrecel backwards. Sarah and I named our property outside Melbourne using the names of our daughters, Cara, Breann and Celine. And Lecerbrac was owned by Sarah and my mum.

Going bush was very useful when I trained for a lot of stud owners and breeders, who wanted their well-bred filly to get a black-type win (Group 1, 2 or 3, or Listed races) to boost the value of their later progeny. You'd take these fillies to the bush, win as bad a race as you could, then look for your mid-week city race, then your black-type race to aim at, and slowly keep lifting the bar. You might then have your black-type race against a good filly who had been placed at that level, but because yours had learnt how to win, regardless of where that was, you were sometimes able to knock them off.

I've always loved country racing, and I think it's important to support it as well. What's more, there was always something in it for me too.

....

Life in Sydney the second time around was richly rewarding and a huge learning curve. I was still a young bloke, though, and still managed to have a bit of fun.

I kept up playing rugby league, with the local Kensington side in the South Sydney Juniors competition. It was pretty fair-dinkum stuff. One big bastard dropped me with an elbow one day. Concussion again. I played on, and went to work the next morning, but this time I did have a splitting headache for a few days. These days you would be off work. Back then I had an aspirin.

Another time some bloke stomped on my right hand. I got our vet Michael Robinson to X-ray it, and he found all these smashed bones. You couldn't do anything about it—just wait for the arthritis in later life.

I wasn't big into the social life, as I had to get up early each day, but I've been eternally grateful for one trip I made to the racing fraternity's pub, the Doncaster Hotel, just before my 21st birthday.

I was sitting with a bunch of blokes when a bunch of girls sat at the next table. Eventually, the girls invited the blokes over. They all went, except for me. I was getting ready to go home, since I had work in the morning. But then this blonde girl came over from their group, maybe feeling sorry for me, and started talking.

It turned out she was a Kiwi who rode trackwork. She had only just stopped off in Sydney on her way home, after working at Kerry Packer's polo establishment in England, so I was lucky to catch her. I felt especially lucky later on when I gave her a lift home and she surprised me with a goodnight kiss on the cheek. I thought: 'This is all right. I'll have to give you a lift again!'

Her name was Sarah Belcham, and we've been together ever since. She became Sarah Moody a few years later when we got married at Eagle Farm racecourse, and she's been a massive part of the success I've had. That's why, when we launched our business, I wanted it called Moody Racing, to include both of us.

Sarah used to ride in hunts, showjumping and jumps racing in New Zealand, and is a fantastic judge of a horse. I value her opinion so much that, when we set ourselves up in Brisbane, if I had the odd bet to get some extra cash coming in, it was because Sarah had ridden the thing in work and said she liked it.

She's a remarkable horsewoman, but also just a remarkable woman. She unfortunately had to stop riding work before long. As I like to say, she was the best trackwork rider I ever had, then I went and got her pregnant.

But later she ran the financial side of our business. We started with just a few horses but she continued to run that when we were at our peak and turning over $20 million a year—having taught herself how to do it.

She's also raised our girls, pretty much single-handed, which is often the lot of horse trainers' wives. We have three wonderful daughters, who, like their mum, are now smart, independent women. I guess that, to a degree, Sarah and I both being from broken homes meant we were singing from a similar song sheet. We didn't have plush childhoods, we knew the value of hard work, and we've instilled that into our kids.

I guess to use the cliché you'd call Sarah my rock, who has been a great support through good times and bad all the way through.

6

Northern Satellite

Throughout my training career I always tried to do a lot of things a little bit differently, as did Bill. So it was fitting that when it was time for me to spread my wings, that was done a bit differently too.

Typically, Sarah was instrumental in this. We both felt like a change out of Sydney, and I sounded out some owners about kicking off with a few horses in Brisbane. I went and got Bill's blessing, with a six-month timeline, and Sarah and I moved into a tiny bedsit to save our pennies. Things were still going to be tight. It didn't help when my car was stolen—though I was even more stunned when I ended up getting it back.

It was around then that Bill presented me with an idea formulated by a banker mate of his, Stuey Hudson. He would open a Brisbane stable, with me as foreman, while keeping his Randwick one going.

It was pretty revolutionary—a satellite stable, especially for an operation of our medium size. Bart Cummings and Colin Hayes had had stables split up, but that was about it. There was also no such thing as training partnerships then. We did apply to the old

Queensland Turf Club to be registered as Mitchell and Moody, but they knocked us back. It was going to be satellite-style.

It might have been Bill's way of looking after me. Or maybe he didn't want to lose me and felt I could bring him more success if I operated independently, but with his horses, in a different and easier racing environment. It made logistical sense too. The stable was notching up more than 100 winners about the place a year, so he was acquiring new horses all the time. He needed boxes to house them.

Bill proposed a partnership. Sarah and I would own half of the satellite stable business, which traded as FW Mitchell, Brisbane, Pty Ltd. I took out a car loan for about $15,000, but never did buy the car. Bill put in the same amount, and that was how we launched the Brisbane stable.

I went up early and rented stables from veteran Queensland trainer Pat Duff at Eagle Farm, then Sarah and I rented a house nearby. Bill then sent up half a dozen horses that had been running in the bush in New South Wales, which he thought were city class for Brisbane.

We soon built up to a dozen gallopers, with other tried horses from clients of Bill's and owners I knew from Queensland. One of them happened to be my mum, with a galloper we had bred together. Mum still had a broodmare called Sarah's Grace, which Tony Facey had given her a half-share in as a Mother's Day present years earlier. I arranged for the mare to be sent to a Queensland stallion called Space Appeal, and the result was Storm Appeal, a gelding who won a couple of races for us.

It was a novel idea, but it worked well, although Sarah, who rode most of our trackwork, didn't hit it off with Bill. She thought he was something of a stuck-up Pommy bastard. He could seem that way to people, though I never had a problem with him. Maybe that was my mum's quality of mixing with different types of people coming through. So there was a little bit of tension between Bill and Sarah early on, but they became mates later.

It was interesting, new and very stimulating. As the stable grew we had to employ staff. A girl called Tina Webb was the first person I employed.

Apart from fast horses, we had to get a fast cat. I'm not a cat person but you need one in every stable, to keep the mice out of your feed (though later at Caulfield so many of my staff would feed them that a mouse would have to walk into a cat's open mouth for a kill to be recorded). We also brought up from Bill's stables these infamous blue heeler dogs, Spot and Maddy. They were vicious bastards, who liked biting people, and Bill was sick of them. They once ripped the shit out of Jimmy Cassidy's new snakeskin boots when he stuck them under our gate. Another time in Brisbane I heard this commotion and went outside to find jockey Doug Messingham perched precariously on top of our gate, with the dogs barking at him from below.

As the horses started getting results, we had the money flow to keep the business going, which was run from Bill's office. Having them look after the paperwork and licensing matters helped. It let us just concentrate on the horses. We were happier living there too. Sarah had a good friend in Brisbane, and I got to see a bit of my dad.

It was an exciting new challenge, and the fact we had Bill's backing, rather than going it alone, was a massive help.

....

I've forgotten a lot of horses from back then but, fortunately, I was still writing things down in my books. They had become a bit different, though. Now we were running the show I thought I should get a big ledger to write down details of our horses' runs.

I've still got it now. It's a big thick 1988 diary, which had obviously been lying around for five years. On the front it shows what I'd decided to name the stable, from the handwritten black texta title: 'FROM THE PLANET LODGE—RACE RESULTS'.

It mightn't look entirely professional, but it was heartfelt. I thought From The Planet deserved some recognition, though the name didn't roll off the tongue as smoothly as, say, Tulloch Lodge. It never got as formal as having a sign made up or anything. It might just have led to people looking at this newcomer to the Brisbane scene and asking 'Where's the planet Lodge?'

At the end of each race day, I'd sit down with a beer and fill in my 'captain's log' with details of each horse's race, jockey, weight, barrier, margin, time, prizemoney and finally, 'comments'—my verdict on the run. I ended up keeping these logs throughout my career, though after a few years I stopped bothering with the comments. In time I ended up having a secretary to do it, even though you could look up all results on the internet by then.

The big book shows our first starter was a filly called Rebisca. She was owned by Brisbane bookmaker Freddie Lanskey, and always had feet problems. It wasn't an auspicious start: she ran twelfth of sixteen in a 1600-metre Eagle Farm maiden. It was the first time, of hundreds, that I legged the very good Brisbane jockey Jim Byrne onto a horse.

In my comments I've written 'not ready'. I'm not sure we were, either, because of our first four starters, three of them were Rebisca. She was at least placed at Ipswich and Gold Coast at her next two.

Our first win was a bit elusive. We had gone two months and eleven starters without one, capped by a tenth of fourteen at the Gold Coast from old Storm Appeal for Mum.

But then finally, on Australia Day, 1994—fitting for this proud Aussie—we got the chocolates when a horse we had brought from Sydney, Endorsement, won a 1350-metre Doomben maiden. Just for extra cheek we got our second winner the next day, with Whyalla also leading throughout at Ipswich.

Were we on our way? It felt like a start, at least.

....

After we had waited two months for that first winner, things started to tick along fairly well. The big book shows I saddled four winners in a row in April 1994, in typical geographical style—one at Gatton, two at Toowoomba and one at Ipswich.

Reading the book now is a great little nostalgic exercise. I'm glad I kept it, or I'd struggle to remember many of the thousands of horses I've thrown a saddle over, given a thankful pat to, or cursed the very name of over the years. It also gives me a chuckle seeing some of the things that went through my head in the comments. Well, I didn't think I should sugar coat it. It was for my consumption only.

Some comments were technically instructive: 'Hung out in straight.' 'Take blinkers off.' 'Tongue over bit.'

I was sometimes less precise: 'Something amiss.' 'Something not right.' 'Don't know!'

At other times the reasons were clear: 'Ordinary.' 'Very ordinary.' 'Plugger.' 'Weak.' 'Weak—sack.' 'Didn't try—retire.'

And at other more disappointing times the comments started to sound like a children's book: 'Dog.' 'Cat.' 'Mole.'

Poor old Aspen Belle—our second-ever starter in Brisbane—had four runs in early 1994. She went from 'disappointing', to 'better', before ending with 'suck' and 'suck'. She doesn't appear again after page one, so I assume she got shipped out. Similarly, eight months after becoming our second winner, Whyalla earned itself a 'SACK!!!' and doesn't appear again.

'No good.' 'Too fat.' 'Racing dreadful.' 'Did not partake.' 'Doesn't try.' 'Doesn't win.' 'Wouldn't win anywhere.' 'A. Joke.'

I would have told the owners, too, if their horse was no good. The best thing is to try to educate the owners that they're better off without the horse, and to get another one if they can. Some trainers talk up horses because they need the numbers in their stables. But keeping slow ones around wastes the owners' money and is bad for a trainer's business. Get rid of the slow ones, get a better strike rate of winners, you'll attract better horses.

That's why I've never bullshitted an owner. Again, it's the way you treat people. You get more respect and goodwill by telling it straight.

I once had an owner take her horse to her property for a spell. A keen rider, she asked if it'd be all right to take it for the odd ride in the bush. 'No problem,' I said. 'And if it should happen to throw you off, don't worry. You'll be able to catch it on foot.'

I also like the one about the trainer who comes to a crossroads with this underperforming horse and asks the owner what he wants to do with it. 'I want to race it,' the owner says, to which the trainer replies: 'You'll probably beat it.'

Occasionally an owner would get the shits and take their horse elsewhere. Mostly they would come back later and say you were right. Then you'd get some nark who'd take a horse away and eventually win a $5000 race in the bush. 'We won a race with that!' they'd say. It's cost them $20,000 to do it.

....

The odd jockey would get in my 'bad book' too: 'Bad ride.' 'Shocking ride.' 'Woeful ride.' 'Disgraceful ride!'

One bloke got a 'shocking ride' for a fifth at Gatton. And a week later he copped a 'disgraceful ride'. I don't mind outing him now because it was my apprentice Tony Haydon. He didn't last long as a jockey—not because of my bagging, but because he got too heavy—but we would have a long association.

I guess I used my people skills to get him back in the saddle in the first place, since he'd quit because of weight issues when I met him. After a few years he moved to Mount Isa, where the weights are heavier, and then he still got too heavy, so he quit and went to Melbourne. I'd later have to use those people skills again to annoy him into joining our operation there.

I'm glad I did. Tony became my right-hand man, a very clever 'mechanic' who was great at picking up problems with horses, and a big part of the Black Caviar story. We still give each other stick about those early days when he rode for me. To be fair, I did spot a 'good ride' I gave him for a win at Gatton (it did take two more years though).

The book reminds me how, when 25 and feisty, I wasn't scared of bagging jockeys for bad rides, and not just in my ledger. I respected what they went through, but I had high expectations. All the hard work of preparing a horse can fall apart very quickly in their hands. As I got older and hopefully matured, I held my tongue and waited till I watched a replay. If my suspicion that it was a dud ride proved correct, I'd maybe suggest a different way the ride could have been executed. But sometimes I'd watch and say: 'Well, he was right. He didn't really have any other option.'

I could usually move on from a bad ride, though I'd sometimes give them a 'suspension' of my own, and not put them on for three months or six months. But I would like to give them another chance if I could. Sometimes it was just because I'd think they couldn't possibly ride it that badly again!

You might sack a rider for good, but not often. Sometimes, in losing, they would learn a lesson about that horse. Put a different rider on and they would have to go through the same learning process. You'd also try to match a rider with a horse, on qualities like temperament or strength, so, even if someone put in a bad ride for you one day, they might be better suited to a different horse the next.

Some horses might need a dominant, strong rider. Others get sick of being dominated. They will run better for a female jockey, perhaps someone who is a bit gentler and has softer hands. On that note, I've never been shy of female jockeys, and there are some great ones around. I don't think it's because they move any better on a horse than the men, just sometimes they're a bit kinder with a horse, and work with them, rather than against them.

Then there's the contentious issue of jockeys pulling a horse up, or 'giving it a run'. It means someone has paid off a jockey to make sure their horse doesn't win. You'd be a mug to think it's unheard of, but I don't think I've come across it often.

When I was young and more volatile, I probably suspected the worst more often. But as I've become older, mostly I just think the jock's made a split-second decision to go here or there and it's gone pear-shaped, and the horse ends up stuck behind other horses. 'Have they given it a run, or just stuffed up?' It's more often the latter. But if I did suspect something, I'd take it up with the jockey, and not involve the owners, since it's often just one person's theory.

It's impossible to prove someone gave something a run. It might also just be a brain fade. It happens sometimes with young jockeys wasting too hard. They're getting around bleary-eyed, dropping piss pills, getting dehydrated and worn out, and their decision-making gets impaired. By contrast, when a jockey's in form their decision-making just clicks. They don't have to think about it.

I might have bagged some jockeys over the years but I do have the utmost respect for them—what they put themselves through just to ride, and then the courage they show on the track. There have been one or two who've done the wrong thing but, mostly, if a jockey can be blamed for a horse getting beat, it's more about judgement than intent.

....

Of course bad comments weren't the only things I wrote (they're just the funniest ones). But one very memorable ex-Sydney horse who did cop a bagging was Magnier. He was regally bred and could do anything on the training track, but had what you might call commitment issues. Over a few starts his report card read 'Didn't try', 'Suck', '?', 'Didn't try' and, worse still, 'Didn't try a yard'.

You had to try to out-think horses like that. You would underwork them in trackwork, so hopefully on race day they'd be rearing to run fast. I don't think I had many tricks up my sleeve then but we did finally squeeze a Doomben maiden win out of him—his only win in 48 starts.

Magnier's best performance was yet to come. We sold him to veteran Brisbane trainer Lyle Plumb Snr, and one morning he came off the track at Eagle Farm and just collapsed. He didn't move. It was all a bit sombre. They took his gear off and put a blanket over him, but didn't get a tractor to tow him away as it was a busy time of morning.

A few old trainers were sitting there, rubbing their chins about what might have killed him when, after about 20 minutes, the horse just got up! Everyone's just shat themselves. The old boys jumped up in fright, and the horse just trotted off. It might have been his final protest to show he just wasn't cut out for racing. It was one of the most bizarre things I've ever seen.

....

My first Brisbane winter carnival was quickly upon us, and it was a brilliant start.

Our biggest cheque in five months had been the $8400 Endorsement won for that first win. But Bill sent up a good mare called Let's Hurry, owned by his father J.D., and she comfortably won the Group 2 Sir Byrne Hart Stakes, earning $64,000. A lovely filly called Aragen, who had won three races in Sydney, came up and won the Group 1 Sires Produce Stakes, and $119,000. This was one occasion where Sarah's trackwork impressions led me to have a bet, at the handy 14/1. She then ran a gutsy second in the Group 1 Castlemaine Stakes, earning another $80,000. (Sadly, a year later Aragen fractured her pelvis in the Australasian Oaks in Adelaide and had to be put down. Sarah and I were shattered.)

Bill also sent up Zetoile, a lovely big mare I'd worked with in Sydney. I had a bit of training to do, dropping her back from two 2200-metre fourth placings to the 1500 metres of the Listed Winter Stakes at Eagle Farm, worth $74,000 to the winner. I freshened her up with a lot of swimming at Brisbane's Nudgee Beach, again with me under her neck, and on race day she won by a length under Danny Craven, despite drifting from 14/1 to a very nice 20/1.

That drop-in-distance win, and the victory of Aragen, felt like an announcement that we had arrived in town. They were important for Bill, too, in the infancy of the split stable.

As time went on, some people had problems with our arrangement, feeling I wasn't getting the recognition I deserved. I was never one of them. I thought it all worked beautifully, and I never felt undervalued. Bill would always give me a wrap and never tried to take the credit. Apart from being the decent thing to do, that was also him promoting his business. I'd be the same years later when I set up a satellite stable in Sydney, run by Clare Cunningham. You want to promote your people, to assure your clients they are very capable and that you're a slick operation.

....

That first year in Brisbane was an especially busy one.

On Sunday, 2 October 1994, Sarah and I got up, worked the horses, went home and got changed, then went back to Eagle Farm and got married. It was a great day, apart from the rain forcing us from the manicured saddling enclosure to the concrete surrounds under the grandstand.

It was a bit of a no-brainer, to put it romantically, that Sarah and I would get hitched. It was, however, slightly earlier than we'd anticipated, because so too was the birth of our first daughter, Cara, in January 1995. That was a big day too. We listened in hospital as our stable's Welsh Miner, saddled by Bill, won the Prime Minister's Cup on the Gold Coast. I remember doing a phone interview with a journo while in the delivery ward. Then, that night, came an even better prize in little Cara. (Perhaps because of the special memories, I've kept that cup to this day. I should admit, though, that somehow it's ended up as a water bowl for our dogs.)

Business-wise, we were keeping the till ticking through some fairly consistent gallopers. We were building in numbers, acquiring more staff and more boxes, which in Brisbane were scattered around the place, a few here and there, mostly in people's backyards by the neighbouring racetracks of Eagle Farm and Doomben.

We had some cherished, honest gallopers, like Flawlessly, who won the Listed Toowoomba Cup in course-record time under my old 'idol' Mike Pelling, and Knight's Run, an old marvel who paid the bills with a hat-trick of wins during a six-week stretch in 1996 when no one else won anything!

In three seasons, starting 1994–95, our tally of winners improved from 31 out of 234 starters to 42 out of 337, to a big leap of 62 out of 386 (a strike rate of one in six). The stable's earnings went from $478,000, to $611,000 to $1,356,000. If that sounds like an extraordinary jump, it's because of an extraordinary horse.

7

General Nediym

The spring of 1996 was fairly unremarkable other than one thing that was big and getting bigger. It was Sarah, who was expecting twins. Breann and Celine would come along in March 1997, and then the fun around the house would really begin.

On the track, things were a little quiet. I was getting a touch anxious for something to turn up. One stinking hot Sunday when I was mowing the front lawn, it did.

A car pulled up and out got a bloke who introduced himself as Ron Ashdown. He was a breeder, who had a two-year-old colt by his foundation sire Nediym, who I also didn't know much about. The dam was Military Belle, by the successful former Lindsay Park sire, Without Fear.

Ron had taken his colt to the Magic Millions sales at the Gold Coast with high hopes, but the horse played up in his box and took a chunk out of his leg. He then only fetched $20,000, with the buyers given the option of returning him if they weren't happy with the leg. They ended up doing just that.

Ron kept the horse, and had gone to find a trainer this day. He went to the Brisbane barn of John Hawkes—who had followed our lead with a satellite stable—but couldn't raise anyone. Our place was nearby, and as Ron was driving away he spotted me, and the rest is a very interesting history. While hard work makes good luck, sometimes good luck happens by itself, and you need it in this game. Had I not been mowing the lawn, had I been inside taking a leak, Ron might have driven on.

....

With Ron Ashdown heading a syndicate of eight owners, General Nediym arrived at our stables not long before his first start. He was a lovely liver chestnut who from day one seemed a very natural sort of horse—a real running type. When we got him into serious trackwork he looked pretty handy indeed. Already I allowed myself thoughts about the Magic Millions race on the Gold Coast a couple of months later.

At his first jump-out, at Deagon, I was ready to be impressed. But in fact there was this little grey horse, trained by Bruce McLachlan, and my bloke couldn't get away from him the whole 300 metres. Though they finished well clear of the others, I thought, 'Shit, this horse isn't as good as I thought', and went home a bit crestfallen. I was less confident than I'd expected to be for his first start—a 1000-metre two-year-old race at Eagle Farm.

While Hawkes' Brisbane stable had missed opportunity knocking with General Nediym, they had a very good two-year-old up there called Guineas, who had won his first two starts. Fortunately, the second one was only a week before General Nediym's debut, so we dodged him, but there was a highly rated filly up against us called Chase The Chick. Because of her, and our moderate Deagon jump-out, our bloke was a hefty 12/1.

I told Ron and his co-owners their horse should go well, without being too effusive. If he went badly, we'd have time to stop and geld him, then get him ready for the Magic Millions. But come race day General just blew us away, bolting in by four lengths, with Chase The Chick second. He'd never get near 12/1 again in his twenty subsequent starts. In fact, he'd be odds-on in twelve of them. I gave him a somewhat restrained comment of 'Class act'.

There was no such restraint two weeks later when he led again under the top weight of 56 kilograms and won over the same course—by seven lengths. His time of 56.9 seconds made it the fastest 1000 metres by a two-year-old ever in Brisbane, by half a second, and was just 0.2 seconds outside the track record. I wrote just one word: 'Freakish!'

I later learnt I'd had no cause for worry at that jump-out. That grey horse ended up being Classic Day, who won a Listed sprint up the straight at Flemington. And, in line with my initial suspicions, General Nediym turned out to be much better than him.

As with his first start, he pulled up in fine order. He'd also won so impressively that he wasn't going to lose his balls either! I'd soon need a fairly big pair myself, as we got to grips with what we had on our hands.

....

For his first two starts General Nediym had been ridden by Phillip Wolfgram, a lovely fella from Toowoomba, not long out of his apprenticeship, who had ridden a few winners for me. For a battler like him to ride one like General Nediym would be a once-in-a-lifetime opportunity.

But after that seven-length win I was, for the first time, thrown into that gut-wrenching situation most trainers come across. General Nediym would soon be running in some million-dollar races, involving huge pressure and the very best jockeys in the country. Not only were we heading for the Magic Millions, our little satellite stable now had the favourite for the richest two-year-old race in the world, the Golden Slipper.

I felt terrible but I rang Bill and said we should get a serious, experienced jockey. It would disappoint me later when owners would want a big-name rider on their horses instead of someone like Luke Nolen before he became well known. But with this horse at that time of his career, Phillip just didn't fit the profile we needed.

This is one thing from ages ago I do remember clearly. I had a knot in my stomach as I fronted up to Phillip at trackwork, but I just had to tell him: 'Sorry mate, you've got the drag here'.

It was the hardest thing I'd had to do in my life. He took it on the chin, but I can still remember the look on his face, and he was just gutted.

I hoped I was doing the right thing, but you just knew that if Phillip had ridden the horse in the Magic Millions and got beaten, the first thing everyone would have done was look at our jockey and say: 'You stupid bastards'. Still, it's always hard taking people's chances away from them.

At least Phillip went on to do well, winning a Toowoomba premiership. His son Travis is also showing great promise as a young rider.

....

With one of the most promising two-year-olds in the country, you wanted one of the very best jockeys around, and there was none better than Mick Dittman.

Mick had moved back to Queensland and, though now 44, he was still one of the best big-race riders in the country. He was an unbelievable jockey who had unbelievable strength on a horse.

So, about sixteen years after I'd first glimpsed him at Albion Park, here I was legging Mick onto Australia's boom two-year-old.

After the unpleasantness of sacking Phillip, I've got to admit that felt pretty good. Dittman rode General in his third race, stepping up to 1200 metres at Eagle Farm on Boxing Day. When horses go so fast over 1000 metres, you sometimes wonder if they'll have the stamina for the extra 200 metres, but at the Black Caviar odds of 25/1-on, he did it easily. Mick bounced him to the front in the eight-horse field and he won by two lengths in 1:11.90, about half a second off the track record, which he might have broken if not eased down.

I had to call Bill again: 'You'd better get up here, this horse is a little bit special'. I probably wanted his input to make sure I didn't fuck it up. When you're handling top horses, you're always worried about something going wrong. And soon I did get a major fright with the horse.

The Magic Millions, worth $570,000 to the winner, was three weeks away when I took the colt to Ipswich to gallop between races. Apart from Deagon, he had only trained and raced at Eagle Farm, so I wanted to condition him to different environments before his trip to the Gold Coast.

I asked Brook Swanton, who did a bit of riding for us, to give him a nice, soft 600-metre gallop. That was the plan, anyway. But this horse just loved to run fast.

Ipswich is a tight track, with an especially tight turn out of the home straight, where they go around beside the primary school next to the course. As I was watching, General appeared to get away on Brook a little and just seemed to get faster, and faster, and faster down the straight. He hit the line that bloody fast, I swear I'd never seen a horse moving at that speed before in my life. He then went into that corner after the post—and I started to panic.

He went wide. Way wide. He didn't run off or act silly—he was just going too fast to take the corner. Everyone else is staring in wonderment and I've just had to close my eyes. I couldn't watch. I thought he might just go through the fence and into the school, he was going that fast.

Thankfully, when I opened my eyes, I saw that while he'd gone to the outside fence, he hadn't gone through it. Talk about a horse being frighteningly quick!

But there were no scares on the big day, with General making it seem pretty unremarkable. I was nervous—something can always go wrong—but Mick was pretty upbeat. He knew what he had under him. We had barrier 13 in the sixteen-horse field, which was a bit awkward, but General Nediym had the brilliance to get straight across to the front and he was just far too good, winning by a length and a half.

It was a fantastic day, and pretty emotional, with Bill and Sarah both there. To win such a big race with a homegrown Queensland product, a horse we'd had in our Brisbane stable who hadn't been through the Sydney system, it was pretty special. The win also prompted a $1 million offer for the horse from Hong Kong, which the owners rejected.

It was all systems go to try to make General the first Queensland horse to win the Golden Slipper ten weeks later, and confidence was high enough that the owners didn't flinch at paying a $100,000 late-entry fee. However, that decision to get a new jockey, even one as great as Dittman, would lead to a regret that still haunts me today.

....

Tony Haydon and I took General Nediym to Bill's in Sydney a week before his run in the Todman Slipper Trial over 1200 metres at the Slipper venue, Rosehill. Mick asked me if he needed a good hit-out, since it had been two months since his last race. I said we could give him a soft run, since he was already having his fifth start and you never needed to do a lot with him, he was so bullish and eager to run. He got that soft run, leading the other six horses home comfortably.

I went home in high spirits, and when he drew barrier 4 for the Slipper, I was cock-a-hoop. He'd bounce out in front like always, use his natural speed, and good luck to anyone wanting to run him down. Except . . .

Mick suddenly didn't want to lead.

He had led in his three wins on the horse, but now, in the world's richest two-year-old race, he wanted to take a sit. As jockeys do for big races, Mick wanted everything sorted out, wanted to know how the race would pan out. He was worried we'd be attacked in a speed battle, convinced that Grant Cooksley would want to lead on the 33/1 shot Sports, and would take Mick on and worry General out of the race.

What do you do? I'm all of 27, not even a trainer, and the best jockey in the land and winner of three Golden Slippers tells you this is what he wants to do. It certainly surprised me, and Bill, considering the horse was so unbelievably brilliant. But Mick would have his way.

They jumped—Sports missed the kick. We were well in front of him after 50 metres but still Mick took a sit on our 7/4 favourite. Chris Munce, one of my favourite Queensland jockeys, scooted over to take the lead on 66/1 shot Regal Chamber. We were behind her, and on our outside was another unbeaten entrant: that other Brisbane horse, Guineas.

As Regal Chamber led, Mick was fighting General, dragging him back and holding him up, but the horse just wanted to go. It might have looked like Mick had got a beautiful run, third on the fence, but that wasn't how the horse liked to race.

And when they straightened, General just couldn't kick. There had been this battle between jockey and horse, and that ended up dulling the horse's brilliance. General Nediym tried hard, pushed up on the fence and hit the lead briefly at the 150 metres, but couldn't muster his usual dash. He was swamped and could only finish fourth, miles ahead of the fifth horse.

Regal Chamber, who had been allowed to zip along, beat us to third. A narrow second was second-favourite Encounter, trained by Slipper specialist Clarry Conners. The winner was Guineas. Of course there was no consolation from the fact the main prize went to a Queenslander.

The horses came back in to the mounting yard. Not a lot was spoken, but the feeling was massive disappointment. We were there, standing around, and we'd thought we'd be celebrating. Mick and I still haven't spoken about the race to this day.

A few thoughts still go through my head. On the Thursday before the race, with me still in Brisbane, General did a little too much work. He might have got away from Tony, who rode him. Or maybe Bill felt he needed more work. He was a deceptive sort of horse, gross but energetic, and I learnt you didn't need to work him very hard. He always blew pretty hard after everything he did, no matter how minor. I think he might have just had narrow nasal passages, or maybe even allergies. Others might have seen him blowing and thought he was short of fitness.

Still, the biggest factor was Mick not letting him stride along. It dead set cost him the Slipper. General earned $100,000 for fourth. The winner got $1.25 million.

I've been beaten plenty of times before and since, and usually it's part of the game. But here we are twenty years later and I still regret not just blurting out: 'Fuck it—just lead!' It's one of those occasions when a situation was over-thought. Again, it usually pays to keep it simple.

....

Funny how things change. Six months after the thrill of legging him onto General Nediym, I had to tell the great Mick Dittman he was sacked from the horse.

While I do value continuity in jockeys, Ron Ashdown and his fellow owners had been as disappointed as I was about the Slipper, and said they wanted a change of jockey. At least with Mick having had his share of success, it wasn't as hard as sacking Phillip Wolfgram. All the same, while Mick didn't go right off his head, he wasn't too bloody happy about it, I'll tell you that.

We engaged Brian York, a beautiful rider who had come from New Zealand to dominate in Brisbane, winning three premierships before moving to Sydney and winning another there in 2002. He unfortunately had to retire prematurely at 41 due to injuries and is now another prominent trainer—of show poodles!

Our plan for General Nediym was a spring campaign culminating in a second tilt at a Group 1. We hoped, having missed out in a Slipper won by Guineas, we'd win the Guineas instead—at Caulfield in October—and boost the stud value of the horse, who had furnished out nicely as a three-year-old colt.

General was able to show Sydneysiders his best in four straight black-type wins. With the 1600 metres of the Caulfield Guineas a possible challenge, we lengthened his Sydney races each time. We started with the San Domenico Stakes (1000 metres), then the Up And Coming Stakes (1200 metres), where he beat Encounter, the Heritage Stakes (1300 metres), where he beat Guineas, and the Stan Fox Stakes (1400 metres).

He mostly bowled along in the first two and won by three lengths or more, but in the last two he pulled very hard and Yorkie tried to restrain him too much. He won each by less than a length, though at least this time it didn't cost us a race.

I took the horse to Melbourne determined that nothing would be ballsed up. And would you believe it, he got a stone bruise. It's one of those annoying things that can happen. You put steel shoes on their feet but still they can stand on a stone and hurt the tender flesh inside the hoof; it becomes very painful.

The bruise became an abscess, and General missed a vital track gallop on the Saturday before the Guineas. He galloped well on the Monday but it stirred the foot up again. All week he was head-bobbing lame. We were bathing him, using poultices, and taking him to Mordialloc Beach to stand in salt water. It took a lot of effort from Tony and myself, but finally he could start in the Guineas, though he was a gallop short.

With a good draw in barrier 5, we convinced Yorkie to let him roll along. Starting at 5/1, probably because of the distance, he jumped well and led, but the problem was a bolter called Danasuria attacked him and gave him no peace. This was what Dittman had feared in the Slipper. But, that being 1200 metres, General could have easily won a speed battle and the race. Here, he couldn't afford to go quite as fast early. The end result was our bloke ended up going too hard. He still kicked in the straight and was three lengths clear at the 100 metres, but got swamped and finished third, three-quarters of a length behind winner Encounter.

It was a phenomenal run, considering the stone bruise and the speed battle, but we'd had two massive stallion-making Group 1s, arguably should have won both of them, and had won neither.

After eleven starts, I was starting to wonder if General would ever get the Group 1 he deserved. It sounds hard to believe, but I'd have that same nagging feeling years later with Black Caviar. Group 1s are hard things to win.

....

By now our family had grown to five and the Brisbane satellite stable had grown to 40. Or I should say 'stables' really, because our boxes were all over the place. I had to dart around a bit to keep on top of everything, but it was enjoyable. We were winning races, without setting the world on fire, and when you've got a good one in the stable it makes getting out of bed a bit easier.

We hoped General Nediym could crack that Group 1 by targeting Melbourne's autumn sprint triple crown—the Lightning Stakes, Oakleigh Plate and Newmarket Handicap. This time, I'd stay with the horse throughout, while Sarah stayed home. I'd have one horse to manage while she had the other 39. Plus three babies. Okay, she had some help. But as I've said, I couldn't have done much without her.

General had come back stronger, more mature, and was in great shape. We felt pretty good about the Lightning. He was a three-year-old taking on older sprinters at weight-for-age, coming in with a nice 54 kilograms.

In an eight-horse field something would have to go terribly wrong to stop us but, finally, it didn't. General Nediym won like an 11/8-on pop should, bursting out first and staying there to win by two and a quarter lengths down the grandstand side.

To finally get a Group 1 felt very sweet, and made us feel a bit vindicated after the two trouble-plagued misses. It felt so good, in fact, that Bill and I went out to celebrate with the owners. Racing can be a bit of a fickle beast, however, and it was at dinner where the trouble happened.

It came from part-owner Dave Jackson, a business partner of Ron's with a big bushy beard. He took a shot at Bill. I can't remember the exact words, but it was essentially that I should get more credit for being the real trainer of General Nediym. It was a real clanger to throw out there, when we all should have been just savouring a Group 1, and on what until then had been a good night out. It was awkward for Bill and me. And it was just out of line.

To clear this up once and for all, Sarah and I were very comfortable with the satellite stable arrangement, though others weren't. A few of the media in Brisbane used to make it hard for me too, writing 'Trainer Peter Moody'. Granted, that situation probably wasn't helped by the fact Bill rarely came to Brisbane and, when he did, he could be a little aloof. It was maybe a sign he didn't like Queenslanders. Sometimes this would even make things a bit prickly between us, and I imagine it'd agitate him reading such things.

Some people wanted to say that Bill was claiming the credit while I was doing the work, but it was never like that. The media knew I looked after and trained the horses up there, but Bill held the licence. I was always mindful to promote the fact that he was the trainer and I was his offsider. And Bill was happy to heap praise and credit on me.

That a few of the media people were a bit reckless about it would have stirred the pot as far as General Nediym's owners were concerned. But when Jackson piped up with his comment at dinner, it was a real sour note. What's worse, it was the start of the rot from the owners towards Bill and me.

....

The Oakleigh Plate at Caulfield was a further sour note after the Lightning wash-up. With not many really hot sprinters around, General got an astronomical weight for a three-year-old in that handicap of 58 kilograms.

Still, he was tough, and he had drawn barrier 2, so we were hopeful. General led but was taken on by a bolter called Ossie Cossie. You'd always have backed him to shake the other horse off but our 5/4 favourite was the first horse beaten, finishing fourteenth of fifteen. In my book I just wrote '?'

We had one theory. Just before the jump, a barrier attendant was in the stalls and General dipped badly in the back. The attendant might have accidentally bumped him, and I reckon the horse hurt his back. We also feared he might have choked down or swallowed his tongue, but the vets found nothing.

Thankfully, General was his normal self after the Oakleigh Plate, and we worked him as normal. We put a tongue tie on, just to eliminate the possibility that he'd got his tongue stuffed up at Caulfield, and in fact he did settle better with it on, working and racing less fiercely.

The bookies had us at 5/2 for the Newmarket after the Caulfield shocker, and at least General only had 55 kilograms this time. Bart Cummings' outstanding sprinter-miler Catalan Opening had top weight of 58 kilograms. Spicing things up a little, he also had Mick Dittman.

This day General Nediym really proved how gutsy he was. Jumping from barrier 11 out of 14, Yorkie crossed and led on the fence. With 200 metres to go, they just all came at him. He was going to get beaten every step of that last furlong, the challengers were coming from everywhere. Finally, three of them hit the line together, but General lasted on the inside to win by a half-head. Second was 16/1 shot Toledo, ridden by a young Dwayne Dunn. On his outside was Scandinavia, God bless her heart. Catalan Opening was fifth.

I couldn't have been more proud of our bloke. He'd now won eleven of fourteen starts and well over $1.5 million, and those two Group 1s were great stallion-making races. He was still only three and looked to have a great future ahead of him. And yet, we never had a good, clear, drama-free run with him for very long. Alas, that would be shown again in his next campaign.

....

By this time I'd pretty much decided the time was right to branch out on my own. I'd been with Bill for ten years, and it seemed a natural progression.

Growing up in the bush, you learned to ride as soon as you could walk. Here's me on the right on the first thoroughbred I had anything to do with, Doubtful, who was a suitably sedate old gelding for a five-year-old to ride. I won a couple of events as a youngster, though I'm sure they just used to tie me on and whack the horse on the arse. With me is sister Fiona.

First Seal? Me and big sister Fiona on one early exotic trip to somewhere near the ocean. Looks like I felt better around horses than I did around seals.

Aged around ten at Charleville Primary, where, in a rare bit of achievement in the education sector, I was school captain in grade 7. It wasn't long after this I started working with trainer Frank Cavanough before and after school. Frank was a cantankerous old bugger who dealt out some tough love. Mum used to make sure I was up at 5 a.m. when he'd come and get me, otherwise he'd sit outside honking his horn and waking everyone up.

With Frank's horse Coming Country, a speedy little mare who won a handful of races. We weren't exactly poor growing up, though that school shirt I'm wearing might still have been the best shirt I owned.

One of my favourite photos: Coming Country after winning at Roma one day in 1984 for jockey Tom Johnstone. There's me, with my trademark pen in my top pocket in case there was something I'd need to write down, and old Frank, looking suitably grumpy. Despite appearances, and the odd belting, he was very good to me.

Here I'd landed in the big time, strapping Tommy Smith's very good horse Lygon Arms. Unfortunately he and Peter Cook were about to run an agonising second in the 1987 Golden Slipper, to Marauding.

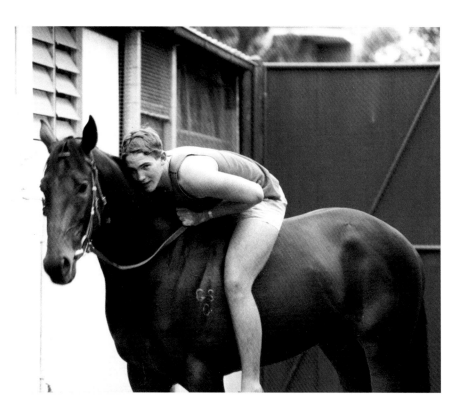

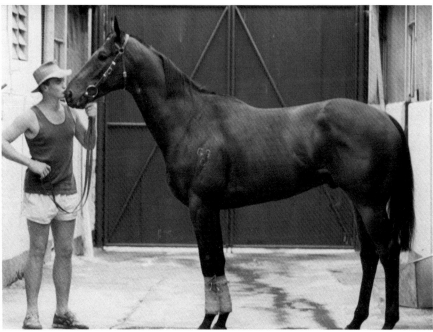

Having a play with Lygon Arms, one of my all-time favourites, at Tommy Smith's Randwick stables.

With Lygon Arms again, at Randwick with Craig Carmody up. Seemingly only a few months after leading around some pretty ordinary horses in the dust of the bush, I was mixing with some of the best horses and jockeys in the country.

I must have done something right in my time at Tommy's, because in 1988 I was trusted to take two horses, including this one, Unforeseen, up to the Magic Millions. I certainly looked the part, for the Gold Coast in the 80s, with the requisite white shoes.

Pretty soon after that I was back in the bush on tracks that looked not a lot like Randwick. Here I am with Scarlet Beau at a meeting place called Nockatunga, a station west of Cunnamulla.

Central Warrego Race Club – 23rd July 1988.

SOLO SAILOR

SOLITARY HAIL – CALL A SAILOR
BAY GELDING 3 YEARS

SOLO SAILOR winning BUENA SONIC MAIDEN HANDICAP of 1400 Metres.
Owned by W.K. & D.E. Goodman.   Trained by P.G. Moody.   Ridden by K.Pope.
Margins: 4 lengths x 8 lengths.   Weight: 56kg.   Time: 1min 26.6sec.
Second: BAZABRI.   Third: THE BLIZZARD.

A long way from Royal Ascot. My first ever winner as a trainer—good old Solo Sailor winning on the red dirt of Charleville eight days before my nineteenth birthday. Training in the bush as a teenager was, however, pretty hard going, and it wasn't long before I went back to Sydney.

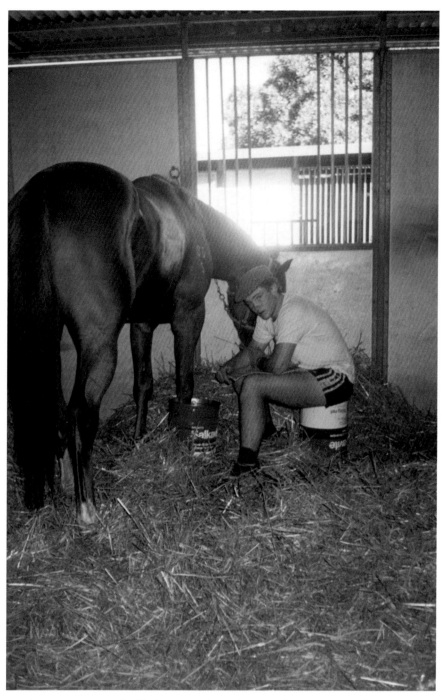

Working as Bill Mitchell's foreman from the age of 19 was great for my career. First, I had a lot of autonomy at a young age. And second, our two stable stars were quite unsound, so I learned a lot about caring for horses and being patient with them. Here I am giving From The Planet the ice bucket treatment.

Celebrating my 21st birthday in Sydney during my time with Bill Mitchell. In the background, with a quite magnificent mullet, is my old mate Brett Cavanough, who'd be with me at Royal Ascot with Black Caviar many years later.

With three of the great women in my life (L to R): Sister Tanya, Mum, and Alison.

Studying the form back in Sydney at the races, in younger, hairier days.

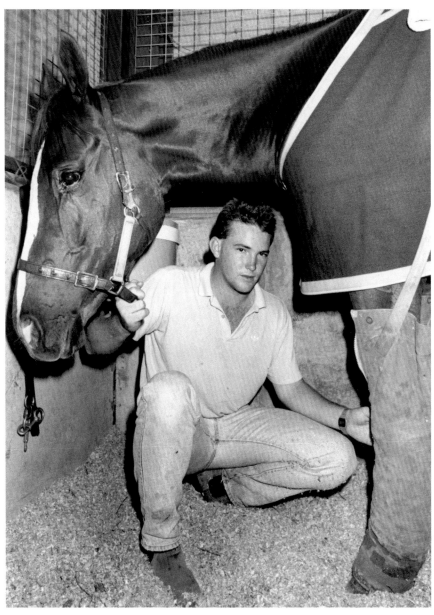

Here's another way of icing a horse's leg. With From The Planet at Bill Mitchell's stables around 1990. We had a good bit of success for a small stable, housed by the Randwick 1600-metre start in what were supposed to be temporary portable stalls, but which were still there in 2016!

It was all go up in Brisbane after moving there to run Bill's satellite stable, and with a rapidly expanding family on the ground. With me, Sarah and the kids are my mum Jan on the right, and Sarah's mum Ann Belcham on the left.

We certainly had our hands full. Sarah is a great horsewoman, and an amazing woman all round really, who's done a tremendous job of raising the girls almost single-handedly, while also teaching herself how to do the finances for a multi-million dollar business. I owe so much of my success to her.

With Bill Mitchell, celebrating our win with General Nediym in the Magic Millions. He was a brilliant sprinter, and gave me my first up-close experience of what it's like to have a real class racehorse on your hands.

Giving the General a pick of grass in Brisbane.

The General and I. You do get attached to horses who do so much for you. Showing racing's fluctuating fortunes, we pretty much fluked getting him when his owner drove by and saw me mowing the lawn in our front yard. Unfortunately we ended up losing him just as unexpectedly as well!

General Nediym was a very strong, muscular sort of horse. I'd never seen one travel faster . . . until Black Caviar came along.

Sarah and me, a good bit later.

Beers with an old friend. The girls and I drop in on Black Caviar in her retirement in the Hunter Valley. (L to R): Celine, Cara, Sarah, me and Breann.

Again, I put a six-month transition plan to Bill, and he was fine with it. We'd sit on it till the end of the 1997–98 season, then tell the owners. It did surprise me a little when Bill said he'd keep the satellite stable going with someone else, but it was working for him, so fair enough.

We would have to divide up the horses but it would still be amicable. Yet some people just couldn't accept that was the case, that I wasn't spitting the dummy and storming off. The only problem we were really going to have was who would get General Nediym.

In the end, the owners decided that for us.

We were eyeing the Queensland Group 1 jewels of the Doomben 10,000 and Stradbroke Handicap, after a first-up run in the BTC Cup at Doomben on Anzac Day.

The first setback came when Brian York turned down the ride. He'd stay in Sydney to ride Might And Power in the Group 1 Queen Elizabeth Stakes instead. He was a great horse and he won, but still Yorkie's decision blew me away. I was probably just annoyed that General would need his fourth rider in fifteen starts.

With Mick Dittman firmly on Ron Ashdown's banned list, we got Grant Cooksley, the Brisbane-based Kiwi who'd ridden Aragen in her Sires Produce win for us, and a few others. Fittingly, Anzac Day was good for General, who won by two lengths.

The hype around General was at fever pitch. Bob Hoysted said in the press he was the best sprinter he'd seen since his mighty champion, Manikato. There'd been a $2 million offer for the colt to go to America. The owners were talking about a European campaign, and about General possibly starting his stud career there.

Two weeks later, he went to the start of the 10,000 as a red-hot 5/4-on favourite. He produced probably the run of his career. Unfortunately, he finished third.

I probably should have stayed in bed that day. First, I suffered a flat tyre on my car and had to stop to fix it. Then I lost my mobile phone.

Then, when the race came, there was more drama because as the field jumped, two crucial things were missing. One was the racecaller's voice. Unfortunately for the club, its PA system chose Doomben's biggest race of the year as the time to break down. Many in the packed crowd weren't even aware the field had jumped. They were left wondering what the hell was going on as the whole race played out in a very bizarre silence.

Even more disastrously, the other thing 'missing' at the start was General Nediym. When the gates opened he slipped a little on the soft, greasy track, missed the kick and settled nearer last than first. In the home straight he weaved his way through and stormed home, but was beaten a length behind another great Queensland sprinter in Chief De Beers, and Clarry Conners' Staging.

I was disappointed, and pretty emotional after the race, but then I was gobsmacked when a few of the owners came to me and complained about Grant Cooksley. They had got it into their heads that he had deliberately done something wrong, missed the start on purpose and given the horse a run.

Now, I'm not going to say the odd horse hasn't been pulled up over the years, but in a Group 1? Worth half a million? Give me a break. The horse just slipped when he tried to bounce. I tried to tell Ron and his fellow complainants this, but I don't think I convinced them.

They weren't disgruntled enough to sack another jockey, but we then struck another hitch a week before the Stradbroke when General gave himself a whack somewhere and suffered a swollen tendon. Scans showed he didn't have a hole in the tendon, which can happen with blunt trauma, but when decision time came on the Tuesday I opted to err on the side of caution, not risk further injury, and get him ready for the spring instead.

I had Bill's approval, of course, and I thought we'd have a better General Nediym in the spring, with more riches awaiting, particularly up the Flemington straight.

First, we had a nice little distraction to attend to.

....

The Queensland Horse of the Year dinner was coming up at the end of the season, and the owners and I booked a table together, thinking General Nediym was a shoo-in to win. I'd given the heads up that I was going to split from Bill, so the question of who would train the horse was looming.

From when I arrived, though, I felt something was a bit off. Ron Ashdown was quite indifferent to me the whole night. I tried to have a little chat about who would train the horse, which was spelling at Ron's property.

'It doesn't matter which of us trains him,' I said. 'The important thing is he's got to get back into work for the spring carnival.' Still Ron kept dodging the subject.

General Nediym was announced as Horse of the Year, Ron got up to accept the award, and the rest of us were all smiles and pats on the back.

Racing is always full of surprises, but then two days later came one out of the blue. Ron said—not to me or Bill but in a Melbourne radio interview—that when the horse came back, he was going to go to Clarry Conners in Sydney.

It felt like I'd been smacked in the guts. I was just flabbergasted, as was Bill when I told him. Not only had it come completely out of left field, but I then learnt arrangements had already been made to send the horse to Clarry even before that day. It's fair to say I was pretty bloody pissed off about it when I spoke to Ron.

'These sort of splits are never amicable,' he said. 'I've got the best horse in the country and I can't risk it being caught up in the middle of this.'

I said: 'So what? It's irrelevant. Either he's in my care or he's in Bill's care. We're not going to walk in with a chainsaw and cut everything in fucken half!'

But the deed had been done. I gave Ron a bit of a gobful. I can't remember exactly what I said but I think I effectively conveyed that I was pretty bloody upset about it. I might have said he was kidding himself and that it was all a fucking disgrace and a joke.

And that was the end for Bill and me and General Nediym—still one of the finest horses I've had anything to do with, and probably the best horse out of Queensland since Vo Rogue about a decade earlier.

After twenty years I've still got a very bitter taste about it, especially the way it was handled.

You think of reasons: the insane suspicion about Grant Cooksley; Mick Dittman's ride in the Slipper. Those things kept being brought up, but it was just racing. Part of the problem is that, when owners get a good horse, it becomes their whole world for a few years, and they can obsess about it.

Had General run in the Stradbroke and stuffed himself, you'd never forgive yourself. The owners would have been within their rights to take him off us. But we erred on the side of caution, thinking of the horse and the owners, and here was our reward.

I assumed it was those radical thinkers Ashdown and Dave Jackson who were driving the decision. Two of the owners were a lovely old couple—Dr Fred Schubert and his wife Joan. He was devastated, and she was actually in tears about it when I saw her next, but it was out of their hands.

I did get a bit of sympathy, even from Ashdown's own brother. Plus, it was a bad business decision for Ron, since I'd had success with a few other Nediym horses I'd bought from him. I wasn't going to be putting many wraps out for the bloke. And Queenslanders being a parochial lot, I don't think he had many friends left in the state after sending General to Sydney.

I would have been happy if Bill had trained him. In fact, with Sarah and I making plans to go it alone, we would have been on a hiding to nothing taking General with us. He had always been a good horse. If he failed to fire for some reason, it could have killed my career.

It all ended ingloriously, and messily. General Nediym had five more starts and won only one. I think Clarry Conners might have been fooled by the fact he was a big blower, and poured too much work into him. The horse had been in line to get an invitation for a big sprint race in Hong Kong late that year, but because of his loss of form he didn't make the field.

His stud career was stuffed up too. He went to Ron's farm in Queensland. A stallion like that should have been in the heart of the breeding action, in the Hunter Valley or Victoria, to help have better mares sent to him.

Ron promised me a breeding right, which is a tradition for trainers, and sometimes jockeys, of stallions, but reneged on that after one season, when the horse was switched to the Hunter Valley. He sired some decent progeny, like dual Group 1 winner Regimental Gal. I bred from him once and got a foal that died. Sort of sums it all up, really.

General Nediym died at stud after a colic attack, at a relatively young fourteen. That was upsetting. It always is when it's a horse you're attached to. At least he became a good sire of broodmares.

Today, I've got a picture on my man-cave wall of me, Bill and the horse after his first big win in the Magic Millions.

He put us on the map, and gave us a taste of preparing top horses for top races.

8

Going Solo

It seemed like a neat bit of timing that after ten years with Bill—five in Sydney and five in Brisbane—I'd finally go it alone.

The satellite partnership had gone well. On the Brisbane trainers' premiership we had finished sixth in our first full season of 1994–95, then fifth, third—to John Hawkes' Brisbane team—and then fourth, with many country winners besides.

I learnt a lot from Bill—on horses, running a business and how to deal with people. Bill was well educated and very articulate. The experience I had with him, his brothers and father, had taught me a lot from the age of nineteen through to 29, had knocked a few rough edges off me and prepared me to carve out my own training career.

Things did get a little strained between Bill and me because, out of the 40 or 50 horses we had in the satellite stable, about 35 came to me. But mostly the parting was amicable. I kept leasing one of the stables we had and Bill kept another one as his satellite stable, this time run by Liam Birchley as an employee. After three years, Liam went out on his own and Bill closed his Brisbane stable.

Like me, Bill ended up at Caulfield, where we'd often be seen ribbing each other in the trainers' tower at trackwork—me calling him a toff and him calling me a scrubber from the bush. He retired in 2005 due mainly to a bad back. He's now racing manager for Segenhoe Stud in the Hunter Valley.

I hope he knows what a positive influence he was on my life, and that I'll be eternally grateful for the opportunities he gave me.

....

It was very exciting for Sarah and me, kicking off on our own and getting ready to have a fair-dinkum dip.

I've always believed in having a go. In fact, Brisbane journalist Bart Sinclair has described me as the biggest risk-taker he's seen in racing, and he's been around for a while. I suppose I've always felt you've got to back your own ability.

We did have our hands full, with three little kids and a career to build. This was when Mum came to the fore again. She had just retired in Dalby, but moved to Brisbane to run the books and help at home. Some staff from the satellite stable had come with us, and we ended up with some very capable people in our small team, such as my foreman, Bruce Deacon, and a young jockey who was apprenticed to me up there who I'd have a long and wonderful association with in Victoria, Linda Meech.

Our main place was still the sixteen boxes we rented at Pat Duff's stable, but again we had to stick horses behind every second house—six behind Hughie's place, four at Dennis and Marcia's, three behind old Bill's up the road . . .

It was a pain in the arse. The houses didn't back onto the track, so we had to hire more staff than we actually needed to walk these horses through the streets. Eventually, an investment group built a twenty-horse barn on the side of the track and we moved in there, which partly helped.

But it was an exhilarating time. I was a young father of three and we had our fate in our own hands. I put some colours together— dark blue, with white striped sleeves and cap—and we were away. (In Melbourne, because of a clash with someone else's, we had to reverse them to my better-known white with blue-and-white striped sleeves and cap.)

Moody Racing's first-ever starter was a grey filly called Resolute Lass, in a Sunshine Coast maiden, on 3 December 1998, ridden by my 3-kilo apprentice Cecily Eaton. She nearly got us off at 100 per cent, but clocked up her third-straight second placing, beaten half a length. Cecily dropped the whip in the straight, though that mightn't have cost us the win. 'Good', was all I wrote, fairly un-momentously.

Typically, our first eight starters were spread over the Sunshine Coast, Brisbane, the Gold Coast, Toowoomba and Lismore (a horse called Terrorist! Good luck trying to call one that today. It was clever, though: by Marauding out of Tourist Visa).

We went almost a month without a winner but finally it came on 28 December, our sixteenth starter. Again, I needed the book to be sure, but it was a gelding called Ebony Way at Eagle Farm, ridden by Jim Byrne. This time I was more effusive, writing 'Very good'.

Soon we would be up to about six winners a month. A lot of our horses were two-year-olds, which was important for our future prospects, but how Mum managed to balance the books in that first year I'll never know. We had a mortgage, having bought a house with some money I inherited from Dad, but we also had to prioritise the stable's many outgoings.

First came the feed man, then the farrier. Then the vets, general maintenance people, the gear suppliers, and the staff's wages. Despite six or so winners a month there wasn't much left for Sarah and me.

At least we both had a strong work ethic and never lived beyond our means. There were never any holidays and, if things were tight, we didn't do anything fancy, like go out to dinner. I might have looked flash driving around, but that was only because Bill had palmed off his 5-series BMW onto me as a sling one day, since he wanted to sell it.

We were helped by some wonderful people, who would stay with us for a long time and introduce us to other clients—like Fred and Mary Lanskey, who owned Rebisca, Rick and Merry Trivett, and Graham and Shirley Milligan. Graham actually paid my wages for about three months, and a few bills. I still can't thank him enough.

....

After setting up, it was time to think about the thing every trainer needs—horses. The 35 I'd inherited from Bill wouldn't last forever and were fairly moderate besides. Like with every business, I'd need to replenish stock.

Up till then I hadn't had much to do with yearlings. That had been Bill's baby. But now I'd have to up-skill. Obviously I had an eye for what a racehorse should look like. Looking at yearlings was more of a crystal-ball exercise. You look at physiques, the way they're put together and the way they move, and imagine what they're going to be like in twelve or eighteen months. I had to learn more about pedigrees as well.

I had great help in these areas from bloodstock agent John Foote. He also introduced me to the right people from the breeding world, first in Queensland, then in that great nursery of horses, New Zealand. I started doing what trainers do—buying horses at auction, then finding owners for them.

I didn't pull off any coups, but didn't commit any major stuff-ups either, though I probably bought a couple of duds, like everyone. I remember one I bought in New Zealand, because, when it got to us the thing had gone blind, having hurt its eye on the plane. There's that glorious uncertainty they speak of again, though I think the horse suffered from a lack of ability as well.

Thankfully, the dodgy buys became fewer, though two decades later I'm still learning. I'll confess to suffering the odd rush of blood at an auction. I'd get home and tell Sarah, who'd be doing the books, and I think she'd silently shake her head sometimes. I guess it's like a husband saying he went a bit overboard buying some golf clubs or something—only yearlings are a bit more expensive, and more prone to breaking a leg!

On the track, I was sniffing out races to turn my honest-but-moderate team into winners. That bore results with the first trainers' premiership I won anywhere, at Ipswich in my initial full season of 1999–2000. I was proud of it too. In fact, I've still got the trophy and I use it every day. It holds my keys by my front door.

In Brisbane, I came eighth with eighteen winners. Satellite stables were all the rage by then, with John Hawkes winning it, Lee Freedman coming sixth and Bart Cummings also featuring. In 2000–01, we were fourth in Brisbane with 28 wins, followed by a fifth with 26. We were consistent, without threatening the big boys, but I did win another Ipswich premiership in 2001–02.

The partnership with Sarah was working well, though we'd try to leave work talk at the back gate that separated our house from our stables. Sometimes it'd spill over if we had something to get excited about. Like Bravisa, owned by the Trivetts, who won three good races and about $170,000 in the summer of 1999–2000. Bravisa helped start the new millennium with a bang—my first city treble, on 1 January 2000—also featuring Apparel and Turnerz.

Not many people would remember Turnerz, but he was instrumental in my career, and I guess a little representative of it. He won two more races after that first one, and I thought, 'Bugger it—let's have a shot at Melbourne!'

Looking at the book now, I think: 'Turnerz, tenth of eleven in a Group 2 at Caulfield. What were you thinking, you dumb bastard?'

Tunerz then ran mid-field at Flemington. He wasn't up to it down there, which I'll put down to my inexperience, but there was a nice twist of fate. I stabled with Caulfield trainer Jim Conlan, best known then for winning the Newmarket with Miss Pennymoney the day Turnerz dudded at Flemington. Jim had stabled with us during the previous year's Brisbane winter carnival.

In Melbourne, he told me he was thinking about leaving Caulfield, and that if I could get a Victorian licence, I could have his boxes. So that ambitious failed trip with Turnerz sowed the seed for the move south.

It turned out to be one of two career-shaping trips I'd make in early 2000.

I went to the esteemed Karaka Sales in New Zealand with hopes of getting some good stock for our stable. I set my sights on this Straight Strike filly, and tried to get her but finished second. However, I recognised that the successful bidders were also from Queensland. It was Ron Wanless, a scrap-metal and waste businessman who had been a big trotting owner, trainer and driver, but had branched into gallopers, and his wife, Judy. I bowled up and introduced myself, and asked if I could train the horse for them.

They didn't really give me an answer. I knew they had horses with a few other trainers, so I thought that was that. But a few months later, Ron rang to say I could train the filly. What's more, I could have a colt they had bought as well, for a considerable $100,000.

The filly turned out to be More Diamonds, who would win two races at Ipswich and Gatton and earn $17,050, ending up in the ownership of my mum.

The colt was called Amalfi, and he'd turn my life around.

....

I would have looked at Amalfi but obviously I wasn't moved to buy him. He was by European stallion Carnegie, who had won the 1994 Arc de Triomphe but was still unproven as a sire. Amalfi looked smashing, and was lovely to work with, but I always feared he'd be on the small side. We called him Daley around the stables, after the manager of the Wanlesses' farm.

We put the colt into a barrier trial at Eagle Farm, and he went okay, but in the manner of a staying horse. I thought he'd probably stay, so I wasn't all that confident about his debut over 1200 metres at Eagle Farm in April 2001.

Here's what began a long, sometimes awkward, but mostly jovial relationship with Ron and Judy Wanless. Judy loves seeing her horses run. Ron, a former Australian polo representative, amateur boxer, national dragster and sprint car champion, and a five-time competitor in the Bathurst motor race, loves seeing his horses run—with a whack of his money on them.

I gave Ron a fairly cool assessment of Amalfi's chances before the race, saying he should finish on well. So Ron didn't have much of a bet on him, if he had a bet at all. The horse blew from 11/1 to 33/1 before starting at 20/1. And of course, he won handsomely, coming from sixth on the home turn under Michael Cahill to score by half a length. I was over the moon, particularly since I trained a double that day with Carbrecel (spelled forwards this time) also winning.

But it wasn't all happy for Ron, who gave me a bit of a bollocking for not tipping the horse. In mitigation, I hadn't said it *couldn't* win.

But, having not had a stayer of that quality before, I probably didn't realise how well they could sprint fresh. It was a learning experience for me too.

Perhaps to ease Ron's chagrin, or maybe just because I was a cocky bastard, I told him: 'I reckon we'll win a derby with this horse!'

I'm not sure that calmed him down much. And at any rate I was probably talking about the Queensland Derby. But seven months later the little colt would exceed all expectations.

9

Group 1 Glory

Just before Amalfi's debut, I'd made my first move on Melbourne. Jim Conlan told us he was ready to leave Caulfield, Sarah and I thought it over for about thirty seconds, then we launched our own satellite stable.

Looking back, I guess it showed a bit of ambition. Normally you'd think a trainer from Melbourne might set up a satellite stable in Brisbane, but here I was, all of 31, and with about 40 horses to play with, doing it in reverse. I'd never believed in biting off more than you could chew. But I did take big mouthfuls.

Sarah and I were okay in Brisbane but we weren't going to retire off it, and Melbourne appealed on many levels.

It is, of course, the home of the best racing in Australia. It's a great launching pad for tackling more moderate races too. Unlike in Sydney and Brisbane, there were all those country tracks—about 40 of them within a three- or four-hour radius of Melbourne—where you could find races for most horses.

Victorian racing was also superbly structured, with lots of fillies and mares races, and lots of three-year-old events. Queensland didn't offer anywhere near as much specialised variety. Furthermore, Melbourne was a great, central launching pad for taking horses on longer missions, like to Adelaide, Sydney or Tasmania.

And whereas Sydney was dominated by a few big stables, like Crown Lodge and Gai Waterhouse, Melbourne seemed more of an even playing field. David Hayes and Lee Freedman were at the top, but others seemed to get a slice of the pie too, like we've seen more recently with Mick Price, Robert Smerdon, Darren Weir and others.

I went to Melbourne to be interviewed by the stewards for my Victorian licence, which I was granted. I took with me Desleigh Forster, who was working for us, to run the stable. I sent half a dozen horses, and we were away.

I'd say people thought we were mad—bringing some horses who weren't exactly Strawberry Road to Melbourne—though I don't think anyone said it to us. I guess I was trying to boost my profile by winning the odd race down south. In hindsight, it was obviously our 'advance party' ahead of a hopeful permanent move. We had the security of the Brisbane stable, so we weren't burning all the boats. Still, we didn't want to go home with our tail between our legs.

The 'first fleet' included Othapus, a mare who had won two of seventeen, but had mostly been running against males. Her owner, Warwick Doughty, was the director of Sydney's Luna Park, so he was obviously up for a bit of fun and adventure.

There was also the eccentrically named gelding Eric, raced by some of the owners of our first winner, Ebony Way, and Australian Olympic Committee president John Coates. Eric had won one of ten, and was a last-start fourth of eight at Doomben. There was Red Aquilla, part-owned by Sarah, who had won an Ipswich maiden and nothing else from eight runs. There was Berlin, a mare part-owned by Stuart Ramsey, the breeder and meat industry baron who had Turangga Farm stud in the Hunter Valley. He became one of my favourite owners and a close friend. This horse, however, had won one of fifteen, with a last-start eleventh of eleven at Doomben.

No Strawberry Roads? More like Struggle Street and Battle Avenue.

On Sunday, 4 March 2001, our satellite stable had its first runners, at Sandown. Othapus ran third in a 2100-metre mares race. Eric came sixth of fourteen in a 1400-metre colts and geldings event.

That was a so-so beginning, but our next three starters all won. Red Aquilla became my first Melbourne winner, taking a mid-week Sandown Class 2 with Damien Oliver aboard. Three days later Othapus won a 2000-metre mares race on a big autumn Saturday at Flemington. Four days after that Eric got up at Sandown. When Berlin won a mares race there two weeks later, we had had seven starters for four wins. It turned out that training winners in the headquarters of Australian racing was a piece of piss.

Well not quite, but we were off to a good start, which helped attract more owners. I started to branch out. I sent Deployment to win a maiden at Moe. I found a mares race in Adelaide that Berlin won. Things were coming together, and pleasantly quickly too.

....

In August 2001, after my best Brisbane premiership finish of fourth, we brought Amalfi back for the spring. He resumed at Doomben over a longer 1350 metres, which had me more confident. I might have even tipped him to Ron, though the 4/1 probably still didn't make up for missing the 33s four months earlier.

Amalfi had grown marginally, though he always had been a strong bugger, and this time he won impressively by more than a length, earning an 'excellent' from his trainer. It was onwards to Flemington.

Two wins in Brisbane might not normally be strong recommend-ation for the Victoria Derby, but I felt he might go all right because he was by a staying sire. In the long run, Carnegie turned out a fairly moderate sire, so we got lucky with this bloke. Here was where having the satellite stable also paid off, because it made such a trip a lot easier.

We'd had a change of manager down there. Desleigh asked to move back to Brisbane. I thought she should stay in Melbourne, having done the hard yards so well, but she insisted. It might have been a bit of a lonely life for her down there.

In her place I put two blokes, Dale Turgeon and Jamie Unwin, a brother of Alan, who I'd worked with at Bill Mitchell's. He was mad as a cut snake, Jamie. Come to think of it, so was Dale. They loved a beer and a good time. I never had a lot of faith in their punctuality, or office-keeping skills, but I knew they cared for their horses.

I'd started shuttling between Brisbane and Melbourne and I was fortunate again with some good people looking after me. The Lewis family ran the Emerald Hotel in South Melbourne, as they still do, and I'd be there most nights for dinner. Their son Andrew was a great bloke to know, and introduced me to many future clients. These included caravan magnate Gerry Ryan, who I'd later train for, and who'd also part-own Americain when it won the Melbourne Cup. I'm thankful for the many people, like the Lewises, who helped me build my training career.

....

I was keen to get Damien Oliver to ride Amalfi through the spring. We had a bit of history. He had ridden that first winner from our Melbourne satellite stable, Red Aquilla, and the fourth one, Berlin. But the very first time I'd asked him to do the steering wasn't so glorious.

In 1991 I had taken a couple of Bill Mitchell's horses to Melbourne and stayed with Damien in a house at the Flemington stables of Damien's master, Lee Freedman.

On the Derby Day ten years before Amalfi's, I'd stayed at Flemington after the last for a couple of beers. I wasn't drunk, though I probably shouldn't have hopped in the car to go get a feed. I was driving along when up the road 100 yards I saw the police pulling people over after the races for random breath tests, and I've shat myself.

I parked the car and, fearing the cops had seen me, I jumped straight into someone's front yard. I crept over a couple of fences, then bolted—running all of the 400 metres back to Damien's house. It's fair to say I blew pretty hard at the end of it.

Damien hadn't had a great day, running second in the Derby on Freedman's Naturalism, but he helpfully volunteered to drive my car home, since he hadn't had a drink. We got to the car and he got behind the wheel and—bang—the police grabbed us both. Even though it had been an hour or so after I'd parked it, they had been waiting. This cop started in on me, telling me I'd been driving the car earlier, which I of course denied. Then they started on Damien to get him to admit I'd been driving, but Damien stuck solid and said I hadn't.

So there we were, a couple of young idiots arguing with the coppers, when who drives by but the king of Melbourne himself—Lee Freedman. He might have had a couple of beers too because he got out of his car and blew up. The cops told him to piss off or they'd lock him up too.

I said to the police: 'Look, just put me on the bag if you're worried about it—I don't think I'll be over!' Thankfully, they didn't. They tested Damien but he hadn't had a drink. Eventually the cops told us to leave or they'd pin something on us.

Ten years later Damien would be my hero again.

....

While Amalfi was shaping up as our stable star, some good things were happening for us that spring. Our sprinting colt Strategic Image won two Listed races at Moonee Valley. And Golden Fawn, a Stuart Ramsey–owned gelding, won the Listed Dulcify Quality at Sydney's Warwick Farm.

I put Amalfi in a 1600-metre race at Moonee Valley in mid-September. Though it was a lot stronger than his Brisbane races, he started at the new-style odds of $5 and ran a good second for Damien, beaten a neck by Freedman's Spitz.

On Damien's suggestion, we put blinkers on from Amalfi's next start onwards to keep his mind on the job. Still, Damien switched to Spitz for their next meeting, the Group 2 Bill Stutt Stakes, also over a mile at night at the Valley. I asked Scott Seamer to come down for the ride. He'd been a dependable jockey for me in Queensland, but would soon become a household name by winning that year's Caulfield–Melbourne cups double on Ethereal.

In the end, Damien missed out entirely when Spitz was scratched, and Scotty rode Amalfi to a handy third. He was a long $11 this time, because of the presence of John Hawkes' good colt Viscount and Rick Hore-Lacy's Dash For Cash, who were first and second.

I wrote that Amalfi was 'looking for further'. He lined up over 2000 metres for his next start, in the Group 2 Norman Robinson Handicap on Caulfield Cup day, when Damien hopped back on and, as $4 favourite, did the job, winning by a neck from Grey Song, and becoming my first group-level winner. Scott Seamer was unplaced on Ecstasy but made up for it in the Cup, beating Damien and Sky Heights *and* surviving Ollie's protest.

Amalfi's win capped a great week, which boosted thoughts of a full-time move to Melbourne. Three days earlier Brief Embrace had romped in at her first start, the Debutante Stakes at Caulfield. She was a bit of a wild child in the stables, but would end up winning $650,000, including flashing home for a narrow second in the Blue

Diamond the following autumn. I can't be dirty on the winner, though. It was Bel Esprit.

....

Brash. Cocky. Boisterous. They're all labels I've had attached to me. Usually the word 'Queenslander' is right behind them. I'm not sure why. Perhaps it's because up north we don't mind our *p*s and *q*s, or our PC, so much.

My outspokenness would get me into trouble from time to time, particularly in the last couple of years of my career. In the last couple of days before the Derby, it certainly got my name in the paper.

'The favourites have had steaks cut out of 'em, week in and week out!' was my somewhat intemperate assessment of the Derby field, when asked by a newspaper reporter. I did gulp when I saw the paper the next day.

Of course it was a great quote for a journo to seize on. Only trouble was, the favourites were Ustinov, trained by the great Bart Cummings, and Viscount, prepared by the formidable John Hawkes. I'm sure they were as taken aback as I was when they saw the paper, thinking, 'Who's this smart-arsed bastard?'

My colourful point was their horses had had tougher, high-pressure preparations, running in big races up to a week before the Derby. Ustinov had had six starts, culminating in a second to Lonhro in the Caulfield Guineas and victory in the 2040-metre AAMI Vase at Moonee Valley. Viscount had had seven starts. After beating us in the Stutt, he'd failed as favourite in the Guineas, then run a good third to Northerly and Sunline in the Cox Plate.

Amalfi had had only four starts in his campaign and I'd taken the low road, the Stutt–Robinson avenue. Again, I was trying to place him carefully, to get that winning mindset going, but I also still didn't really know if he was good enough to win the Derby. The bookies clearly preferred the 'high road'. Ustinov was $2.35 favourite in a twelve-horse field, with Viscount $3.20 and Amalfi $6.

Amalfi might not have been the best in the field, but he was set specifically for the race. Mind you, his lighter preparation meant I had to pour the work into him. But he coped well, reassuring me his toughness would help him get the 2500 metres and, I hoped, make him the first Queensland horse to win the Derby.

The problem would be keeping Damien Oliver. He had had a serious offer to ride Tommy Hughes' Grey Song, with the owners promising to double his standard 5 per cent of prizemoney if he won. I'd need to make the same offer to secure Damien. Trouble was, Ron Wanless was overseas representing Australia at polo. I couldn't reach him, and Damien needed to know.

I was keen to keep him, but feared he'd show loyalty to a Melbourne trainer, rather than this Johnny-come-lately. But if there's one thing Damien loves more than riding horses, it's a dollar. I stuck my neck out and guaranteed him the bonus out of my 10 per cent, thinking winning the Derby would be worth that much in advertising anyway. Damien stuck with us. Ron later said he'd cover the extra 5 per cent, so I'd won on all fronts.

With Sarah in Brisbane with the kids, Mum came down for what we hoped would be our big day, and we caught the train to Flemington. That was one thing about Melbourne—distances. In Brisbane, you lived at one track and next door to the other. In Melbourne, driving across town was a pain compared to the train. It also helped that no one knew me.

I left the riding up to Damien, as I've never been a huge fan of giving jockeys instructions. As the old saying goes, the good ones don't need them, and the bad ones don't listen. At the same time, my T.J. Smith years taught me you mostly want your horses up on the pace. So when they jumped, I was a bit shocked that Damien drifted well back from a good alley.

With 800 metres left, we were still ninth, but they'd gone quick so I thought we'd be catching them at the end. Still, it took Amalfi a good long while to get going. Ustinov and Viscount weren't going to win (maybe I was right about the steaks after all!) but still in the way was this 60/1 bolter Zarek, ridden by Greg Childs. He and Amalfi knuckled down at the 200-metre mark for a real ding-dong run to the line.

I'm not a big shouter normally, but I was giving Amalfi a big gee-along that day. When they passed us at the 150 metres, it was still anyone's race, but our boy kept coming and coming, and finally Damien just lifted him over the line. I was confident we'd won—I don't know why, since it was a short half-head—but we still had to wait.

Finally, the judge put it up: number 3.

I was now a Group 1–winning trainer.

It was just surreal.

It was all a blur, but I was pretty animated. I think I grabbed Mum and gave her a good twirl around, and the same for Judy Wanless. It was a helluva feeling. Easily my biggest thrill in racing to that point.

I only had one starter that day so I had time to savour it and enjoy it. I gibbered to the press, had the presentation and some photos. I can't remember if Bart or Hawkesy shook my hand, but they probably did. It was just an unbelievable feeling—winning one of the biggest races on the Australian calendar.

Various thoughts went through my head, like that it would've been nice for Dad, Frank Cavanough or Tony Facey to have been alive to see it. I gave Sarah a call, and we were pretty emotional.

But my biggest memory is how great it was to have Mum there. After all the shit she'd been through her whole life and not getting looked after by any bastard, and doing it very tough along the way, to have her beside me as we won the oldest classic in Australia, and then on the dais with me—that was pretty special. I know she was proud and pleased. That was the icing on the cake.

As Mum likes to say, we caught the train to Flemington that day, but we didn't catch the train home! We all got taxis to Crown Casino. Damien came along, and we had a great night.

Later, I got home and added my latest and biggest winner to my captain's log.

'Outstanding effort.'

....

Three days later I caught the train again to Melbourne Cup day. It was a bit different from Derby morning. On Saturday, no bastard knew who I was. On Cup day, heaps of people were coming up to pat me on the back. My arm was nearly shaken out of its socket! So that felt pretty good.

I only had one starter on Cup day, too, so I could enjoy it as I watched Scotty Seamer win the big one. My horse Levante came second-last in the last. Oh well.

The following autumn, I thought about Amalfi resuming in the Australian Guineas at Flemington, but first-up over 1600 metres wasn't the done thing, although it is now. Instead he contested the 1400-metre C.F. Orr Stakes. He went well for fifth but disaster struck when he injured a tendon. He would be out for eighteen months.

When he resumed in Brisbane it was for a different trainer, my mate Kelly Schweida, but after four more unsuccessful starts he was retired.

There was a high attrition rate from the Derby that year. Viscount only had one more run. Ustinov had twelve more but didn't win. We did some stats for this book, and, of the twelve starters, seven of them had only eight or fewer more runs.

This raises the contentious question of whether the Derby crocks young horses. Is it too searching a test for spring three-year-olds? It seems hard for me to argue, seeing what happened to Amalfi, but I've got some different thoughts.

Some Derby winners have gone on, like Elvstroem, Efficient, Nothin' Leica Dane, Mahogany and Stylish Century. Others haven't, but I don't think it's because they are worn out or get slower. Those other horses who didn't mature in time for the Derby end up getting bigger, stronger and better than those who were earlier developers. The late maturers come on the following year and it turns out there's some handy ones, who outshine those who raced in the Derby. Similarly, a lot of Golden Slipper winners look like they don't improve after the Slipper.

But you could argue the job's been done, the money's in the bank. In fact, in a quirky stat, the $812,500 Amalfi earned from the Derby would remain the second-biggest whack of pure prizemoney any of my horses ever earned. (The top one may surprise. Black Caviar's biggest pay was the $1.2 million for winning the 2011 Patinack Classic, but half of that was a Global Sprint Challenge bonus. Manighar's $1.25 million from the BMW at Rosehill in 2012 stands as my No. 1).

Amalfi went to stud but didn't do anything there. I think he ended up serving more polo mares than thoroughbreds.

Still, on Derby Day 2001, the little colt put us in the spotlight. He was the catalyst for us in deciding that after eight months of having a satellite stable in Melbourne, it was time to flip that around and move down permanently. It was now or never.

10

The Science of Training

In the autumn of 2002 I made the biggest move of my career—switching full time to Melbourne. It had become a bit of a no-brainer, partly due to ambition, and partly because I was sick of all the shuttling. I went down first to set some things up. Sarah and the girls followed a couple of months later.

Already there was Tony Haydon, who'd left us in Brisbane to ride work for Lloyd Williams in Melbourne. Dale Turgeon and Jamie Unwin had moved on, and I'd convinced Tony to run it. It took me a couple of weeks to work on him but I'm thankful I nudged him into his niche in the end. He became an integral part of our success, and our association would run to nineteen-odd years in the end, before he became a trainer himself.

We ended up a bit like an old married couple, bickering or taking shots at one another a fair bit, but we were both able to move on. Tony reckons the best thing I taught him early on was never to carry a grudge. I hope if I've ever given people sprays I've been able to quickly carry on. He also said recently that, while I could push my staff hard,

I'd also know when to throttle off, and that I knew how to get the most out of my horses and my people, which I hope is also true.

I kept Brisbane as a satellite stable for another year but then we threw all our eggs into Caulfield. I had the eight off-course boxes I'd got from Jim Conlan. In an interesting twist, I had to pay my rent to a company connected to Horty Mokbel, the brother of controversial Melbourne identity Tony Mokbel, so Horty was more or less my landlord for several years until I moved out of those stables.

Before long I got sixteen more boxes on course at trainer Russ Cleland's place. This was a lot more presentable to clients, and meant you didn't have to walk your horses on the roads. Still, it was a little similar to Brisbane initially in that I had other boxes about the place.

We mostly had our ex-Brisbane horses, but we also had owners like Stuart Ramsey, and Phillip Esplin from Twin Palms Stud, also in the Hunter. They used to love sending these well-bred fillies to Brisbane to win a race. They were even keener to have them win in Melbourne, to boost their breeding value.

The important thing was to be recognised as a Victorian stable, to let people know we would stick around. It helped that Brief Embrace won the Blue Diamond Prelude and ran second in the Blue Diamond. Strategic Image had won a couple of Listed sprints at Moonee Valley. We also started to springboard from Melbourne in the way I'd imagined. We took another Wanless-owned horse, Moonah Brooke, to win the Group 3 Tasmanian Derby, and a few months after that Strategic Image won a Group 3 for us in Adelaide.

I quickly started going to the bush, drawing a bit of ribbing from my fellow Caulfield trainers. At first, believe it or not, I was too tentative to say anything back, but the horses started winning, so that was the main thing. And as the years went on you saw more of my fellow city trainers heading to the bush too!

My existing owners quickly realised their Queensland horses were good enough to compete in Melbourne in their own age groups. Then we started attracting Victorian owners and things started gradually building up.

....

Sarah says she remembers I didn't just want to be a horse trainer—I wanted to be an extraordinary one. I can't recall making that vow exactly, but I suppose moving to Melbourne only three years after getting my licence showed I wanted to give things a shake.

One thing I did want to get into, where I might have differed from some, was the whole concept of applying sports science to racing, modelling what we would do with horses on what human athletes would do.

I'd always been a big admirer of a couple of prominent sports coaches who happen to also be Queenslanders—Wayne Bennett in rugby league and John Buchanan in cricket. They had started studying the people they trained more, looking more into the mental side of it. They had brought in whole new levels of professionalism, and were open to new and possibly unusual ideas. I wanted to take that approach with horses.

Bennett had ramped everything up in terms of professionalism, with relentless attention to detail. I looked at football and how the training had really evolved. From the days of going to training twice a week, playing the game and walking off, all of a sudden there were ice baths, warm downs, stretches, and so on. I tried to put that into practice with my horses: give them a good warm-up before they worked or raced, and then a good cool-down afterwards.

John Buchanan used science and professionalism to turn a struggling Queensland side into world-beaters. He then achieved similar success with the Australian side. He was the first bloke to turn up in the coach's box with a laptop, and he was doing a lot of computer work and statistical analysis.

I wanted to take that approach with my horses, but I was—and still am—a bit of a dinosaur with computers. So I took some advice from Des O'Keeffe, who was a jockey manager and is now chief executive of the Victorian Jockeys Association. He said: 'You're gonna get very big and be very successful very quickly. Make sure you surround yourself with the right people.'

Jeff O'Connor was a young bloke who'd been an apprentice jockey and had worked at Racing Victoria. He'd also even dabbled in acting, and had a couple of walk-on parts in *Neighbours* and a couple of other things. (It still bugs him that he auditioned for a part in *Gallipoli* but missed out, despite all the horse-riding scenes. Maybe he was a rubbish jockey!)

Jeff had an unbelievable passion for, understanding of, and love of racing. When I met him he had just finished setting up the Australian Racing Museum. He could turn his hand to anything, really—training, running a race club, anything.

He was also smart enough to talk his way into my organisation. He could see I was growing, and suggested I hire him as racing manager. At first I said I'd be right, but before long I said we should talk. When he joined, in 2004, we had about 100 horses on our books and 30 to 40 in work. We grew to have about 350 on our books and 100 or so in work, using up to four stables at Caulfield.

A bit like Buchanan, and contrasting me somewhat, Jeff was a pretty studious, serious sort of bloke who balanced things out a bit. He handled client liaison, but most of all he was my statistician. He could work a computer and had a beautiful ability to map out programs for horses, figuring out how to place them to best advantage.

In this period I started to hone what I think, on reflection, was probably my best attribute as a trainer: that capacity to teach horses how to win. I was never afraid to run good horses in bad races. Again, the odds didn't matter to me. This especially helped in relation to the breeding world.

After I retired, some prominent stud people gave me a good rap for my impact on the breeding scene, which was nice. Any successful stable will end up sending a lot of winners off to stud, of course. I guess what these people meant was that I was always very mindful that a lot of my owners, often big breeders, raced fillies with an eye to breeding from them later, so I'd try to look after them to enhance their horse's stud value. The knack was to recognise the animal's capacity, work towards it, and stop when it was reached. I retired a good few fillies and mares who had one race for one win. It was 'job done'; they might not have reached much higher, and they were better off in the breeding barn before they spoilt their record and devalued their progeny. In other cases you might have a well-bred filly who didn't show any ability. You might advise the owners that she go to stud unraced, and maybe she'd throw a horse with ability. With the colts, you were always looking for those good, recognised 'stallion-making' races, though I was probably associated with more quality females than horses who became successful stallions.

Of course, any trainer looks for black type to enhance their horses' stud value. I'm proud that, while I got to celebrate 53 Group 1 winners as a trainer, I also had 44 Group 2 wins, 65 at Group 3, and 106 Listed races. (Mind you, while I was always looking to add value, I'm not saying there weren't times when I might have decreased it with the odd wrong choice as well!)

With Jeff O'Connor and me, it was a great blend of two worlds. I selected when and how I wanted to go with horses, and Jeff would do the rest. He got us to a new level in terms of form assessment, assessing races, barrier draws, times, where our horses fitted into the food chain, and things like horses' weight-carrying ability. It was amazing to find you'd get a 500-kilogram animal and some of them couldn't carry 56 kilograms, but find a race where they'd only get 53 kilograms and they could do it. Then you might get a horse weighing 440 kilograms who can carry 60 kilograms. It's a mystery why, but we'd clearly define it for all our horses.

Of course any crusty old trainer might just say this is knowing your horses. But we soon had a huge team, and it was harder to be across everything. If I could get others to focus on certain areas, I could concentrate on getting the horses race fit, and mentally fit.

Jeff and I grew and learnt together. We set programs in place, like how quickly I could bring different horses to fitness. The older ones would need a week or two more of fast work, since they got fit more slowly than the young ones. Again, regimented programs like we had were crucial to knowing, managing and getting as much success out of our big team as we could. I also found I could use Victoria's superior barrier trial and jump-out system to assess whether our horses were ready to start racing.

Jeff fitted my approach of wanting to surround myself with young people. I'd never have that old veteran type in the stable to guide me. I wanted people my age or younger, with, I hoped, fresh ideas and open minds.

I was happy to experiment and have an open mind, such as with horses' first-up runs. Traditionally you'd resume over 1200 metres or 1000 metres, but I became more inclined to resume a horse over a distance it liked. If a horse liked 1600 metres, with its fitness in place you wouldn't be afraid to start them off over that trip. Along with racing horses in the bush, this is something you see more often among city trainers now.

I also learnt it's easier for a horse to win first up over 1400 metres than over 1200 or 1000 metres. In the 1400s, a horse would often get a rest in the middle stages, whereas in the shorter races they'd go flat out from start to finish. So sometimes you could take a 1000-metre horse and win a 1400-metre race with it first up, but you couldn't take that horse and win a 1200-metre race with it, silly as it sounds.

I was evolving my style as well. A lot of trainers might have tended to be in the coffee shop or back in the stripping sheds, but I liked being in the middle, watching my horses. Even if they weren't galloping I'd study them and see what I could improve on, or look for any ailments as they were cooling down or warming down. I'd also have a day a week doing what the stablehands do, like hosing horses down or giving them a roll in the sand, to give you another perspective.

I really got into the swimming of my horses. I'd seen John Size emphasise this in Sydney and Brisbane. It was particularly good to get results out of older, tried horses.

In Brisbane we could only use the pool in the afternoons for some reason. In Melbourne, my horses would swim twice a day every day, except after fast work, as a form of controlled exercise. They got fitter, increased their lung capacity and worked different muscles—strengthening their back and hindquarters in particular. As humans know, swimming's a great overall body work-out, with no pressure on the legs or joints. With horses who were crotchety, or sore, or who tied up with muscle acid, we'd swim them and it'd loosen them up.

We would also give our horses, like footballers, a warm-up *and* a warm-down at trackwork, usually with light trotting. I had seen people like Neville Begg do a lot of warming up, but never saw many doing warm-downs. I found it let horses catch their breath, get more composed before they went off the track.

I started to do a lot of leading them off ponies—old horses you'd have at the stable for this kind of work. A lot of trainers used ponies, but more as a mate or a sedative than a training tool. Once my horses were fit, I didn't want them to have a jockey on their back the whole time, so they'd be led off a pony for long walks, trots and canters. I rotated my ponies too, as another way of keep things fresh.

That was the big key—variety—preventing that staleness and mundanity that can easily come in a big-city stable. When my horses came out of their box in the morning, I wanted them to not know what they were going to do: gallop, trot, swim, walk, work the reverse way, maybe even go over jumps—whatever. In fact, I even ended up starting a few over jumps, winning six out of 22 all up for a fairly decent strike rate of 27 per cent.

I was never scared to try something out of the box. For example, I once made the papers over the race-day plan for my Caulfield Cup hope Testafiable in 2006. He was a bit headstrong but I worked out he usually went better after a road trip. Trouble was, he only had 300 metres to travel to Caulfield. I plotted a cunning plan to just stick him in the float and have someone drive him around for a few hours on race morning so he'd think he was going somewhere. In the end he was injured on the Friday and was scratched, but I tried the idea out later —with him and other horses—and it got results.

Sometimes I'd take a horse and gallop it on the morning of a race, over 400 or 600 metres. People would question it, but it often worked to calm the horse down a bit, take the edge off. I'd actually seen Bart Cummings do it once or twice. It used to work a treat on a stayer we had in Brisbane called Flaxmill Bay, who won us a Rockhampton Tatts Cup.

When horses really did travel, for a genuine trip away, there were tricks you could try with that too. If we had horses go to Sydney, after we worked them the reverse way at Caulfield, we started sending them up on the float on the Thursday night; they'd race on the Saturday and be back home Sunday lunchtime. Some people thought this was a bit rushed, but there were ways to help make sure they were well settled for the journey. I'd ask the float driver to just pull over somewhere halfway up, park the float and go have a cup of coffee. While he was inside, all this horse urine would just start streaming out of the float. Horses won't take a leak if they're in transit, because they're keeping their balance while the float's moving. So if the float went all the way to Sydney without stopping, the horses could arrive there in a bit of a state because they hadn't been able to take a piss for ten or so hours.

We would tailor our feeding regimes, generally in line with the old saying that you feed to your work and work to your feed. If a horse is a big eater, you generally work them harder. If a horse is a lighter eater, you work them lighter.

And then there was gear. I'd sometimes take these tried horses like Stuart Ramsey used to buy and change what they had had on them. If they'd been wearing blinkers or tongue ties, I took 'em off, gave them a change, hoping to get them into a frame of mind where they didn't need such gear.

You keep horses fresh and happy that way, and generally get better results. If you didn't just run them every day, hopefully on race day they'd be happy to be going for a run, not thinking, 'Not another bloody run!'

....

Apart from Jeff there was my assistant trainer Tony. He might have lacked confidence in his own ability, but was tremendous running the stable. He had a great eye for detail in getting to know the horses, working out problems and offsetting them.

We had a great understanding with our vet, Peter Angus, who became an integral part of our team. There was also our farrier, Matty Martin, who did his apprenticeship at our stable. And there was our horse chiropractor, Michael Bryant, who became a great friend and one of the keys to my success.

I'd met Mick years earlier in Queensland through Kevin Thomas, the trotting heavyweight. Mick came from neither gallops nor trots, but greyhounds. His father Ned was called the Bart Cummings of dog trainers, and Mick started out as a greyhound chiropractor. In time his healing hands found their way to horses.

He always had a brilliant knack of feeling his way around a horse, working with its skeletal and muscular system to identify and fix problems, or potential problems, and how we could guard against them to keep a horse racing. He was a massive part of the success of Black Caviar, with all of her issues.

Crucially, I was also introduced to Peter Clarke, who had a pre-training property where he worked on gallopers and trotters at Murchison, near Shepparton. He invented and built water-walkers, like a doughnut-shaped pool, in which a horse goes round and round in water halfway up its shoulder, getting fit without bearing all its weight through its legs and joints. At their peak times, horses would walk up to 4 or 5 kilometres a day in the water-walker. On top of that, Peter kept the horses in paddocks, as opposed to stalls, so they would walk an extra 4 or 5 kilometres a day in the paddock as well.

I ended up sending just about all of my horses up there. They would then be used to the water-walker if we needed to send them at any time, for injuries or just to change things up.

Peter worked our horses up to a good level of fitness without having a saddle on them. When they came to us in Caulfield, I could then have them at the races in a relatively short five or six weeks, which is great when you've got a big team that you have to keep rotating. His low-concussion techniques meant they were still really keen on running as well. Again, he was crucial to Black Caviar, who often needed some extra special care.

....

Water-walkers have come to the fore in Australia now because we're training this finer, softer horse. Alongside this tide of greater professionalism, everything has seemed to have become finer and faster in sport. That's why records keep getting broken everywhere—swimming, athletics, horse racing, whatever. There are no Tony Locketts or Artie Beetsons in AFL and league these days.

If you look at a horse now and a photo of a horse from the 1970s or even 1980s, they're chalk and cheese. They haven't got anywhere near the bone in them now. Partly this is European stallions, breeding out the tougher colonial-bred horse that evolved in tougher Australian conditions.

The other thing is inbreeding. Let's be honest, if racehorses were humans there'd be that many cousins and inbred types running around it wouldn't be funny. Black Caviar had Vain on both sides of her pedigree. Vain was her dad's grandfather, and her mum's great-grandfather. It'd be like looking at your mum's and your dad's family photos and seeing the same old bloke standing in both sets. They call it line-breeding if it works, inbreeding if it doesn't! Perhaps the modern horse's greater fragility than 30 years ago is also a result of those extra generations of inbreeding.

There's also the outlawing of anabolic steroids in Australia, which started to happen with greater restrictions on their use from about fifteen years ago, until they were banned entirely, both in and out of competition, in 2013. When the ban came—as a reaction to a high-profile case involving the Godolphin stable in England—the Australian Racing Board boasted it had gone far beyond most other jurisdictions. They also said it was done in consultation with trainers' associations. I thought it was to the detriment of our industry. It reduced the longevity of the horses.

The Australian horse industry is borne on the back of the gelding. Whether it was teamsters in the earlier 1900s, pony clubs, polo or racing, we gelded our horses to make them more manageable, tougher, and more honest competitors. We used to then replace their balls with hormones, which generated muscle growth, enabled them to be trained harder and faster, and aided recovery and the repairing of injuries. A gelding could come back from a spell earlier and start earning money for the owner, who is the lifeblood of the industry. But when anabolics were banned it gave you a more fragile gelding.

This is possibly a reason we've seen so many mares at the top in recent years, from Sunline, to Makybe Diva, to Black Caviar, Atlantic Jewel and Winx. They have been great horses, but maybe the rise of the mare is because of the disadvantaging of the gelding since the days of Better Loosen Up, Super Impose, Saintly, Might And Power, Northerly and the like.

We've all had to adapt along with the evolution of the thoroughbred, which is why swimming and Peter Clarke became such keys to my success.

....

Trackwork was busy, and often frantic as our stable got big. I'd be working my stopwatches and monitoring, often timing three or four horses galloping at the same time. One or two would finish and then you'd look back up to see who was coming round the turn, or who was starting off at the 800-metre mark.

It kept you on your toes, that's for sure, but life in the Caulfield trainers' tower was usually fun. There was a good camaraderie among everyone and a good bit of funny banter flying about, though I'll admit there are a couple of stories about me not being too jovial on occasion. There was a certain chair that went out the window one morning. And possibly a fax machine. Usually this was a result of someone fucking up in trackwork. Sometimes that someone was me!

Maybe I hadn't looked back quickly enough to time a horse starting off, or something like that. It could become a bit of a juggling act.

One thing that was handy here was that over the years I'd developed a good eye for a horse. People have commented on this—how I could see just about any old horse going by and tell you which one it was: 'That's that three-year-old of Robbie Smerdon's' or whatever. Without giving myself a rap, it's just something I acquired along the way from a lifetime of looking at them. I reckon I'm probably better at recognising horses than people!

It really kicked off when I was at Tommy Smith's, looking at all these trainers and trying to take everything in to pick up things and see what they were doing with their horses. Then later at Caulfield it was always exciting around carnival time. I'd be keen to get a good look at the likes of Northerly or other big guns who were at Caulfield, like Elvstroem or Haradasun. I guess I just familiarised myself with them. There's the head, of course, but it's not just about 'a bay with a white star' or things like that. Let's remember you're often seeing them before dawn, when you're just looking at a silhouette. There's mannerisms—like if they dance and prance you might know it's such-and-such—or you look at their gait and the way they move. Perhaps they've got this smooth, floating galloping action, and you know who it is straight away. Steve Waugh had a very distinctive walk. It's the same sort of thing.

Then later on you can also start to recognise horses' offspring. It's like when people might say, 'That boy looks like John Smith's son'. I'll go to stud farms now and think, 'I bet that filly's a daughter of so-and-so'.

....

Early on in my time in Melbourne I made another great and long-lasting association, this one by accident.

Luke Currie was a jockey who rode a bit for me, but had weight troubles. One day—the big book says 3 May 2003—we had a couple of maidens in a Saturday meeting at Sale, but Luke couldn't ride them. There was a jockey called Shaun Nolen kicking around who I'd seen riding in Queensland a bit earlier, so I asked Luke about this Nolen bloke, and he said, 'Yeah, he's going all right, give him a crack'.

So I rang this number I was given for Nolen and spoke to him about the rides. On the Saturday I went to Caulfield and watched on TV as these horses—Sydney's Quest and Umagold—finished second and first at Sale.

A full three weeks later, I saw Shaun at Geelong and thanked him for riding that winner for me. He said: 'What are you talking about? I wasn't even at Sale.'

I was pretty baffled, but then he said: 'It wasn't me, it was my brother Luke.'

And that was how it started: L. Nolen and P. Moody. I did end up meeting him in person a couple of weeks later, and we would go on to become the most successful Australian trainer–jockey partnership of the modern era, and very close to the most successful of all time. (It's hard to say definitively who the top jockey–trainer combo in history has been, since the old records are a bit sketchy, but a reasonable bet would be George Moore and Tommy Smith first, with Luke and me second. With Moore winning ten Sydney premierships from 1956 to 1969 while Tommy's No. 1 rider, they most likely had more winners than us, certainly at city level. Mind you, they were together a bit longer too, at around eighteen years to our thirteen.)

Starting with Umagold, and of course including his association with Black Caviar, Luke would ride 774 winners for me from 4009 rides at a strike rate of 19 per cent, or one in five, and prizemoney of $48 million. Amongst our achievements were 31 Group 1 winners.

We were an instant success. Luke's third ride for me was a win on eventual Group 1–winner Sky Cuddle at Kilmore, and his first twelve rides for us brought five winners and two seconds. I felt comfortable enough with him to put him into a Listed race in Adelaide on Niagara Falls for ride No. 11, and he duly won that.

Luke's place strike rate for me was 45 per cent, or almost every second horse, which fitted our stable really well. Again, we weren't in it for the punt. We were in the game of placing our horses where they were best suited, so if they didn't win we hoped they'd come second, third or fourth and earn some prizemoney for their owners.

I maybe could've created a similar record with other riders, but the loyalty and respect Luke and I had for one another worked un- believably in our favour. We just gelled. We just got on. We're both from the bush, Luke having spent time as a youth between Swan Hill in Victoria and Jandowae, near Toowoomba. In fact, how's this for coincidence? Like myself, Luke played representative rugby league as a kid in Queensland (though he wasn't a big boofy prop like me of course, but a chirpy full-back). He played in a rep carnival in 1992 as I had a decade before, but while mine was held on the Gold Coast, when Luke played it was hosted by Charleville. The visiting kids were billeted out, and the twelve-year-old Luke Nolen stayed with none other than my mate and patron David 'Crockett' Power! Considering what would unfold for Luke and myself, that's a bit spooky. (In another coincidence, I used to play footy in the backyard as a kid with a young Andrew Bensley, the radio and TV pundit who started his career at Charleville's 4VL. When he interviewed me at Flemington after Amalfi won the Victoria Derby, it was pretty surreal.)

Luke and I had a great understanding, we thought similarly about the way we worked with horses, we could take the piss out of each other and our relationship meant we could ride out the bad times together. There were a few spats. He likes to remind me how I left a minute-long spray on his voicemail after one ordinary ride. He gave me one back another day when I may or may not have asked if he'd given one a run at Kyneton. But we could blow up at each other and then move on quickly, as I'd like to think I did for most jockeys, or other people I worked with.

Luke also said to me one day: 'For a bloke who never rode in a race, by Christ you can read them!' (What this also meant, he confessed, was that he or other jockeys could never bluff me about what had gone on!)

There are other blokes with superior records to Luke's—Dittman, Beadman, Cassidy. We've got guys now who would hold their own anywhere in the world—Damien Oliver, Dwayne Dunn, Craig Williams, Hugh Bowman, Blake Shinn. Then there are a lot of good unheralded riders, and that's where your Luke Nolens come along.

Luke was the perfect jockey for me. Was he the best jockey I've seen? No. But was he the best jockey I've worked with? The stats say yes.

The thing I loved was it didn't matter if you were at Bairnsdale or Flemington, Luke got the same job done. And it wasn't just the stats. Luke was a real team player. He'd make suggestions even if to his own detriment, like suggest we use a claiming apprentice instead of himself. Jim Byrne's a good jockey, but he could celebrate a win and forget about the ones that got beat. I'd rather find out what went wrong with the losers.

As a rider, I'd back Luke against anyone. He was certainly the perfect jockey for me, because we just had a great relationship. That's something that's priceless in racing. What's more, we found each other at the right time in both of our careers, when we were both ready to hit our peak.

....

After a few years the machine we'd assembled in Melbourne started roaring but, in the first couple of seasons after that watershed with Amalfi, the big prizes proved elusive.

Brief Embrace took me within a neck of a second Group 1 in the Blue Diamond in the autumn before a close sixth—beaten less than two lengths—in the Golden Slipper. And in spring I came close to back-to-back Victoria derbies when Ain't Here was third, a long neck behind Helenus. But for two years after Amalfi I didn't have a Group 1 to my name. Or a Group 2, for that matter.

Still, success isn't always measured in Group 1s, as Ain't Here proved. Bred and part-owned by Philip Esplin, Sarah and I bought a third of him for $10,000. He was well bred, and we had all planned to sell him overseas after a trial. But we couldn't get the price we wanted.

He had ten starts for us, won three and was placed in three big ones. And after the Derby we managed to sell him for a very tidy profit to Hong Kong, where he won two Group races for David Hayes.

While money had been tight, that sale brought Sarah and me our deposit on our property, Carbrecel, where we still live.

Out by the Dandenong Ranges, I call it our little slice of western Queensland bush outside the bustle of Melbourne. Sometimes, on long drives home from Caulfield or, worse still, night meetings at Moonee Valley, I envied my fellow trainers with their trackside houses in town. But as soon as I stepped outside the kitchen for a beer and bunger while looking over the hills, I knew I wouldn't swap it for the world. I also love our little community of Belgrave South, and have been known to play the odd game of Aussie Rules for the local side (they played in jumpers in Black Caviar's colours for one match), and a fair bit of cricket (I may be tall for a wicketkeeper, but at least other blokes have to do all the running).

We traded quite a few horses overseas in those years—including the aforementioned Garth and Lecerbrac—which was important for getting a bank to buy stock and build up business.

....

Ancient Song was one of those horses of the sort John Size used to have success with. She came to me from Stuey Ramsey as a tried five-year-old, with the idea of breeding later on at the Turangga Farm stud he had just acquired.

By Golden Slipper winner Canny Lad, Ancient Song had shown early promise in New South Wales, winning at Group 2–level some eighteen months earlier, but had lost her way.

The mares can switch on and off a bit. Is it seasonal? Mental? Wear and tear? You're never sure. Are they hurting somewhere you can't find? It's one of the biggies in our profession—trying to work out why horses won't push themselves to the limit anymore. Getting them physically fit is common sense. Working on them mentally, keeping their minds fit, is the challenge. You've got to think how they think. Ancient Song's form showed she could run. We had to get her to want to.

She was one of these test cases, probably the first of several tried females I had success with, in fact. We had to turn her back into a blank canvas. We started by changing her routine and getting her fit on Peter Clarke's water-walker. And it had results. In fact she came close to winning her first four starts for me. First up, in the spring of 2003, she took an average 1000-metre handicap at Moonee Valley under lights. She rose to the Group 2 Dodo Sprint on Caulfield Cup day and at $31 ran a one-length second, to Blur.

So I was feeling pretty good when she went to the Group 1 Salinger Stakes up the straight 1200 metres at Flemington on Derby Day. I'd tried taking the blinkers off her in trackwork that week to help relax her to run out the 1200 metres. It seemed to work, so I left them off for the race. I'd got Scotty Seamer to come down and ride her, and he and I were both happy when some rain came to produce a soft track, which Ancient Song, a $10 shot in a fourteen-horse field, didn't mind at all.

She was a natural on-pace horse, and Scotty bounced her out to lead on the flat side from barrier 8. Travelling well, inside the last 100 metres she still held a handy break, but then Damien Oliver's ride Into The Night came at her down the middle of the track. He gave us a big fright but thankfully Ancient Song, looking like she loved running again, held on to win by a neck.

It was my second Group 1—a long two years after my first—and it felt great to get that monkey off my back. Scotty was over the moon too in winning a Group 1 again at Flemington, where he'd had his Melbourne Cup glory two years earlier.

I was starting to like Derby Day. I'd also started Brief Embrace in the Salinger, and she raced a tidy fifth. That week I also had my first Melbourne Cup runner in Schumpeter, though the owners were keener to run him than I was, and he came second-last at $201.

Unfortunately we didn't get another win out of Ancient Song and she retired the following year. The best of her progeny was the Lonhro mare Tampiko, who I trained to win the 2011 Prime Minister's Cup on the Gold Coast.

11

Close—but Few Cigars

The year 2004, when we had all our ducks in a row, was the year things started to really happen. With me training them, Luke Nolen riding them, Jeff O'Connor, Tony Haydon, Peter Clarke, Mick Bryant, Sarah and a few others playing their roles, there was a real buzz about the place.

We were clocking up a lot of miles, saddling up a lot of runners and leading in a lot of winners. The big book shows that in two weeks through Christmas–New Year 2003–04 we had 24 starters and eleven of them won—from Benalla to Caulfield and Stony Creek and a treble at Ararat—with Luke riding seven of them.

February brought a patch of 28 starters for 12 winners, including the Group 3 Hobart–Launceston cups double with Zacielo. That was particularly helpful for us in setting up, as Sarah and I also owned most of him and he earned $250,000 for those wins. That's why, beside the great Black Caviar, you'll see a picture of the honest stayer Zacielo on my man-cave wall. Eighteen months later I asked Sarah if she wanted him in the Melbourne Cup but, unlike many owners, she didn't want him running if he wasn't a chance, which says a lot about her approach. He contested the Bendigo Cup instead and ran twelfth, so she's a good judge.

We got the Kilmore Cup with Marbine, the Wangaratta Cup with Schumpeter, and a couple of black-type city races in Melbourne and Sydney, but ran frustrating seconds in a couple of big ones, with Ancient Song in the Oakleigh Plate and Star Of Gretchen in Adelaide's Australian Oaks.

Only two years after setting up in Melbourne, I trained 100 winners in a season for the first time, finishing sixth in the 2003–04 national trainers' table with 130 winners, at a 20 per cent strike rate. I won the Victorian country premiership, was second on the Melbourne table—with 47 wins to Lee Freedman's 82—and a fairly close second to the same man on the Victorian overall table, with 114 wins to his 132. To have those sorts of results so early on in Melbourne felt terrific.

Late in 2004, we also got a more solid physical base by taking a large chunk of the stables vacated by the legendary Angus Armanasco, behind Caulfield's 1400-metre start on Booran Road, which was split amongst a few trainers. We kept boxes in a couple of other places to house our growing team as well.

It was busy, and getting busier, and very enjoyable. I was getting my name in the paper, which was good for attracting clients, while also networking and hopefully putting into use any people skills I'd developed.

One horse I really fancied was Sky Cuddle, a lovely big chestnut by Snippets that Stuart Ramsey had bred. We called her Serena, because she had a good-sized rump like Serena Williams, and she always showed ability. So I was disappointed when jockey Danny Nikolic bagged her after her debut at Flemington in January 2003. I'd thought she'd gone okay. The big book shows she came eleventh of eleven! Stats aren't everything.

My faith was restored when she resumed from a spell for a win at Kilmore (Luke Nolen's third-ever ride for me) and a second at Ballarat. She worked through her grades until, at her eighth start, she contested the Group 2 Tea Rose Stakes at Rosehill in the spring of 2003, finishing fifth. A year later she broke through for black-type success in a Group 3 in Adelaide, which was good for Stuey's breeding ambitions, and it was time to aim higher.

A sixth in a 1400-metre Group 3 on Derby Day mightn't seem great form for the Group 1 Emirates Stakes, but she'd finished well so we decided to return to Flemington a week later for the big mile.

We had a few problems. She'd only got 49 kilograms, which was great in one sense but also meant she was second emergency.

Thankfully the track ended up a heavy 10 and four horses were scratched, getting us a start—but by race morning we still didn't have a jockey. Luke and Chris Munce had been riding her, but the 49 kilograms was too light for them. We'd scratched our heads but couldn't think of any other senior rider. There was only one option, but he was headed to Geelong.

Baby-faced Jason Benbow, all of eighteen years old, was a good young rider from Traralgon who was temporarily apprenticed to me on loan from his trainer dad Ben. He'd begged to ride Sky Cuddle at the light weight, but as a 3-kilo claimer he was still pretty wet behind the ears for a Group 1. He'd hardly even ridden in town much. But with only hours till the race, that didn't matter anymore. We had to get him. Trouble was, he'd taken rides at Geelong—ten of them!

I had to get busy. I got permission from the stewards to contact the trainers of Jason's rides to get him excused from them. Thankfully, six were scratched anyway because of the wet. Three trainers agreed, but Jason couldn't get off his mount in the first. At least he was able to ride that—finishing eleventh of eleven—then belt up the Princes Freeway to Flemington in time for Sky Cuddle.

Mind you, on paper it still looked like we were little chance. The bookies had us at $51, with Grand Armee heading the market and Wangaratta hero Lad Of The Manor on the second line.

Sky Cuddle had only been placed once on a heavy track, at Ballarat, so we had to cross our fingers a bit. But she'd drawn well at barrier 3 and had no weight. She'd worked well that week so, not for the last time, I thought we had a genuine hope with a long shot in a Group 1.

Stuey and I were, however, mindful of Jason's inexperience, so we said to him before the race: 'When you think it's time to go . . . count to ten and *then* go'.

Jason bounced her out well and she raced about sixth, and then around the home turn they all spread right across the track. To his credit Jason waited and waited. He actually told us later that he'd counted to eleven! Sky Cuddle came on in the last 200 metres amid a cluster of horses, then dived through the pack and got her head down on the line to get the chocolates, upsetting Lad Of The Manor by a head.

It was a fantastic day. I was over the moon for Jason, who was all smiles and had his dad there boasting about having bred a Group 1 winner. I was also delighted for Stuey and his wife, Trish. Stuart had owned Group 1 winners before—Ancient Song for one—but this was the first one he had bred and owned. Coming another lengthy twelve months after my second Group 1, it was an important win for me for many reasons, not least repaying Stuart's faith in me.

It was great for Jason, although a dozen years later that remains his only Group 1. He was the big story that day but, in hindsight, I wonder if ambition got ahead of ability. He never really reached the levels he or any of us had hoped for him, though he was the man for us that day.

Sky Cuddle only won once more, at Group 2, in thirteen starts, but perhaps saved the best till last—in that unforgettable 2005 Cox Plate when everyone took off down the side in the vain hope of upsetting Makybe Diva. While everyone else burnt themselves out, poking up through the middle was Sky Cuddle, at $101, getting fourth and $135,000.

Makybe Diva—what a horse she was. When her very astute trainer David Hall went to Hong Kong after her first Melbourne Cup in 2003, I got a lot of horses from his stable, and I'd hoped Makybe Diva would be one of them. I'd already trained for her owner Tony Santic, and would do so in the future with Headway and others, and I asked him if I could train her. She was that good I reckon she could have won a Newmarket up the straight Flemington 1200 metres.

But sadly, Makybe Diva went to Lee Freedman. I think I was still too much in the up-and-coming brigade to be handed a superstar like her. We'll never see anything like what she did again, winning three Melbourne Cups.

That Cox Plate fourth was a good performance by Sky Cuddle, by her patient jockey Greg Childs, and by me if I say so myself, since I had to train a bit more staying ability into her for the 2040 metres. Oddly enough though, Sky Cuddle would be one of only two starters I ever had in the Cox Plate, the other being King's Rose, an unlucky seventh to Pinker Pinker in 2009. There should have been a third, but that's a bit of a sore point.

Sky Cuddle went to stud after that race but had no success. I trained both her foals, full sisters by Stuey's stallion Zizou, but they weren't blessed with the ability of their mum, who I'll always remember very fondly.

....

The winners were still coming at a steady rate in that 2004–05 season, though not quite as frequently as the season before, as I contented myself with second place to Darren Weir in the Victorian country premiership, and fifth place in town, with 33 city wins.

But while the winners were ticking over, 2005 was a year of close to but not quite at the top level.

Caulfield's big autumn day was agonising for myself and Luke Nolen, as we almost caused upsets in the meeting's two Group 1s. Seidnazar ran second at $30 in the Blue Diamond, though comfortably beaten, while Segments very nearly pulled off a huge boilover in the Oakleigh Plate at $150. This was a classic escapade straight from my textbook.

Segments was another tried mare owned by Stuey Ramsey who was like General Nediym in reverse—she was transferred from Clarry Conners to me. Though her earlier good form had tailed off, I found her to be a fast little mare. The Oakleigh Plate might have been ambitious—she was massive odds in a ten-horse field—but I did say to Stuey: 'I don't think this is the silliest thing we've done, y'know . . .'

After Luke had her well positioned in third place, Segments got to the lead in the straight. A hundred metres out she still had me and the bookies cheering, but she was just collared late by Fastnet Rock. Still, she became a handy mare for us, winning the Group 2 Schillaci Stakes at Caulfield in the spring that year.

Our Group 1 placings continued, with Vouvray second in the Ranvet Stakes and third in the BMW, Sky Cuddle third in the George Ryder, and Douro Valley second in the South Australian Derby.

By the end of the year it felt like I was close to something big but couldn't quite grab it. Around Christmas, I saddled six winners out of eight city starters, including four in one night at Moonee Valley in Alto Adige, Napa Sky, Jarrod and Recline. A couple of weeks later I repeated the trick with another quartet at Kilmore. The stable at least got a great payday, though no black type, a week after that when Testa

Rossa gelding Tereschenko won the Magic Millions three-year-old race on the Gold Coast and $583,000. He looked very promising—having won four from seven—but it was a good thing he struck when he did. He went right off the boil and only had one more placing, a third—at Ballina.

On into the autumn of 2006 and some big near-misses continued. One of them had been Testafiable, another son of Testa Rossa who we just called Ross. He was one of those yearlings I'd bought after trading a few horses overseas.

Testafiable finished second in the Group 1 Queensland Sires Produce Stakes at Eagle Farm in the winter of 2005. He wasn't advanced enough for that year's Victoria Derby, but he won the Group 2 Carbine Club Stakes over 1600 metres on Derby Day instead. We took him to Sydney for the following autumn, where he was third to Headturner in the AJC Derby. Yet another Group 1 placing!

Testafiable was a frustrating horse in a few ways, including that he again brought up the trainers' worst nightmare—the headstrong owner. Funny enough, I got on really well with his majority owner, Gold Coast quarry businessman Rod Kennedy. He'd been with me for a while, and part-owned my first-ever winner Ebony Way. We could have a beer and a chat. I actually liked the bloke, and I think he liked me, but when it came to the horses he just did my head in. He was very forthright. He'd always be on the phone, telling me what races to enter, which jockeys to put on, saying the jockeys had been up to no good, even telling me what gear they should be wearing. 'No, you don't put that gear on my horses. Stick a ring bit on him, or a nose roll', or whatever.

It just drove me mad. I'd say to Rod: 'Imagine if I came into your quarries and told you what to do with your business and how you'd feel. You give me these horses to train and you tell me how to train them, what jockey to put on it, even what gear to put on the bastards!' I'd been through it with Rod with Zacielo, but thankfully Sarah and I were majority owners, so we got the final say.

In fact there were a few colourful owners around at the time, as we were expanding and getting new clients. Douro Valley ended up with Flemington trainer Danny O'Brien when I suggested to one of the part-owners, who was rather opinionated, that he might like to take his horse and get out of my joint. The horse had come to me from my Caulfield neighbour Colin Little, and ended up being switched to a fourth stable.

Tereschenko was part-owned by John Cappellin, the flamboyant Melbourne businessman who owned his sire Testa Rossa. To be honest, I hadn't thought he was good enough to contest that Magic Millions race, and after he won it, Cappellin delighted in reminding me. 'You didn't even want to be here!' he said.

He delighted in reminding me of that many times later, too. Our relationship deteriorated, you might say, to the point where one day at Caulfield, there he was poking his finger into my chest in the mounting yard. Needless to say, I told him to take his horses out of my stable (and his finger out of my chest). His horses might have left anyway, since shortly after that Cappellin was jailed for fraud.

This is the lesser-known side of training. You spend a lot of time trying to handle people—and often trying to get them to pay their bills! You'll bust your arse and finally win a race with a shit horse, only to see its owners reinvest in a better horse and send that one to another trainer. Or you'll see your owners swooped on at the races by an agent working on behalf of another stable. Building and holding your clientele is a challenge. The bad owners mean you really treasure the good ones, like Stuart Ramsey or the Black Caviar syndicate.

My relationship with Rod Kennedy was one of the most tumultuous I had—but it did bring my long-awaited fourth Group 1, nineteen months after Sky Cuddle's.

Three weeks after the AJC Derby, where Testafiable was a bit underdone, we sent him to the South Australian Derby, where'd I hoped to go one better than Douro Valley's second the previous year. There were a couple of hitches to overcome.

Testafiable had had four riders in five starts, most recently Craig Newitt at Randwick, but Rod wanted yet another change, which wasn't surprising but was annoying. Luke Nolen was coming to ride some for me, but Rod wasn't a fan of his, so on went Greg Childs. I liked Greg as a rider, but the horse wasn't getting that continuity of jockey that's so important.

While Testafiable was a $3 favourite after his Sydney run, the other worry was the weather. With the Derby on a Sunday, I'd flown in on the Saturday night from the Gold Coast where Vouvray had run in the Group 2 Hollindale Stakes (another second!). When I got into Adelaide it was pouring, and there was talk they might call the meeting off.

Luckily for me, they raced. Testafiable didn't mind the wet, and Greg turned in a beautiful ride—getting to the fence mid-field from the outside gate of 16—and the horse did it smoothly, winning by almost two lengths. Poor old Luke, who came third, twelfth and twentieth on my horses that day, finished second on Empire Gold.

Ironically, it wasn't too long after that that I couldn't stand it any more. I was training a good filly for Rod as well, La Vie Amour, but one day I just cracked and rang him up and told him to get his horses out of the joint.

The owners do pay the bills. But every now and then you'd say, 'Fuck this, it's too hard. Take your horses somewhere else and do what you want with them.'

It was funny. I liked Rod, but I couldn't stand him. He was too overbearing, and one of those owners who could never just enjoy it. It wasn't until about eight years later that I agreed to take another horse for him. Perhaps by then I had a bit more clout to dig my heels in on things.

12

The Scandinavian Connection

Though our stable was expanding, we hadn't really had those big gun horses you needed to count yourself up with the Freedmans and Hayeses of this world. But at last I was about to get a good 'un, who was special in more ways than one.

Magnus was bred and raced by Rob and Yvonne Crabtree. Rob raced a lot of horses, including Magnus' dam Scandinavia, who had run third to General Nediym in the Newmarket.

Magnus, or Riley (since he was broken in by trainer Mark Riley), won his first start as a three-year-old only narrowly at Werribee under Jason Benbow, but was showing enough that after a spell we sent him to Sydney in the autumn of 2006. He won there as well, and after a second at Caulfield we were eyeing some big races for him that spring. He ran second in three of five black-type races that campaign, so we tried him in the Group 1 Salinger Stakes on Derby Day, but he only came tenth. He was flat in that race, so I took him back to our farm for a spell. But on the Wednesday morning he was bucking and squealing and full of beans, and I'd also just heard that nominations for the Group 2 Age Classic that Saturday had been extended due to a shortage of entries. So I rang Rob and we pretty much talked each other into it. I got Sarah to give Magnus a trot at home, then took him to Flemington on the Saturday and he won by a long neck under Luke Nolen. *Then* he'd earned his spell.

Starting an autumn campaign of Group 1 sprints, Magnus unfortunately ran into a good one in Miss Andretti when second in the Lightning Stakes. Again, Rob was an owner who liked changing riders and was never a big wrap for Luke for some reason. So Steven King was aboard for his third in the Oakleigh Plate, Dwayne Dunn rode him to a narrow fourth in Miss Andretti's Newmarket, then Damien Oliver got on for his next run—the Galaxy.

It was switched that year from Randwick to Warwick Farm, on a Sunday when it poured with rain. When they went into the barriers, you could hardly see them, though at least the track was only soft. And Magnus couldn't have been more courageous. After running on the pace, Damien sent our stallion to the lead 250 metres out. Gai Waterhouse's smart Bentley Biscuit came on his inside but Magnus beat him off. John O'Shea's favourite Fast And Famous then came on the outside, but Magnus dug deep again, and got to the line half a neck in front.

It was Group 1 No. 5, and 'only' ten months after my previous one. In fact, I came close to a Group 1 treble that autumn, with Ambitious General—a good stayer despite being by General Nediym—second in the Rosehill Guineas and AJC Derby.

With Magnus it was time to aim higher.

It was time to have a crack at Royal Ascot.

....

Before that, there'd be a trip home to Queensland for the Brisbane winter carnival. That brought another Group 1, but it was also my saddest day on a racetrack.

Stuart and Trish Ramsey had given me another tried Sydney mare called Cinque Cento, who we just called Wildy, since she was a bit headstrong. She was good early, running second in the Queensland Oaks, but she had gone pretty cold. While she went winless in her first four starts for us in the spring of 2006, the next autumn we got her going. She won a 1200-metre Group 3 at Caulfield, then ran a couple of fair fifths in the Group 1 Coolmore Classic and George Ryder Stakes at Rosehill, then won the Group 2 Queen of the South Stakes in Adelaide.

With Stuart's great approach to tackling big races despite the odds—like Sky Cuddle's $51 Emirates win and Segments' $151 Oakleigh Plate second—we targeted another Group 1 in the Doomben Cup a month later, where Cinque Cento would start at $21.

But after a couple of weeks I got a terrible phone call.

Stuart and Trish had been great supporters of ours, and had treated Sarah and me and our girls as part of their family. Likewise, we were very fond of their seven daughters. But now came some news that I just couldn't believe. Their daughter Sherilee, just eighteen years old and one of the babies of the family, had, without warning, died in her sleep.

It was just awful. She was a beautiful girl, just out of school, very fit and in the prime of her life. But she'd gone to bed one night and didn't wake up. It was later discovered she had a heart disease.

Stuart and the whole family were devastated, as you'd expect. But we decided to continue with the plan with Cinque Cento.

The event had been billed as a match race between Gai Waterhouse's Desert War and John O'Shea's Reigning To Win, but Cinque Cento was given the run of the race in the eleven-horse field by Steven Arnold. He's a beautiful rider, a tall bloke but with great hands and balance, and he got her up in the first two or three while Desert War led. Steve sent Cinque Cento up to the leader 600 metres out, and while he later said he feared he'd gone too early, she held on to win by half a length, from another long shot in Gaze. Desert War was sixth, while Reigning To Win dudded.

It was pretty surreal afterwards—a feeling I've never felt before or, thankfully, since. The Ramseys were in tears as all the emotion just poured out. I was tearing up as well. And though Stuey could hardly speak, to be able to get such a win for them felt so special. It was a lift we all needed at such a horrible time.

....

Since Magnus now had a Group 1 under his belt to boost his stud value, Rob Crabtree and I thought we'd have a throw at the stumps at Ascot. We'd follow in the hoofsteps of Choisir and Takeover Target by running in the Group 2 King's Stand Stakes over 1000 metres and, provided he came through that, the Group 1 Golden Jubilee Stakes over 1200 metres. A few compatriots were going in Bentley Biscuit, Miss Andretti and the wonderful Takeover Target, so at least we weren't going it alone.

I was excited. It would be a great learning experience, and I'd never been to Europe before. Magnus had matured into a good Group 1 sprinter and, though he was probably fourth pick of the Aussie quartet, I thought he'd be competitive.

The horse went over early with our stablehand Angelica Sunset, and I flew in ten days before the first race. We stabled at Newmarket along with Lee Freedman, who'd travelled with Miss Andretti, and Takeover Target and his trainer Joe Janiak, who knew the ropes and was a good man to know. Two members of our party hit it right off—Magnus and Miss Andretti! You wouldn't believe they were stallion and mare. It was amazing how well they took to one another.

The trip ended up being a great dress rehearsal for what I'd do with Black Caviar five years later. In fact, we stabled at the same place, which was trainer Geoff Wragg's at the time but would be Jane Chapple-Hyam's by 2012. But while Magnus settled in well, that's more than I could say for his trainer on his first night of this big adventure.

I was staying above a shop in Newmarket, where there were two little flats upstairs, with me in one and a young couple in the other. On my first night in town I had a few beers with some old mates, including Mark Wallace, who'd spent time in Sydney and was now a trainer over there. I got back to the flat about 11 p.m., and though I hadn't had that much to drink, with the jetlag kicking in, I just fell into bed. I reckon I would've slept for a day or two but I woke up in the early hours of the morning and needed a leak.

I went into the dunny and, this being one of those tiny English flats, you just about had to back yourself into it. There was a door or two to get through and I was still half asleep but, in the end, I've had my leak, come out, come through the door and closed it, then turned around to get back to bed.

Only then I discovered I wasn't in my bedroom. I was actually standing out in the corridor between the two flats. And the door had locked.

And I was completely in the nude.

You bloody idiot!

I'm standing there, nothing on, there's this other little flat next to mine with the young couple in it, I'm suddenly wide awake and thinking: 'What the fuck am I going to do now?'

I thought of a plan of action, although it was fairly rudimentary. I'd just kick the door off its hinges and pay to get it fixed in the morning. Well, it was one of those big old English doors that must have been about four inches thick! I was there pounding away, kicking harder and harder, in the nude, the adrenalin pumping, but it wasn't going to budge. I was probably lucky I didn't hurt myself. That would have been a story to tell, turning up to trackwork on crutches or something.

I went downstairs and stuck my head out the front door. I'm thinking it was about 300 metres to Mark Wallace's stables. Could I dash across and make it there without anyone seeing? But it was about 4 a.m. in a horse town, so people were going to be stirring, and by then I had even less than a rugby league front rower's pace, so I thought the risk was too great.

I went back upstairs and just stood there for about half an hour, wondering what to do, when I heard a click downstairs. I panicked.

Thankfully, I discovered it was just the newspaper being delivered through the mail slot. I went down and got it and thought: 'At least I've got something to wear!'

Finally, despite the early hour I decided there was nothing else for it but to knock on the door of the other flat. I'm there knocking and knocking, thinking: '*Please* let the bloke answer—not the girl!'

The door opens—and of course it's the young lady, and I'm standing there with a newspaper over my old fella.

'I'm Peter Moody, I'm a horse trainer from Australia and I've got a horse in the Group 1 at Ascot coming up . . . I'm in a bit of trouble here.'

She took a second to get over the shock, then went and got the bloke. And that was how I met Phil Harlow, the man who would be our driver five years later when we were stuck in the car park after Black Caviar's win. Some introduction!

It turned out Phil was a handyman. He tried to get the door open—after kindly giving me some gear to wear—but he couldn't. We had to wait about another hour before he could go and get the spare key from the owner.

Phil was in fact a handyman who did a bit of work around the various stables in town. So word soon spread. Every time I was outside and a string of horses went past me every bastard would point and laugh: 'There's that Aussie who locked himself out of his room in the nude!' There'd be wolf whistles and all sorts of piss-taking.

I'd always laughed when I'd heard about things like that and thought: 'What bloody idiot would ever do that?' Well, now I knew.

....

Like the first time I saw T.J. Smith's, being in Newmarket was like a dream (and I don't mean that dream where you discover you've got no clothes on).

It's horse heaven. Just unbelievable. A town set up solely for horses, with stables and training tracks everywhere. I say tracks but they're called gallops—3000 acres of grass surrounding this town where horses run over rolling hills and so forth. Everyone could tell you the history of their stables—that they dated back to the 1700s or 1800s, and who had been in them before.

I met some amazing people. The great jockey Lester Piggott was a mate of Geoff Wragg's and he dropped in for a beer and chat with Freedy and me at the stables, and to have a look at our horses. I spent some time with Luca Cumani, the trainer I'd met on one of his many visits to Australia. And Lee and Janelle Freedman looked after me very well, with the odd dinner and things.

A lot of the trainers I met were 'sirs'. There was Sir Michael Stout, Sir Henry Cecil, Sir Mark Prescott. In fact, one thing that struck me was the class system there, which we of course don't have in the more egalitarian Australia. There were all these strappers and stablehands calling me 'guv'nor' and 'sir' and 'Mr Moody'. 'Can I bring you that saddle Mr Moody, sir?' I was a bit uncomfortable with that. I was mid-thirties and these stablehands were twenty or thirty years older than me, with years more experience than me, but they felt obliged to call you 'sir'.

Someone asked me if stablehands in Australia did that and I nearly fell over. 'Call you "sir"?!' I said. 'They'd more likely call you a cunt than sir!'

But the place was just amazing. In that environment, it all just makes sense—everything about preparing thoroughbreds for racing. It's so different from Australia, where the city's going on around you, where horses often have to be led through suburban streets and you're watching out for cars and so on. If we could somehow replicate something like Newmarket in Australia, it would be terrific.

....

Because Newmarket revolves around the thoroughbred, people work their horses at more convenient hours, starting at a relatively sane 6.00 a.m. But we were still doing the Australian thing to try to normalise things for our horses, and working them at 4.00 a.m. The tracks weren't officially open then, but no one minded. We were done and dusted by the time the locals got up.

The Poms wondered why the hell we did that, and it's a question you get asked all the time. The simple answer is that it's been going on for 150 years. Trainers used to like hiding their horses in the dark to get a better price on race day. Some had day jobs to go to. Admittedly, we don't need to worry about odds these days because the prizemoney's decent. But also, at Australian tracks where you're in the middle of a metropolis, you still want to get everything done and dusted before the public come out. Caulfield is a funny one too, because it becomes a public park at 9.30 a.m., with people jogging through and whatnot. The early starts didn't really bother me—though I still set my alarm for 3.05 every morning because I couldn't bear the thought of getting up at 3.00 a.m. And, like Tommy Smith, I always wanted my horses first on the track every day.

There were a couple of things I did struggle for in England. One was a good beer. I couldn't cop the room temperature stuff, and didn't get very far on the bitter and ale. Eventually I found my beloved XXXX over there—but only in these big tall cans you could get in service stations. I ended up sticking to Dutch drop Grolsch, in the green bottle. The other thing was a swimming pool. I think there were only two in the whole of Newmarket, but Clive Brittain, a trainer across the road from our place, had one and he let me use it for Magnus.

Though most gallops were hilly, I stuck to the flattest stretches we could find for Magnus to keep it like home—a tip Joe Janiak passed on after Takeover Target had won the King's Stand and been third in the Golden Jubilee the year before.

Joe's a great story—the hobby trainer who bought a broken horse on its way to the knackery for $1200 and turned him into a champion who won $6 million. We were all cheering him on, that's for sure. That's the Aussie way—everyone's got a chance of getting that good horse.

People joked about how you had Joe the taxi driver from Queanbeyan with one of the best sprinters in the world, but I was certainly prepared to learn from him.

....

Just going to Royal Ascot for the first day of their carnival was a real buzz, though I must admit getting into top hat and tails for the first time felt a bit weird. I felt a bit better, though, when I got to the course and everyone had the same gear on.

It was also the first time, other than on banknotes, that I saw the queen. I'm a republican but if you're not moved by being just a few feet away from her you wouldn't be human. (I'd have to wait a few years until I actually met her though.)

Miss Andretti, with Craig Newitt up, was favourite for the King's Stand at £4 while Magnus, with Damien Oliver on board, was £15, but I was confident our little boy could run well, because he always did.

Magnus travelled well behind the two pacesetters, and when Olly took him to the lead 300 metres out I felt pretty good. But then his girlfriend Miss Andretti flew home on his inside and won by almost two lengths. Magnus battled on to get third, with Takeover Target fourth. Bentley Biscuit didn't fire.

With our horses pulling up well, Lee, Joe and I decided we would back up four days later for the Golden Jubilee. Miss Andretti was favourite at £3 but, with rain about, Magnus firmed from 10s into £7.50. I think people thought he was a wet tracker because of that Galaxy win, though he was better on top of the ground. We were optimistic but neither Magnus nor Miss Andretti handled the quick back-up, finishing fourteenth and fifteenth. Takeover Target ran well again to get second, only a head behind Newmarket local Soldier's Tale.

Magnus stayed in England with Angelica for the Group 1 Nunthorpe Stakes at York two months later. He started at £7 but didn't do much for Kerrin McEvoy under the hefty 62 kilograms on the set weights scale, finishing ninth. I wasn't that disappointed with the whole exercise. It had been an unforgettable experience and Magnus had done okay with his third place.

But still, I wanted to go back and win.

....

Magnus came home and turned in his usual honest campaign in the autumn, finishing second in the Oakleigh Plate and Newmarket, a close fourth in the Galaxy, then a disappointing fourth in the T.J. Smith at Randwick. But he recovered well from that so we opted for a second Ascot mission. This time, we'd go via Singapore for the Group 1 KrisFlyer International Sprint.

In hindsight, maybe we just weren't meant to go to Singapore.

For starters, during Magnus' quarantine time at Sandown, he had to work one morning in this pea-soup fog. He spooked at something, threw Angelica off and bolted. I got on this quad bike and went off into the fog to look for him, but couldn't find him anywhere. After about half an hour I was getting into a panic, especially since Eliza Park Stud had just bought into the horse with plans to stand him as a stallion! I was really starting to fear the worst when, finally, I tried up in the 1800-metre chute—and there he was, calmly having a pick of grass.

Next, Sarah and I missed our flight after getting stuck in traffic crossing Melbourne, and had to wait in an airport hotel for eight hours till the next one.

Finally, I got my first look at Singapore and thought I was gonna die. It was that hot and humid, I was just sweating buckets the whole time. It bloody near killed me, let alone the horse.

Then Magnus ran super in the big race, but Damien Oliver was caught three wide without cover on him. We just got done by a half-length—by the remarkable eight-year-old Takeover Target.

After we had arrived in England, there had been some trouble in a build-up press conference over that old chestnut of anabolic steroids. Prominent Scottish trainer Mark Johnston had had a go at Takeover Target, and by extension we Aussies, because it was known that Joe gave the gelding steroids to help cope with his significant travelling. While not allowed in Britain, that was perfectly legal in Australia then, though, as I mentioned earlier, unfortunately it isn't now.

I fired a shot back by saying: 'If someone like Mark Johnston wants to live two hundred years ago and do things the way his father and grandfather did, that's up to him'. I also thought it was a bit rich since I found the drug-testing regimes in Australia far stricter than in England.

At least I was able to add some levity when one journo, perhaps forgetting Magnus was soon to be retired to stud, asked if he had had steroids too. 'No,' I said. 'He's got his steroids between his hind legs. And that's going to earn him a lot of dollars in three months' time.'

At Ascot, Magnus and Olly only ran eighth of thirteen in the King's Stand, at £5.50. Takeover Target finished second, before a fourth in the Golden Jubilee.

And that was it for Magnus. He retired as my second million-dollar winner, just pipping Amalfi with $1.1 million. He was very consistent, though funnily enough he only won four out of 24, and didn't win again in ten starts after that Galaxy breakthrough. He has also produced consistently at stud, with his progeny headed by Group 1 winner Malaguerra.

Perhaps most importantly, I'd walk into a yearling sale a couple of years later and spot this filly out of a daughter of his mum.

13

A Bitter Pillar

By 2007–08 we were in full swing. We'd been in the top three on the Victorian overall premiership five years in a row, and were regularly just off the leaders in the city. Around this time we took over Angus Armanasco's stable entirely and still had a couple of other spots. With 100 to 120 horses in work, we were now the biggest at Caulfield. That sounds great but it was starting to do my head in. We were getting too big, and I was struggling for enough quality staff. I decided to scale back.

I wrote to my clients saying I was bumping up training fees by around $10 or $15 a day, to around $100 a day. It was the smartest thing I ever did. Some took their horses elsewhere, but most were happy to pay the extra. I edged the numbers down to about 80 in work, and about 350 on the books in total, but I had a better concentration of quality horses and more affluent owners. Instead of getting cast offs from Lee Freedman and David Hayes, suddenly I was getting first pick at the yearling sales. That move, borne out of frustration, allowed me to make that transition to winning premierships; I've got no doubt in the world.

That spring of 2007 we won a few Group 2s and 3s with the likes of Hidden Strings and Pillar Of Hercules, so things were going okay. But we did have a bit of a drama with Pillar Of Hercules, a horse who ended up in the news for the wrong reasons, and gave me some unwanted attention as well.

I had bought the colt at the Sydney Easter sales in 2006, knowing Horty Mokbel was looking for a horse. Horty ended up taking three-quarters of him while we kept one quarter, which was put in Sarah's name.

As I've mentioned, Horty was indirectly the landlord of the first stables I had rented at Caulfield. It's well known now, of course, that he, like his brother Tony, ended up going to jail, but still I never had a problem with Horty. I didn't have much of a relationship with him but what there was was purely business. I paid my rent bills, and he paid his bills to me as an owner.

In any case, when Pillar Of Hercules was getting ready to race in 2007, it was my understanding that Horty sold his three-quarters to an associate of his, Tom Karas. Tom saw that most of the horses Sarah and I owned raced in Sarah's name and thought he would do the same, putting that 75 per cent stake in the horse under the name of his wife, Irene Meletsis.

Pillar Of Hercules progressed well, winning his third start, at Moonee Valley, and the Norman Robinson Stakes at Caulfield at his sixth start, which put him in the market for the Victoria Derby. But a few days after the Robinson the police stepped in, saying they were investigating whether that 75 per cent stake was really owned by Horty, and whether it was bought with the proceeds of crime.

I had no knowledge of anything to do with that, or of any impropriety to do with the horse. I could only take Horty and Tom Karas at their word that the former had sold to the latter, as I tried to concentrate on training the horse. The case in fact brought a good call from the Australian Trainers' Association for authorities to more strictly check the bone fides of owners, since trainers can't be expected to. If a bloke comes and says he's got a horse he wants them to train, most trainers are going to take it with open arms, rather than have the time or resources to run a background check on the owner first.

In the end, the case caused a sensation as the police and Racing Victoria stood Pillar Of Hercules down from racing, pending the investigation. The police's Purana Taskforce, which investigated gangland activities, wanted Irene Meletsis out of the horse. They took the extraordinary step of ordering a public auction for this one galloper, to be held the day before Derby Day (which would clear it to run the next day) with 75 per cent of the proceeds going to go to Victoria's Department of Public Prosecutions, and 25 per cent going to Sarah and me.

The auction took place at Caulfield and was a pretty unusual event, being an auction for just one horse. I was told that hadn't happened since the great Shannon was auctioned off in 1947.

By this stage I'd decided Pillar Of Hercules was too immature for the Derby anyway, and I'd entered him for the Mackinnon Stakes, which would also be run the next day, instead. I thought he had great potential, so I still hoped to keep him in the stable.

Having been bought as a yearling for $475,000, Pillar Of Hercules was sold at the auction for $1.8 million, to Dean Watt of Dynamic Syndications, who beat other interested parties including Gai Waterhouse. That counted as a nice windfall for us, and Dean, who I'd do a fair bit of business with, let us buy back into the horse with a 10 per cent stake.

In another twist, the major shareholder in the syndicate Dean put together was Bill Vlahos. Several years later Vlahos, acting for his investment group BC3 Thoroughbreds, would buy Black Caviar's half-sister for $2.6 million, and then her half-brother for a record $5 million. He'd then get into trouble for, among other things, not paying up for the colt, who in the end had to be put down due to sickness before he could race. Eventually Vlahos had to declare bankruptcy in 2013. (The filly, Belle Couture, raced only four times, for trainer Danny O'Brien, recording one win before being retired.)

The whole Pillar saga was obviously a bit unsettling for me, as you might imagine, and disappointing. Our kids were young, and yet here was my photo on the front page of the paper amid these stories about police investigations. I was relieved when the auction went through and the whole business was done and dusted.

The next day Pillar went round in the Mackinnon, but weakened to finish ninth. And while there were high hopes for the horse, evident in his hefty sale price, he unfortunately went right off the boil and never won again in 22 starts. He ended up having three poor runs for Chris Waller in Sydney in 2010, then didn't race for another three years before one last start as a nine-year-old gelding for Adelaide trainer Michael Hickmott. The horse certainly had an unusual career.

....

Aside from the Pillar distraction, we were improving all the time, and I was building up to bigger success with Riva San, whose big team of owners sent her to me out of the blue. She was a nondescript filly who we just called 'Darl'. She was small and skinny—you would have fitted three of her into Black Caviar—but just kept defying her weak looks.

After a stakes win in Adelaide, she was fourth in the Group 1 Thousand Guineas at Caulfield, second in the Wakeful Stakes, then an average seventh in the VRC Oaks. We thought she would mature enough for the Queensland Oaks the next winter, but she over-achieved again, winning that and the Queensland Derby a week later to complete a Group 1 double on a memorable day for me in more ways than one.

Watching from Singapore, where I had Magnus, I saw Riva San had no luck when ninth in her Oaks lead-up. Her rider, Luke Nolen, had worse luck later that day when he had his face smashed, amongst other injuries, in a fall off the ironically named Antidotes. Scott Seamer climbed aboard for the Oaks and at $25 Riva San relished the heavy track and won by a neck.

No filly had won the Oaks–Derby double for sixteen years, but we felt the Derby field wasn't that strong. This time Riva San was fancied at $6.50, though Bart Cummings had the $3 favourite in Moatize. Riva San would also have to carry her third rider in three starts, with Jim Byrne replacing the suspended Scott Seamer.

I was flying to England for Magnus that night, so I was home on our farm, which was boggy like Eagle Farm. I was packing my bags when I heard this wailing outside. We kept some cattle on the farm, and I went out and found this steer had fallen down the bank of a creek and broken its leg. My neighbour, Ian Brown, and I had a look and decided to put it out of its misery. After that, we got a tractor each and tried to tow it out.

Well, we got into all sorts of trouble. With the mud and the slope, the wheels of the tractors were spinning madly, there was mud flying everywhere and ropes getting tangled up. Then I looked at my watch and said, 'Shit, they're about to run the Derby!' We stopped, with the unfortunate dead steer halfway up the creek bank, ran up to the house covered in mud, and watched Riva San win impressively by two lengths, despite clipping heels and nearly falling at the 800 metres, giving me Group 1 No. 8.

I then finished pulling out this dead steer, had a long shower, and two hours later flew out to Royal Ascot. It was quite the day.

It was nice to win those two Group 1s with a couple of jockeys I'd had success with up there in my early days, although Riva San didn't kick on. Perhaps she'd done all the development that small body would allow. Still, she was good for us and continued my success with mares. But I was about to get a very special one indeed—that first real superstar I'd been longing for.

14

A Premiership and a Superstar

In the spring of 2008 I missed the big city prizes but got amongst the country cups, winning the Moe Cup with Reggie, and the Horsham–Terang cups double with Macau Causeway. He was owned by Hong Kong's Deborah Ho, daughter of one of the richest blokes in Asia, Stanley Ho. Horsham and Terang might not have been among the places Deborah was used to, but it's nice to win.

The book shows that out of nine horses I saddled over three days in September, seven of them got up. Two were special.

Astro Gains won a Mornington Class 1. Two years later, on Melbourne Cup day, in a carefully executed coup, he would win me my one and only Charleville Cup! I drove him up and met co-owner David Power halfway. Crockett took him home and he won the cup a few days later, adding the Roma Cup at his next start.

The other special one had more mainstream success. She was Typhoon Tracy.

'Cyclone', as she was of course called, was bred (very fortuitously) by her owners John and Fu-Mei Hutchins of Hutchins Thoroughbreds.

She was out of Tracy's Element, an Australian-bred mare who won four Group 1s in South Africa. John and Fu-Mei bought Tracy's Element from Vinery Stud on condition they also got a free service to her by Vinery's American shuttle stallion Red Ransom. The resulting foal was Typhoon Tracy.

I'd known their bloodstock manager in Queensland pretty well, and I think due to my record with mares, they sent me this one.

And she was just beautiful. Words can't describe what a lovely horse she was. She was great to do anything with, effortless to train and just a pleasure to have around. She was even like a cherished family pet. Sarah still ranks her as her favourite of all our horses, partly because of her nature, and partly because she was our first superstar.

Most of the great mares—Sunline, Makybe Diva and Black Caviar—have been big robust things. Tracy was more like a super-model. The pretty ones often aren't as tough as the big-bodied ones, but Tracy belied that. She was a little petite, but had a lovely stride, a wonderful action and, of course, loads of ability. And while you always felt proud if you took over a tried horse and improved its results, Tracy was in our system from day one, which felt good.

I always thought she'd do well, though five Group 1s and an Australian Horse of the Year title was beyond my wildest dreams.

Tracy kicked off that September patch for us at Moonee Valley on AFL Grand Final eve, winning the appropriately named Kevin Sheedy Plate over 1200 metres with Luke aboard. She started at $6 but won like she was 6/1-on, by five and a half lengths.

She came back in the autumn of 2009 and kept on winning—a Listed race at Caulfield, a 1200-metre fillies race at the Valley, then the Group 3 Schweppes Trophy over 1400 metres at Flemington, crossing from barrier 16 and winning by more than three lengths. That convinced me to go for a Group 1 next start, the 1500-metre Coolmore Classic at Rosehill.

Our stable was really hitting its peak. All those years of learning, listening, working, saving, and making strategic moves were starting to pay off. I had built a good team around me, had a good business model and was ready to take the next step and be a dominant force.

I was still enjoying my country racing, of course. For example, a few days before that Typhoon Tracy win at Caulfield (the same day Reward For Effort won his debut), I was a world away watching a gelding called Markus Maximus win us a maiden at Stawell.

But there was a lot of excitement around Tracy.

She got into the Coolmore, a quality handicap for fillies and mares, with 51 kilograms. That was great for her, but too light for Luke, so we engaged Glen Boss. We drew wide again, 14 of 16, though it's not so crucial from that start. It certainly made no difference to Tracy.

She jumped beautifully, crossed over to lead, got a breather from Glen down the side, but then got onto the wrong leg around the turn and lay out in the straight. A couple came at her and, while she was actually headed by New Zealander Culminate at the 200 metres, she just gritted her teeth and beat her off, winning by half a length. This latest Group 1 really took my breath away.

....

Just after the Coolmore came a treat from racing's mixed bag of fortunes. That horse who debuted at Stawell in January? In April, he won a Group 1.

Markus Maximus. Boy, did we get lucky. I bought him as a yearling in New Zealand, and he was comfortably the slowest horse who won me a Group 1, or possibly any other trainer for that matter. I don't want to sound harsh, because I know his owners loved him. I liked him too, the big, rough-looking bugger. But he was very moderate.

After Stawell he won at Mornington, then ran three placings in town. We were scratching for a suitable staying race, so we thought, why not have a crack at the WATC Derby at Ascot? He hadn't even started in any kind of black-type event, but I figured the race wouldn't be overly strong, despite its Group 1 status.

I didn't make the trip to Perth but Luke went to ride Markus, an $8 chance behind a couple of locals and David Hayes' Berlioz at $7. He sat just off the pace and travelled well, Luke took him to the lead on straightening and it all looked fairly simple. Markus hung on by a neck from Berlioz.

I'll admit, I started thinking some silly things: 'Shit, this thing might be better than I thought!'

He wasn't.

The horse didn't improve an inch. In fact, he never won another race. Highlighting his great fortune further, only three years later the WATC Derby was demoted to a Group 2.

His big birthday in Perth was sandwiched between Typhoon Tracy's Coolmore and Black Caviar's debut. It takes all kinds to make a stable.

Typhoon Tracy was the flag bearer, and could have been anything. In fact, I would have had more confidence in Tracy becoming a world-beater than a young Black Caviar, since I was always worried about that big girl hurting herself.

But in spring Tracy came back and, against open company, she was beaten. Three times—third, second and, worst of all, an eighth over the 1800 metres of the Underwood Stakes. Her shortage of dash was possibly because I was training her with the 2040 metres of the Cox Plate in the back of my mind, but still I was a bit gutted. We'd lost the 'picket fence'—the 11111 beside her name in the form guide—and I thought 'Oh well, fairytales don't happen after all'. Black Caviar at least proved that wrong.

Thankfully, Tracy rebounded and would win her next five starts, four at Group 1. Dropping back to female company and to 1400 metres in the Group 2 Tristarc Stakes at Caulfield, she won by almost three lengths over favourite Hot Danish. She met that Sydney mare again in the Myer Classic (1600 metres) on Derby Day. This time Tracy was favourite at $2.20 and she just brained 'em. She burned a bit of petrol early from gate 12, sat three wide for a bit, but then got a nice trail and bolted in by nearly five lengths. She had more than earned a spell.

Her Myer Classic gave me Group 1 win No. 13. The twelfth had come only a couple of hours before, with Headway taking the Ascot Vale Stakes. To get a Group 1 double on Derby Day was pretty amazing stuff.

....

Headway was a funny little filly, a fat, dumpy yearling who we called Chatter after her mum Chatelaine, who I'd trained at the end of her career for Stuart Ramsey, who bred from her. Tony Santic, Makybe Diva's owner, used to like going to the yearling sales and catching up with Stuey in his Turangga Farm tent for a bit of steak and a spot of red wine, and he was there at the 2008 Sydney sales while this pudgy little yearling was out in the yard. Every time Tony went outside for a smoke he saw her, and she looked better each time. So he ended up buying her for $175,000 and sent her to me.

Unassisted by wine goggles, I initially didn't like her. She showed little ability, but then she got fitter and passed every test on the way up.

Her career somewhat mirrored that of Reward For Effort, who I bought at the same sale as Black Caviar with long-term business associate Dean Watt of Dynamic Syndications. I bought the horse for $190,000 from breeder David Moodie, with whom I'd have a long and mixed relationship.

Around the time Reward For Effort was winning on debut before a second in the Blue Diamond Prelude, Headway started off with a second at Seymour—where we found that, like her mother, she didn't like being hit with the whip—before a mid-week win at Sandown.

Ten days after that, Reward For Effort lined up as a $16 roughie in the $1 million Blue Diamond, which was supposed to be a match race between unbeaten filly Rostova and the Hawkes horse Real Saga. I had added winkers to try to keep our flashy colt's mind on the job, and he responded brilliantly, sitting three deep just off the pace and kicking to win by a length and a quarter from Real Saga, with Rostova fifth.

At last, Luke and I had combined for a Group 1. We had won some before, separately, and run a heap of placings together, but it was very pleasing to win our first as a duo. We couldn't dream it would be the first of 31 together!

Headway stepped up to Listed class and won the Pol Roger Stakes at Caulfield for Luke at $14 to earn a trip alongside Reward For Effort to the world's richest two-year-old race, the $3.5 million Golden Slipper at Rosehill.

While Headway continued to fly, winning the Sweet Embrace Stakes at Randwick, Reward For Effort had to be scratched from his lead-up run after we found mucus in his throat. He recovered to win a barrier trial, and we thought he was our best chance in the Slipper. But then it rained.

A $9.50 chance, he jumped well from barrier 3 but, when Luke asked him to go in the straight, he couldn't quicken in the wet and finished seventh. Our $26 shot Headway, however, had no issue with the wet. Under Glen Boss she turned in a super effort to fly home for second and $620,000, two lengths off the long-shot winner Phelan Ready.

From there my two horses' fortunes diverged. Reward For Effort injured a suspensory ligament before his spring campaign and was out for sixteen months. He still came back and won his only start as a three-year-old, the Listed Monash Stakes with Luke aboard at Caulfield. He won his next start six weeks later in the new season, taking the Group 3 Concord Stakes over 1100 metres at Rosehill.

He didn't win again in four tries and was retired to stud, where he's gone all right. He was a genuine Group 1 horse, a stakes winner at two, three and four, which not many can boast. Unfortunately, we never saw the best of him.

Headway didn't win in six more starts, but wasn't far off. For a horse I hadn't initially thought much of, she won a Group 1—before her contemporary Black Caviar did—and $1.1 million in prizemoney. She was very good for us—once we'd trimmed that gut off her.

....

Typhoon Tracy resumed in the 2010 autumn more mature, ready to tackle the males and take that next step to greatness. And she looked every inch a superstar with a hat-trick of odds-on Group 1 victories with Luke aboard.

She won the 1400-metre Orr Stakes at Caulfield by almost two lengths, smashed the six-horse field in the 1600-metre Futurity, also at Caulfield, then easily beat the females again in the Queen of the Turf Stakes over 1500 metres at Rosehill.

We were keen on her in Australia's biggest mile, the Doncaster Handicap at Randwick, despite the third-biggest weight in the twenty-horse field of 56.5 kilograms, and barrier 14. But trouble struck. The horses I'd taken to stable at Randwick that autumn picked up a virus. Some people said it was related to the equine influenza that had rocked the industry in 2007. Some were getting their horses vaccinated against EI, but others weren't, and all of mine got crook. We had to take Willow Creek out of the Sires Produce. Hanks missed the AJC Derby, and in the end his feet rotted away.

Typhoon Tracy wasn't herself, but against my better judgement I ran her in the Doncaster. She was $3.30 favourite but, with a hot pace on, she just never got in the hunt, finishing fourteenth to Rangirangdoo.

This marked a bit of a turning point for me. I admit I'd got caught up in the moment a bit by starting her. She was the favourite, and I felt the public would probably want to see her run, but I should have scratched her. I soon decided that that would be the last time I'd bow to any outside pressure to start a horse somewhere, no matter how special the race, or the horse.

For Tracy, and the rest of my weary Sydney visitors, it was time for a spell.

....

While the end of that Sydney trip was disappointing, there were a couple of sweet moments coming up.

First, I was crowned Melbourne's premier trainer. In fact, I'd been assured of it for a long time and bolted in, my 83 winners almost double the number of second-placed Robert Smerdon. I was also Australia's leading black-type winner, my 28 two more than Gai Waterhouse's.

What did that feel like? If there was no emotion, if it was all about the process, you might think it was just one of those stats you pick up in the course of being a successful horse trainer.

But in truth it meant a lot, and made me extremely proud.

I'd become the first trainer from outside the Hayes and Freedman empires to win the premiership in the mecca of Australian racing for 32 years. The last time it wasn't Colin Hayes, David Hayes or Lee Freedman, it had been Geoff Murphy—also the last Caulfield trainer to win it—in 1976–77, when I was a snotty-nosed seven-year-old! It felt a bit like Brian Mayfield-Smith ending Tommy Smith's 33-year reign when I was starting out in Sydney.

I was proud of my staff, and my family who'd supported me. And, looking back now, I'm also mindful that we won this before Black Caviar was a superstar. Our horses were firing, the staff were motivated, and we had a terrific support base of clients.

After David Hayes had returned from Hong Kong in 2005, he'd gotten into this fierce rivalry with Lee Freedman. They'd eat one another and eat their young, and everyone else got the crumbs off the table. But people had forgotten about the rest of us and we were able to slowly sneak up. Granted, Hayes and Freedman were in transitional periods back then, but our premiership was a powerful achievement and a testament to what we'd built. So were the three premierships that followed!

I was also pleased to win it from Caulfield. When Makybe Diva's first trainer David Hall had left for Hong Kong in 2004, I had actually taken steps to move into his stables at Flemington. People kept telling me it was the place to be, including Freedy, who is, of course, a bit of an outspoken character. He had been there, and Caulfield, but when he moved to his private complex at Rye on the Mornington Peninsula he told me: 'You'll never win a premiership training out of Caulfield, son. It's not a good enough training centre.'

But I was just starting to find my feet and I really enjoyed it there, so I stayed.

Over time there'd always be a bit of banter between Freedy, David Hayes and myself. People would say, 'Lee's got this magnificent place at Rye; David's got Lindsay Park in South Australia' and blah blah. So every time I'd win a race I'd say: 'It just goes to show you don't need the fresh salty air or a view of the vineyards to be training good horses'.

When I did win that first Melbourne premiership, the first bloke on the phone next morning was Lee Freedman.

'I'm ringing you up to congratulate you, son,' he said. 'You've proved me wrong, and well done.'

We've had a few disagreements over the years, but that meant something to me. Particularly since I'd taken his title, it was really special.

Another thrill at the same time was Luke coasting to his first Melbourne jockeys' premiership, with 66 winners, fourteen more than his nearest rival. He won the next two as well. Reflecting our stable's attitude, he also topped the Victorian charts overall with 125 winners.

On top of that, Typhoon Tracy won Horse of the Year, and easily too, with 98 votes, ahead of Starspangledbanner's 61, and Cox Plate winner So You Think's 35.

This was my first of four successive Melbourne premierships, and began a run of three straight Victorian overall titles. The last of those helped me become top trainer in the country for the only time in 2011–12 with my best-ever haul of 209 winners, making up for back-to-back seconds to Peter Snowden. These were very satisfying years indeed.

....

Another horse I was excited about was Anacheeva.

By Anabaa, he was a full brother to AJC Derby winner Headturner, but no one else wanted him. He had failed some veterinary tests— apparently his legs looked ordinary on the X-rays—but I never really got vets to check on yearlings anyway. You often find the problems detected are easily fixable. I backed my judgement and bought him with one bid at $110,000.

In his first preparation, Anacheeva won a Sale maiden, came sixth in a two-year-old at Flemington, then stepped up to the Group 1 Champagne Stakes at Randwick, where he went really well to get fourth. He returned in the spring and just blitzed them. He won first up in the McKenzie Stakes at Moonee Valley, took out the Caulfield Guineas Prelude, then went to Group 1 again for the Caulfield Guineas. With Luke riding, he was never going to get beaten, sitting third on the fence and going on to win by a long neck.

Anacheeva wasn't flashy but was a tradesman who got the job done, and was probably then the best three-year-old in the land. He was a winner at two, and a Group 1 winner at three. I suggested to his three owners they could cash in by selling him to stud but they were keen to keep racing him.

But when he returned in the autumn, his third in the AJC Derby was his only placing in five starts. Then in August 2011, he failed in the Memsie Stakes and went amiss. He needed to be retired to stud, but it was now too late for him to stand that season. He would have to spend a year on the sidelines, meaning that when he did start standing at stud, his Caulfield Guineas was a fading memory.

It's often a toss-up between retiring colts early or trying to win another race. This time we lost. Still, he'd earned close to a million dollars from twelve starts. He's now standing at Chatswood Stud in Victoria, alongside Reward For Effort.

....

Everything I did with the five-year-old Typhoon Tracy in the spring of 2010 was geared towards cracking one race—the Cox Plate. The Moonee Valley 2040-metre feature is not only one of Australia's 'Big Four', but is also our race of champions, won by many of the dominant horses of their era. I'd given it a nudge when Sky Cuddle ran fourth in 2005. I'd toyed with the idea with Tracy the previous spring. But now I felt we had a great chance to win it.

Tracy resumed with a solid fourth in a quality Memsie Stakes behind the previous year's Cox Plate winner So You Think. I put her into the 1600-metre Feehan Stakes to get her back to the Valley for the first time in twenty months. I got Luke to ride her back, to give her every chance to finish off with the longer trip of the Cox in mind. She was a solid second, two lengths behind Whobegotyou.

I took her to Flemington for the Turnbull Stakes over 2000 metres, essentially the Cox Plate distance, and she came from well back to finish super in fifth, one and three quarter lengths off Zipping.

I was tickled pink. And knowing how horses take a lot of benefit from their first try at 2000 metres in any given preparation, she was right on target for the Valley. But, out of the blue, owners John and Fu-Mei Hutchins said they had gone off the Cox Plate. Instead they wanted the 1600-metre race at Flemington she had won the year before, the Myer Classic.

I was gutted, really disappointed. I really wanted Tracy to run in the Cox Plate, and of course I'd trained her up for it. I'm not sure if it was their choice or they were advised by someone. I'd normally be able to persuade owners in a certain direction, but John and Fu-Mei were adamant.

Now, instead of three weeks between the Turnbull and the Cox, Tracy had four weeks till the Myer. Then it poured, and the track was a heavy 8. She had never been on worse than soft and was definitely better on top of the ground, as most good horses are.

Tracy still started odds-on and put up a super effort but ran into that good wet-tracker from Sydney, Sacred Choice, who beat her by four and a half lengths into second.

Because I had trained her for the 2040 metres, that might have taken some of the gloss off her. Sure, I had four weeks to train her for the 1600-metre race, but I'd really geared her for the longer journey, long and slow rather than short and sharp, and probably taken some speed out of her.

We had been holding her back to get her to finish off, but thinking, if she drew a good alley in the Cox Plate, we could race up on the pace. On the day there was no speed on and So You Think got it handed to him on a platter. I'm not saying Tracy would have won it, but she would have got the on-pace soft run with him and had a shot at him, and on a good track.

We'll never know, but I do know that not running her remains one of my biggest regrets.

....

Tracy came back the next autumn and ran third in the 1200-metre Group 2 Australia Stakes at the Valley at odds-on. Even though Whitefriars and Undeniably were allowed to control the race, being beaten by those two suggested she wasn't going as well as we had thought.

She went into the Orr Stakes again two weeks later and produced a very game effort to win, as even-money favourite, in a sixteen-horse field. It was her sixth Group 1 but she'd only just got there by a short half-head.

Afterwards, she was buggered. She hadn't gone off the boil completely, but I could tell she wasn't the horse I'd had previously. We had still planned to take her to the Futurity Stakes but for the next two days I spent a lot of time with her. You get to know your horses, and she was just out on her feet. That spark in the eye was missing. She wasn't injured, but it was just: 'Hey Pete, I've had enough'.

I rang John and, though it might have seemed strange given that she'd just won a Group 1, I said, 'I think time's up'. He said to give him five minutes then, when he rang back, he said: 'You know her better than anyone. If you're telling us that, then we'll retire her.'

I wasn't scared she'd go on to tarnish her reputation; it was just that she was too lovely a mare who I didn't want to do the wrong thing by. So off she went to stud, our first superstar: twenty starts for eleven wins, six at Group 1 level, and $2.4 million in prizemoney.

....

Eighteen months later, soon after our triumph at Royal Ascot with Black Caviar, John Hutchins rang me. I was expecting news of Typhoon Tracy's first offspring, since she'd been in foal to top-line Irish stallion Street Cry.

I remember the phone call very clearly—I was walking around the front lawn of our Caulfield stables—but unfortunately for all the wrong reasons. Typhoon Tracy had had the foal, but had died in doing so.

I was gutted. It certainly put a tear in my eye. She was such a beautiful mare. I'd seen her in the Hunter Valley when I went up to look at some yearlings, and she was looking great. That was one of my saddest days in racing, for sure.

The foal was raised by a nanny mare, and John and Fu-Mei ended up keeping him, causing a bit of a sensation when he was passed in at the yearling sales at $2.1 million. He was called Last Typhoon and I trained him. But, just as fate was cruel to Tracy, racing's great lottery didn't do much for her son. He had won two of seven in the bush by the time I retired.

My office was like a shrine to Tracy, with five of her Group 1– winning photos dominating the walls. She was special to us in many ways. And because of the attention she attracted as Horse of the Year, she helped prepare me—as much as anything could—for the far bigger cyclone ahead.

15

Nelly

One good thing about my logbooks is it's easy to know where I was at any given time. Take these couple of weeks in early 2008.

On 23 February, Magnus ran second in the Oakleigh Plate. On Saturday, 1 March, Cinque Cento failed in the Futurity Stakes. The next day was better—wins at Pakenham and Terang. No starters on the Monday or Tuesday, and on Wednesday I got a winner at Sandown.

But the Tuesday—4 March 2008—was one of the most momentous days of my life. I went to the Inglis Premier Yearling Sales at Oaklands, near Melbourne airport, and bought a horse.

I actually bought a few who went all right at that four-day sale, including Reward For Effort and Set For Fame. But it was on the Tuesday I bought the yearling who would become the best horse in the world.

Four days later Magnus came second in the Newmarket and I was down in the dumps. Life on racing's roller-coaster . . .

....

I hadn't gone especially to look at Black Caviar, or 'Lot 520' as she was plainly known then. I'd circled a couple of others in the sale catalogue. But when I got out there a couple of days before the sale I turned a page and my eyebrows popped up.

You look for things that worked for you in the past. I turned to Lot 520, offered in the Swettenham Stud draft on behalf of the relatively new Gilgai Farm, a couple of hours north of Melbourne. I saw she was closely related to Magnus. Her mother, Helsinge, was a daughter of Magnus' mum, Scandinavia. So I went to have a look.

Helsinge apparently had soundness issues, which is why she was unraced, but when I saw her first daughter—what are the words?— I was just in love with her. She was a lovely, strong filly, with an unbelievable action. She was a big, heavy girl, but she just had this fant- astically economical, smooth movement to her. You're only watching them walk, not run, but she had a nice overstep—how far the hind foot goes past where the front foot had been. Not massive, but nice. But the way she moved just took my eye.

You develop your skills when looking at yearlings, assessing the fundamentals, trying to predict how they will develop. I've bought lots that others wouldn't consider; likewise, I've seen others buy horses I wouldn't look twice at. Most look for a nice head, a deep girth showing lung capacity, the length of the hip and the size of the engine room— the hindquarter. People also look for the big, massive walk. I look for a good walking horse with a good action. When Black Caviar walked, her whole body worked in unison. Every part of her moved.

I also go on first impressions and a gut feeling. If I like what steps out in front of me, I don't need a second look. I'll look and see if I can work with what's there. Most good horses over the years have had some physical fault, like the pigeon-toed Galilee, or the parrot-mouthed Dulcify. Black Caviar would go down as a horse who was offset in the knees—one slightly lower than the other—but that was fine.

I always make my own shorthand notes in the catalogue. For Lot 29, Reward For Effort, I wrote, 'Good size and body up behind, turned slightly near foreleg, slightly parrot mouth, good walker'. 'Parrot mouthed' means a horse's teeth don't meet in unison. The horse can struggle to eat, but this can by rectified. Similarly, a problem like a slightly turned foreleg is something you can work with. You'll often back a horse's athletic ability to overcome that kind of fault.

Probably my biggest statement is 'CE', for 'correct enough'. Since I've kept the catalogue, I can tell you that, after putting a big circle around the mention of Magnus as a prominent relative on the page with Lot 520's details, I wrote: 'Good size and body. CE. OK. Q.' The Q was something I didn't dish out often. It stands for 'quality'.

It doesn't always work, but I knew I was in love with her. Now I had to figure out how to buy her.

....

I spoke to a few clients before the filly was due to go under the hammer (at sales, you usually inspect the yearlings a day or two before the auction), but couldn't gain a lot of interest. I spoke to Stuart Ramsey but, like a couple of others, he bought yearlings with breeding in mind, and this pedigree wasn't going to be strong enough.

Black Caviar was by Bel Esprit, a quality sprinter part-owned by AFL great Kevin Sheedy. (I hadn't had much to do with Kevin—though I did train a fairly ordinary horse called Sheedy!) Bel Esprit had been fast, winning two Group 1s, but hadn't done much at stud. In fact, the average price of his yearlings would fall that year from about $65,000 to $30,000. In fact, it's pretty stunning to think now, with hindsight, that a year after this yearling sale Black Caviar's full brother, Moshe, was bought as a yearling for just $70,000. That price would have been a bit higher only a few weeks on, after the filly's racing debut.

The dam, Helsinge, was out of Scandinavia and by Desert Sun, the sire of Sunline. That was okay, though a little untested. Helsinge went on to also throw four-time Group 1–winner All Too Hard, by Casino Prince, and Black Caviar's full brother Moshe, who won three out of five before going to stud. The pedigree looks magical these days but, back then, not so much.

I then thought of Sydney businessman Neil Werrett. I'd trained for him before and raced a couple with him. Every year Neil and some friends would do a houseboat holiday on the Murray River near Echuca. They'd talk about buying a horse together, but never got round to it. In 2004, Neil's wife Dee unfortunately passed away from cancer. The next time the group went on the houseboat, they said: 'We've gotta buy this horse before we lose any more of us'.

So with Neil, the time was right. He said his group had wanted a filly, for breeding purposes, and he likes to remind me now how I rang him and enthusiastically said I'd found him one 'with a big arse' that he should buy. I went to the sale knowing his syndicate had a budget of $100,000.

It's funny to think now—and you can still watch the auction online—but at first no one stuck their hand up to buy Black Caviar. Auctioneer Peter Heagney calls for $100,000. No one says anything. He calls for $80,000, then 'Fifty, surely?'

Finally, it kicked off at $30,000, and before long it raced up to $100,000. This filly had caught some other eyes as well. Neil Werrett was on the phone to the bloke standing next to me monitoring events, and possibly getting a little edgy. But he also knew how keen I was.

Rising in $10,000 increments, the bidding became a battle between myself and a two-man team—Troy Corstens, son of trainer Leon and now a trainer himself, and Kevin Kelly, who both used to source bloodstock for a Melbourne owner called Peter Carrick. They went to $150,000, and things were getting tense. I went to $160,000; they fired back at $170,000. Now the collar was really tightening.

I'd had rushes of blood before. I had paid too much for some, and offered too little for others, which hurts for a long time. I'd really wanted to buy Samantha Miss but couldn't go to the $1.5 million. She ended up winning three Group 1s for Newcastle trainer Kris Lees. Then there was a colt, nineteen lots before Black Caviar— his breeder, Tony Santic, had tried to talk me into buying him, but I didn't want him. Troy Corstens bought that yearling for $120,000 and with Leon training it became the superb sprinter Starspangledbanner.

But this big, dark brown filly pacing around before us felt special. Things stalled for a bit at $170,000. The auctioneer even called 'Going once . . .' But then I've jabbed my hand up for $180,000 to finish it off.

Bang—they fire straight back, at $200,000. I said, 'Bugger this', and went ten grand more. I waited for the comeback, but as the seconds ticked by there was none. They couldn't go again.

I'd won.

I guess, when you look at some other prices paid around the time, it wasn't that extraordinary a number, but it was a high price for a Bel Esprit. I'd certainly blown Neil's budget, but in a sign of what a pleasure he'd be to deal with throughout, Neil said he'd still take her, and figure out the money later.

As I stepped outside Troy and Kevin approached me to ask if they could buy half of her, but Neil wasn't interested.

And that was that. She was ours. Now we had to see if she was any good.

I like the end of the sales footage, when the auctioneer realises who has bought the horse.

'Oh! Peter Moody!' he says. 'Thanks very much, Pete. Very best of luck with that filly.'

Since we'd burnt his grandfather's caravan that day in Charleville, Brett Cavanough and I had drifted apart for a decade or so. But he ended up down south, and we'd picked up from where we left off. Brett had also become a trainer, but also had a strong business in breaking horses in. I got most of mine educated for their racing career with him. The day after I bought Black Caviar, I sent her to Brett's place at Albury.

She was just another horse going through his system. Dark brown and big, her only other defining feature was the brand on her shoulder—'GF' and '4/6'—for Gilgai Farm, and the fourth foal born there in 2006. Fittingly, she was actually broken in by another Charleville boy who worked for Brett called Kent Wade. She seemed a passive type who stood in the corner and didn't say much—hardly a sign that the boys were in the presence of greatness.

Neil Werrett sorted out the ownership. He'd retain half of the filly and the rest of the syndicate would split the other half. People have asked if I wished I'd retained a share, but that's not how our business operated. Almost everything I bought was for sale.

Eventually I met the other seven owners, Gary and Kerrin Wilkie, Colin and Jannene Madden, her sister Pam Hawkes, and David and Jill Taylor. Jannene and Pam's family went way back with Neil's. Their grandparents had been friends in south-east Melbourne, so it was a tight-knit bunch of lovely people.

Each owner submitted five suggestions to Gary about what to call the horse, and it was Pam who won. A geography nut who loved looking at maps, she saw the link from Scandinavia to Helsinge, a town in Denmark near where they apparently get a lot of black caviar.

We used to laugh that one of the unsuccessful suggestions was the rather more ordinary 'Fish Eggs'. On top of that, Helsinge was nearly named 'Like Billio' by Gilgai's farm manager, who reasoned that since she wasn't going to race the name didn't matter. Wouldn't that have been great to hear after the twenty-five starts of this Australian folk hero? 'Fish Eggs, by Bel Esprit out of Like Billio . . .'

Gary and Kerrin's daughter Shannon came up with the colours: salmon, with black spots to represent the caviar.

....

As with all her career, we had to be patient with Black Caviar early on, watching for the strain her bulk put on her joints. She was moved around a lot in her first year with us. That helps get the animals used to different environments, which helps if they're going to travel as a racehorse. It also helped ensure she developed okay physically.

The newly minted Black Caviar had a couple of spells at Cheval Park near Pakenham with my horse chiropractor mate Michael Bryant. She had her first look at a racetrack on 3 June 2008, when we brought her to Caulfield for a couple of days. She went to Quentin Scott, a wily old horseman who did a lot of my pre-training, who took her to nearby Cranbourne for the odd bit of light work. His reports were positive, though not through the roof.

The filly returned for a few weeks of stable life in the spring but then, in a sign of some things to come, she hurt her chest muscles and had to be turned out for a spell. She must have showed me enough to get me a little excited by then, because Neil Werrett reminds me now that I rang him a little disappointed and said: 'Oh well, we can't win the Golden Slipper with her now'. He was a bit surprised to learn I wasn't joking.

Eventually, the big girl came back to Caulfield in February 2009 to get ready to race. We put her in the fillies' barn, where she had mates like Typhoon Tracy and Avenue, and she got Box No. 1 at the front of the row. This wasn't special treatment. She was just becoming a very big girl and that was our biggest box.

Had Black Caviar had any idea, she would have felt this was a good stable to join. Three days earlier, that colt I'd bought at the same sale as her, Reward For Effort, had won the Blue Diamond. The night before that, Typhoon Tracy and Avenue had won. A few weeks later Tracy got her first Group 1, then Markus Maximus won the Western Australian Derby.

Black Caviar was a lovely filly from early on, promising in her work and with that great movement I had seen at the sale. But she was big, a huge eater, and with a nature that demanded a good bit of awareness. Not silly, but like a bull at a gate. Because of her size, we'd have to be careful.

Like every horse, we looked at her and gave her a nickname. I can't remember who it was—it might've been me—but in any case, and for whatever reason, we decided this one would be called Nelly.

....

Finally, on 30 March 2009, Black Caviar had her first competitive outing, in an 800-metre barrier trial at Cranbourne. I was feeling good enough to suggest the owners should come and watch, saying: 'You might have some fun with this filly'.

Their trip wasn't wasted. She trialled super. From barrier 1 of 9, she came out like a rocket and led them on her ear. If you look up the video now, you see her doing what she'd do in her races—basically pulling Luke Nolen away from the field. She won untouched by five lengths, with the caller saying prophetically: 'She looks pretty smart'.

Three weeks later, on 18 April, it was off to the races.

I had a dilemma. We had another one ready to debut in Set For Fame, who I'd also bought at that Premier sale. The options for two-year-olds that day were a race for fillies and males up the straight 1000 metres at Flemington, or a 1200-metre maiden at Hamilton.

I liked kicking my horses off in the bush but Jeff O'Connor and I found there was only one horse among the twelve at Flemington who'd won a race, a gelding called Kwassa Kwassa. I was concerned over how young horses can get overawed by the Flemington straight, but we thought Nelly was faster than Set For Fame and should go better at the shorter trip. So Black Caviar went to Flemington for the second race on the card, the Cromwell Handicap, and Set For Fame went bush.

Their races were five minutes apart, which caused a memorable moment with my friendly rival Lee Freedman. After I'd saddled Black Caviar, he and I watched the Hamilton race on TV in the Flemington trainers' room.

'It's a pretty nice filly, this,' I said. We watched as Set For Fame, ridden by my former apprentice Linda Meech, bolted in by seven lengths.

'Jeez—you're not wrong!' Lee said.

I said: 'The one here at Flemington goes just as good, if not better'.

Ten minutes later Freedy's come back and said: 'You weren't kidding, were you!'

Nelly started a $3 favourite off that barrier trial—the only time she was not odds-on. Since Luke was suspended we gave the ride to sixteen-year-old Jarrad Noske, the baby-faced Perth apprentice who'd come over for a three-month loan period with us. We didn't think Black Caviar would be too demanding a ride. In fact, I only gave one instruction: 'Hang on'.

I was confident, though with that nagging concern about the straight. But Black Caviar soon laid any fears to rest, crossing from barrier 10 to sit second outside the leader, easing to the front 300 metres out, and coasting home by five lengths. Though untouched, her time was fair at 56.63 seconds.

I was excited enough to put the normal wariness aside in the post-race interviews: 'She's a damn good filly I think!' I said. 'I really look forward to her future.'

I wasn't quite thinking 25 out of 25, but I was getting a little hopeful. Still, whenever she went flat out I was excited and scared, feeling it wouldn't be hard for a big heavy horse like that to go so fast she'd hurt herself.

Though she was a future best horse in the world, I wasn't even at the races when Black Caviar got into the black type at start two. Mind you, that'd be the only day I didn't saddle her. Intriguing though she was, we had a business to run, and Morphettville was where the big racing was on 2 May 2009. I went there to saddle Astro Gains and Fitoussi in the South Australian Derby, with Luke Nolen aboard the former. There was some frustration when Astro Gains and Fitoussi came second and third, behind Victoria Derby winner Rebel Raider, though at least Astro Gains would later get me that Charleville Cup!

In Melbourne, Jarrad Noske rode Nelly again. We hadn't intended to go chasing black type so soon, but the only suitable race two weeks after her first was the Blue Sapphire Stakes, over 1200 metres at Caulfield. Her rise to Listed class didn't deter punters, who made her a $1.50 favourite in the ten-horse field, with the next best thing at $11.

She had half a kilo under top weight at 57.5 kilograms, but there looked little doubt over the result. Watching from Adelaide, I did have a heart flutter as she butchered the start. That would become familiar. She was smart and eager, and she always tried to anticipate the barriers opening. Sometimes it cost her. She'd try to leave the gates that fast she'd nearly fall arse over head with the energy of it all. Usually though, it wasn't a big problem for a horse like her.

She was a couple of lengths off the leaders as they bounced, but soon Jarrad had her going out wide. She led after 300 metres, got to the fence after another hundred, rounded the turn under a tight hold and then brained 'em, breaking 1:10 for the 1200 metres, untouched, by running 1:09.76. (We wouldn't really take that much notice of her times throughout her career. Thankfully she usually wasn't pushed right out.)

Watching on TV, I noticed one thing really clearly: how, with her action, she looked to be going slower than the other horses. It became a great thing about watching her, like watching Ian Thorpe swim or Usain Bolt run. It was that beautifully economical action and giant length of stride, which I'd got hints of at the yearling sales. It was pretty exciting to see it come to fruition.

I also have a quiet smile to myself if I see the replay now, hearing the surprise, or even astonishment, in caller Greg Miles' voice at how easy it seemed.

'But she looked to be cruising in the early part of the straight, Black Caviar,' he said, then suddenly: 'She's three lengths in front, and did it very, very comfortably'.

As she won by six, it sounded like Greg was feeling there might be something special here. So was I.

....

A few days later I got a phone call. It was big-time owner Nathan Tinkler.

'I've got a filly for you to train.'

'That's good,' I said. 'Who is it?'

'Black Caviar.'

I laughed, but he was dead serious. Tinkler had got rich from mining and made a splash into racing through his Patinack Farm operation. It all went belly up later on, but back then he was used to getting what he wanted.

'Tell the owners I want to buy her,' he said. 'I'll give 'em whatever they want. Whatever it takes.'

I laughed again and said: 'She's not for sale'.

'Everything's for sale.'

'The people who've got her won't sell her.'

Tinkler insisted I call them, but I knew what the answer would be. That's because advertising guru John Singleton had just rung as well. He was very smart about it.

'No one would ever sell a horse that good,' Singo said. 'But I'll give the owners an open cheque to buy a half share in her.'

I contacted Neil Werrett and Gary Wilkie but there was no interest in selling. While Singo and Tinkler had come direct to me, which is what you're supposed to do, Neil and Gary would field some offers too, including from some of the biggest breeding establishments in the world. Neil, who knows about crunching deals as a successful property businessman, said she wasn't for sale at any price.

Tinkler would later get a replica. He bought Nelly's half-brother, out of Helsinge, for $1.025 million, outbidding myself and Neil Werrett. As we all know, the horse was All Too Hard. He finished second in a Cox Plate but won four Group 1s. The irony is that three of those wins were under the part-ownership of Neil Werrett's Vinery Stud, after Tinkler had to sell out when his empire collapsed.

Things were getting busier. My phone was ringing a lot more, with old mates and other people calling to check up on this filly. I'll admit Sarah and I were getting a little excited. At the same time we had a good team, with the likes of Typhoon Tracy, Reward For Effort, Headway and Avenue. Still, it was so far so good for Nelly, as Jeff O'Connor and I planned our next move.

Black Caviar had come up too late for the autumn riches, but the Brisbane winter carnival was looming. But after a couple of days' thought we opted to take our time and wait for the spring. After a few weeks on our farm, Nelly did her pre-training at Quinny Scott's again before returning to Caulfield in mid-June.

She began her three-year-old spring a little in the lap of the gods. We had to find out what kind of a racehorse she'd be: the type for the Group 1 Thousand Guineas over 1600 metres? We didn't know. We knew we had a good filly who'd won her first two and created some interest. We also knew she'd won twice, virtually in the off-season. And though a stakes race, the Blue Sapphire wasn't high profile.

But I had started allowing myself the odd fanciful thought. The horse she flogged in the Blue Sapphire, Demerit, had looked okay. He'd go on to win the Caulfield Guineas Prelude. The third horse, Carrara, won a Listed race at the Brisbane carnival. This suggested ours was pretty good, but you still needed to see her come back and do it again.

Nelly made her comeback in August 2009. It was great, but didn't tell us much. She raced just four other horses in a 1200-metre Listed three-year-old fillies race at Moonee Valley, the Crockett Stakes, as a $1.20 chance. The race was special for one major reason. It was the start of the double act of Luke Nolen and Black Caviar.

As I legged him up for a fairly undaunting assignment aboard a horse who'd become one of the greatest ever, I allowed myself a joke: 'Now Luke, make sure you don't get beat on this thing after it's won its first two'.

There wasn't much danger of that. Black Caviar missed the kick clearly again, but was soon outside the leader Noesis. Rounding the home turn she just clicked and, with the ears pricked, skipped three lengths clear in about half a second. She cruised home by almost four lengths in a reasonable 1:11.15. Three races later Carrara franked the form by winning the Listed McKenzie Stakes.

In a sign of the growing interest in this filly, the post-race interview went much longer than usual. Maybe we were scratching for things to say after such an easy win, but one thing I told interviewer Bruce Clark was that it was good to see her go to sleep beside the leader, which suggested she could be versatile. She could have sat at the back and won. I also said, while she'd made a game of it up the straight, we still didn't know how she'd react if something one day put pressure on her.

I made the comparison to that other great sprinter General Nediym, remembering that day I was scared he might run through the fence at Ipswich.

'In terms of raw ability, I've only been involved with one similar and that was General Nediym,' I said. 'You look at them and it's like a car going around a corner too fast and you're watching and waiting for something to fly off. To match his deeds, she's got a long way to go, but she's got a lot of raw talent.'

While she did have a long way to go, it was shaping as a fun ride. I also mentioned there were some nice options for her at Moonee Valley. One was the Manikato Stakes, the big weight-for-age sprint. The other was the Cox Plate.

The latter might raise eyebrows now. Black Caviar never raced beyond 1400 metres, and the Cox Plate is 2040 metres. But I was keeping everything open. I was just thinking good horses go in good horses' races. The Cox Plate, where three-year-old fillies get only 47.5 kilograms, was the cream of the crop.

In the end I jumped off both Valley options. Next, she'd stick to three-year-old company, though against males this time, in the Group 2 Danehill Stakes up Flemington's straight 1200 metres.

....

By this time we had a standing as one of the biggest stables in the country, which was recognised again when we were given another good rising three-year-old in the Sydney sprinter Wanted.

The Fastnet Rock colt had some interesting part-owners: Gary Johns, the father of rugby league stars Andrew and Matty Johns, as well as prominent owner Eddie Hayson. He's been a fairly controversial figure, and would end up declaring himself insolvent and lose control of a high-profile brothel he owned. Another owner was *Sydney Morning Herald* track clocker Mick Fagan, which was why Wanted was just known as 'Mick' around the stable.

Though I never had a problem with the owners, they had changed their trainers a bit. Wanted debuted for John Hawkes, before going to John O'Shea. He had him for four runs topped off by a tenth in the Golden Slipper in which we had come second with Headway. He then transferred him to me.

I'm not complaining, but having another good sprinting three-year-old created a juggling act involving Black Caviar. However, Wanted would still race against her first up, in the $250,000 Danehill stakes.

It was shaping as Black Caviar's biggest test, ahead of some more rich sprints in the following weeks, so she was longer than her previous start at $1.45.

It was looming as a massive day. I had Typhoon Tracy in the Group 1 Makybe Diva Stakes, but she was beaten a lip by Vigor. We also had Avenue and the handy Annenkov at Flemington, but they finished second and fourth. We had Speedy Natalie as a chance in the Furious Stakes at Randwick, but she flopped. Had Black Caviar not won, our promising day would have been a disaster, apart from Cortona winning us a maiden at Warracknabeal.

Nelly won, but it was still almost a disaster.

With Luke riding her under 54 kilograms in the set-weights-and-penalties conditions, and Brad Rawiller steering Wanted under 55.5 kilograms, I took my place in the stand to watch the nine-horse race. When the gates opened, my blood ran cold.

Even watching the replay years later makes me shudder, as you hear the alarm in Greg Miles' voice: 'Oooh—Black Caviar really knuckled. She began terribly today!'

From barrier 2, she had again scrambled to lunge out of the gates. This time it was bad. All those enormous physical forces at play, the dynamics of the start on her big, eager body, more or less boiled over. Her forelegs splayed out, she dipped down at the front, then as all this pressure came from her rear to propel herself forward, she lost her balance to the left.

Thank God for a very ordinary gelding trained by my mate Mick Price called Point Pain, jumping from barrier 1. If he hadn't been there, Nelly could have come down completely, and 25 out of 25 wouldn't exist. Black Caviar scrambled for half a stride, then, in overbalancing, she bumped Point Pride with her rear. That horse got knocked about three spots to the left, which I'm sure Mick wasn't happy about, but it was this that kept Black Caviar upright.

To most, the race unfolded smoothly. Black Caviar won of course, though not by any great margin. In fact, after she settled in a narrow lead and pulled clear at the 300 metres, Wanted got clear and looked like he might pressure her. Luke actually had to give Nelly a couple of hits with the whip and she stayed strong to win by three-quarters of a length. While most were marvelling at this unbeaten filly, I watched her come back with my heart in my mouth.

Horses are fragile things and, though there had been no super slo-mo replay to analyse just what had happened at the start, I feared I'd seen it all before. Those types of stresses on a horse's body will often cause an injury. I'd watched for it during the race, but though she appeared to travel strongly enough, you don't find out until they cool down.

'I just hope she hasn't hurt herself,' I said in the post-race interview. 'Hopefully we've still got a horse.'

I mumbled some other stuff—she wouldn't get away with that in top-level races; and that the Manikato Stakes or the 1600-metre Caulfield Guineas were possible targets—but my mind was racing. I was desperate to go over her.

We had already detected one issue with her, involving the muscles in her chest. It was nothing dramatic, but if she did have any soreness, it would be there. And that was exactly where all the pressure was at the start that day.

I had my fingers crossed that we'd dodged a bullet.

....

We hadn't.

In the hours after the race Black Caviar came up very tender when you felt her chest. We didn't yet know for sure but, while she'd done an amazing job just to finish the race, let alone win, there was a chance this could be career-threatening.

At the least, everything was up in the air again.

Still hoping to race her again that spring, we sent her to Mick Bryant's the following day. Mick identified that she had torn muscles in her chest coming out of the barriers. At least muscles hadn't been torn away from bone, but there were tears within the muscles, something she'd have problems with because of her size and speed. Mick worked on her for a week, using mostly ultrasound, then we sent her to Peter Clarke's at Murchison, to keep her fit on the water-walker. The Manikato Stakes and Caulfield Guineas were out, but there was a chance of starting her in open class in the big sprint at Flemington on Derby Day, then known as the Salinger Stakes.

Peter had her for another two weeks, during which the picture started to look a little less bleak. But it was clear this spring campaign, when she had promised to really show how good she was, was over.

We brought her home for a month on our farm. Here was another reason I loved living semi-bush. We had to run the rest of our big team of course, but at home I could see her every time I stepped out for a smoke. I could see her from the kitchen window. Mind you, that wasn't going to stop her hurting herself.

I'd get to know her better in this period. Structurally, her joints were okay. Her problems were all muscular, again with the strains at play in her massive body. We bought a hand-held laser to work on her, to help repair the chest muscles by promoting blood flow, like an ultrasound. We also used to feed her eggs, because the lining of the eggs was good for muscle healing.

While we had plenty of reasons to celebrate, like Typhoon Tracy and Headway's Group 1 double on Derby Day, those weeks were tense. In the end, though, the injury settled down, and I breathed a huge sigh of relief.

16

A Champion Makes Her Mark

Black Caviar returned in the autumn of 2010 with the world at her feet and our stable burning towards our first premiership. Wanted was giving me headaches, though I guess of a good kind. I thought he could win the Group 1 Lightning Stakes at Flemington, so I wanted to keep him and Black Caviar apart. In Nelly's absence, he'd gone well in three Group 1s, running fourth in the Manikato, seventh in Headway's Coolmore Classic, and a gutsy three-quarter-length second in All Silent's Patinack Classic.

Hindsight shows I should have run Black Caviar in the Lightning. She'd have got a prized Group 1 at her fifth start. But I decided to send Wanted into the autumn treble of the Lightning–Oakleigh Plate–Newmarket. Winning a good stallion-making race like the Lightning would mean more to his breeding prospects than to Black Caviar. So I decided to take the low road with her to Moonee Valley—the Group 2 Australia Stakes, then the Group 1 William Reid Stakes. In the end I was lucky to get the Group 2.

Wanted tried hard in the Lightning but was beaten a long head by David Hayes' Nicconi. Though you'll pull the wrong rein many times in racing, I did kick myself, because by then it was obvious Black Caviar would have won hands down. She'd resumed eight days earlier at the Valley, where things took on a familiar pattern. She scared everyone away for the $200,000 Australia Stakes, with only four other horses turning up. With only 53 kilograms under the weight-for-age conditions, while the other four older males had 58.5 kilograms, it looked pretty straightforward for her.

The race marked a couple of firsts. It was the first time Donna Fisher strapped the horse. She would continue to do so for the rest of her career as the pair of them became great mates. Donna was the perfect fit. Nelly didn't like standing still. She liked to be kept moving. But it didn't have to be at any speed, just cruising along, and that was Donna to a tee. Her manner was to just poke along, unruffled, at the one rhythm all day, and Nelly would poke along with her all day at the same rhythm. They made a great pair, like the human and equine versions of each other. You'd watch them parading before the race and you'd sometimes have to check to see if they were moving. But as long as they were moving in some form, Nelly was happy.

As for the other first, Luke had come up with a solution to Nelly's tardy starts. She was such a big thing that being in the barriers felt claustrophobic and uncomfortable for her. Plus, she always wanted to jump so quick. We wanted to have her more relaxed, so Luke suggested we use a barrier blanket. For the uninitiated, the horse goes in with the blanket wrapped around them from behind, and it is attached to the back of the gates. When the horse jumps, it jumps out of the barrier and the blanket. It relaxes the animal, makes it feel more snug. Thanks to Luke, that would do the trick for the rest of her career.

Around this time Nelly also formed a bond with someone else who would play a role in her story. Glen Darrington was a former jockey and a mate of Luke's who'd become a barrier attendant. Luke asked him to look after our girl behind the gates one day, and this started an association that had Glen not only putting her blanket on behind the gates but actually going into the barrier with her, standing on the rail beside her and keeping her calm till they jumped. It would help guard against that habit of hers of bursting too hard out of the barriers, which risked injury.

Though employed by Racing Victoria, Glen became such a part of the routine that we ended up getting special permission for him to work with her at the start of her two later races in Adelaide, and even at Royal Ascot. You might call it unusual circumstances for an unusual horse.

This Moonee Valley outing was also Nelly's first go under lights, and her first against open company. This was reflected in her veritable bolter's odds of $1.70. I thought she would go well, but there were some worries. There was Here De Angels, a good sprinter for trainer Mark Kavanagh. Plus our mare was first up, and coming back from an injury. In fact, before the race I said something to the media. No one could have predicted that I'd be wrong (not in every instance of course, but in this one at least). In any case, I'm damn glad I was. 'Black Caviar is going to get beaten some time,' I said. 'If it is Friday night, so be it.'

In the end, though, it was a procession. Black Caviar at last made a good start, from barrier 4. Here De Angels took the lead but Nelly sat up outside his hindquarters. There might have been some wondering what the gelding could produce approaching the home turn, but Nelly pulled away easily. With Luke showing her the whip—waving it where she could see it but not hitting her—she strolled in by more than two lengths.

I was hugely relieved. She had been going well at the stables, but you are never happy till you see them race. I commented post-race how great it was to see the improvement in her. She was now three and her bones were still developing but she had gone up again ability-wise. Yes, it was a small field. Still Luke and I were thinking: 'We've hopped on a pretty big ride here'.

She was attracting real attention now, drawing people to the races even then. And when you've got a good horse, everything's on the radar. I said I might get her vaccinated to go to the Dubai World Cup two months later for a $2.5 million sprint on dirt. I also considered the Newmarket three weeks after the William Reid. She was good enough, and would get a light weight. There was the Brisbane winter carnival. I even had a return to Royal Ascot in mind, since it was a fair way off in June.

For now, we'd be back to Moonee Valley in three weeks for that Group 1, in the $500,000 William Reid, while also keeping her away from my other sprinters.

However, disaster was about to hit us out of the blue again.

....

Four days before the William Reid, Black Caviar galloped at Caulfield and worked very nicely. But the next morning Tony Haydon called, saying he had felt some heat and swelling in her right foreleg. I went to the stable full of dread.

I saw her, and she didn't look 100 per cent right. I felt her, and it didn't feel good.

We sent her for scans and X-rays, hoping for the best. But the news was even worse than I'd feared. Not only did she have a minor tear in the suspensory, but she had pulled a small piece of bone away where the ligament joins on. The curtain came down again. She would miss the autumn. Dubai was out. Brisbane, Ascot, the works. Worse still, it was looking like this horse, shaping up as the best I'd trained, might face a whole career plagued by injury. I just couldn't bloody believe it.

These were some pretty dark days indeed. I had to call the owners, which felt bad. They'd been great, and patient, but had only seen her once this preparation, and not even in a Group 1.

I was really kicking myself that I hadn't run her in the Lightning. I thought: 'You fucken idiot! You've just broken down the best horse you've trained, and she's still not even a Group 1 winner!'

I was beginning to wonder if it would ever come. That sounds dramatic, but we know how elusive Group 1s are, and how much can go wrong with a horse. The frustration and the worry were massive— not to mention the self-flagellation.

There was some consolation in that her injury again wasn't career threatening. I did make the comment that if she was an old gelding you probably would have pushed on, and the thought did cross my mind. But, with a horse of this much potential, we weren't going to muck around. Though she was emerging as a headline act, we still had a fabulous support cast. I was desperate to win a Group 1 with Nelly, but at least we weren't sweating on her paying the bills.

Still, as she left our stables for more rest and rehab, I was churning up inside.

....

With Black Caviar gone, we put Wanted into the William Reid. Just to aggravate me further, he was second again, to Anthony Cummings' Turffontein. Wanted was the type who would loom up in the straight and then just sort of wait. He'd had that Lightning shot to pieces, then Nicconi nabbed him down the outside.

Wanted continued to the Oakleigh Plate, with Luke Nolen replacing Brad Rawiller. This time he finished a half-length fourth to that one I'd missed out on, Starspangledbanner.

I was starting to despair about Wanted as much as Black Caviar, but finally he got that stallion-making Group 1 in possibly the biggest sprint there is—the Newmarket. What a day Super Saturday was at Flemington that year!

It was a nineteen-horse field, and I guess it showed how we were going that I contributed four of them, with Wanted, Headway, Duporth and Tickets. Wanted was a $13 chance behind Starspangledbanner, Nicconi, Turffontein and the straight-loving All Silent. I was optimistic about Wanted under a light three-year-old's weight of 51.5 kilograms. But as the race loomed, so too did some massive black clouds.

The weather started getting wild, and it was looking like hailing. I was hoping it would stay away for the race, but my mind was also 30 miles away. Not only was Black Caviar at our farm, she was sharing a paddock with Typhoon Tracy. They were a fair couple to have in your backyard, but I was worried the storm that was about to hit Flemington would end up hitting our place as well. So as Wanted was getting onto the track, I was getting onto the phone to Sarah, hoping she was home.

Watching the replay now, Wanted won at what looked less like Flemington and more like Armageddon. Unusually, they all came down the middle, staying away from the inside and outside. To his credit, Wanted got to the lead for Luke and just kept kicking, fighting off Starspangledbanner, then David Hayes' Eagle Falls, to pull away and win by a length. Headway did all right in sixth, with Duporth ninth, and Tickets sixteenth.

And Wanted did it just in time, because when the horses were coming back to scale—KABOOM—the hailstorm hit.

It was phenomenal, as you can still see now on YouTube. There were hailstones as big as golf balls, and some horses got hurt by them coming off the track. Fourth placegetter King Pulse slipped over on the hail twice, then bolted away down the tunnel and was badly injured smashing into a fence. Wanted also broke free in the tunnel but, thankfully, he was quickly caught by clerk of the course John Patterson. Flemington turned white, while the rain was also bucketing down. They had to call off the last three races, postponing till the following week the day's other Group 1s, the Australian Guineas and the Australian Cup. (I had Set For Fame in the Guineas, but had to wait a week to see her run second.)

Meanwhile, on the other side of Melbourne, the storm hit our place. Thankfully Sarah was there and got Black Caviar and Typhoon Tracy in under our big back shed just in time, because it was murderous out there too. Sarah and our daughter Breann were there holding the horses and couldn't even hear each other shouting over the noise of the tin roof. Fortunately Black Caviar and Typhoon Tracy were a sensible pair. They stood there and waited out the storm.

Despite our troubles with Black Caviar, I was delighted for Wanted to win the stable's sixteenth Group 1. He ran again a month later, for a fighting fourth in the T.J. Smith at Randwick, before being retired to stud. He was a rig, rather than a full stallion. This meant he was operating on just one testicle, but tests had shown he was fertile. Still, Wanted hasn't done great at stud, with one stakes winner to the time of writing. At least it was well named—Dead Or Alive.

....

In that month that we had her at home, we kept Black Caviar restricted until she healed—in a small box in a small paddock so she couldn't go galloping around and aggravate the injury. Horses will do things like run to the corner of a paddock then suddenly have to jam their feet down to pull up, or duck and dive. In general, they don't do controlled exercise. For Nelly, it was a bit hard to be confined because she was such a big girl and could be a bull at a gate.

While the injury wasn't that huge, I worried about how she'd come back. It's important that these suspensories heal correctly, especially for big horses. You want the fibres of the ligament to align well so they will be strong into the future. If an injured horse isn't exercising in a controlled way, the tendon fibres might not knit in an orderly, controlled way. Given the type of horse we had on our hands, patience and TLC were going to be everything. It would be a slow process.

Nelly went to Peter Clarke's for three months of rehab and building fitness on the water-walker, then three weeks back with me, another three weeks at Peter's, then into Caulfield for a few weeks of trotting and cantering, to get her used to being at a track again after six months away. She went back to Peter's as we worked her up slowly, using low-concussion methods to get the weight off her. She was such a big girl. She was tall, though not freakishly so, at 16.2 hands, but she was just built. She just had this massive bulk, which you could see from the fact her beautiful big rump was so much bigger than those of all the other horses. Most horses average about 480 to 500 kilograms. Nelly was always about 570 to 580 kilograms.

She was a huge eater. When she was in the paddock, she'd start on her feed bin, then go and chase a few other horses away from theirs and grab a mouthful of theirs too, then get back to finishing her own. But being a good eater, with an egg mixed into her feed, helped her recover quickly from all those little muscle tears and so forth.

Another thing we learnt was she used to be in season what seemed like all the time, or 'on heat' in dog language. She lived on Regu-Mate, this treatment to suppress the heat. So she could get annoyed and would like to be left alone, which was another good reason for having her in our Box 1. She'd only have one horse next to her, usually Typhoon Tracy or Avenue. Some horses didn't like that box because they always wanted to see what was going on. But Nelly would never be sticking her head out.

Finally, eight months after Black Caviar had hurt herself, we brought her back to Caulfield to get ready to race again. She'd had ticks of approval from everyone—Peter Clarke, our vet Peter Angus, and Mick Bryant. She won a trial at Cranbourne on a heavy 10. It was good to know she could handle the wet, though she would actually never race on worse than a good track. So, with great relief, but of course the ever-present trepidation, I was able to map out a plan—for the spring carnival, and hopefully that long-awaited Group 1. First, she would resume in the Group 2 Schillaci Stakes over 1000 metres at Caulfield.

....

There was a lot of attention on that run on Caulfield Stakes day, which was a royal day for racing. Bart's great horse So You Think won the Stakes. Gai's top mare More Joyous won the Toorak Handicap. I claimed the Caulfield Guineas with Anacheeva, and took out the last with Avenue.

And Black Caviar won the Schillaci.

It was a bumper crowd and expectations of Black Caviar were high. It felt like a lot of people had come just to see her race and were happy to watch her go round. The field wasn't strong, with only seven rivals headed by Blue Diamond winner Star Witness, but, perhaps because of her lengthy lay-off, Nelly was a relatively long $1.80.

I was holding my breath: 'We've got possibly the best horse in the country, but is she gonna stay in one piece?' Thanks to that suspensory, we had reached the stage where every race she had through that period was about hoping she'd get another one. Thankfully, this was in fact where things finally started to go smoothly, where Black Caviar could take a step up and really grab the country's attention.

She jumped well from gate 2, got to the lead early and, as she thundered along, I was relieved to see she still had that explosive kick around the home turn. She went on to win on her ear by two lengths, with Star Witness only fourth.

'Black Caviar's back, as brilliant as she left!' said Greg Miles. He wasn't wrong, but as I told the owners, my biggest thrill would come if I saw her walk out of her box in the morning in one piece.

Morning came and I called Tony down at the stables and held my breath. But the coast was clear. It was on to start No. 7.

It still wouldn't be a Group 1. We'd be patient again, and go into the Schweppes Stakes, a 1200-metre Group 2 on Cox Plate Day. Not only was Nelly stepping up in distance, even though it was just a six-horse field, she would be meeting a better class of horse.

While the Black Caviar phenomenon was building steam, there were still people prepared to doubt her. People will always look for chinks in the armour, or reasons a horse isn't up to the hype. She was 'a Melbourne champion', hadn't won a Group 1, hadn't been tested in Sydney, et cetera. Well now the Sydney form was coming to have a crack at her. Hot Danish, the superstar mare from the Les Bridge stable, would be lining up, as would Melito.

Unlike us, Hot Danish had runs on the board. She had won two Group 1s and won away from home, in big races at Flemington and Doomben. But she was also seven years old. Gerald Ryan's four-year-old Melito had also won twice at top level, and interstate.

Now also four, Black Caviar was rising up the ratings, worked out by handicappers for assessing horses for races. From being benchmark 76 at her second start, she'd quickly risen to 111.

Hot Danish was 117, with Melito 114. They were good mares and Black Caviar was having just her seventh start, and second run back from injury. I'd be lying if I said we weren't feeling our way, though the punters were having none of it. Nelly was a raging $1.40 chance, Hot Danish was $6 and Melito $12.

Deep down, I did think she would win. She was on familiar ground at Moonee Valley, where she'd performed super before. She liked the Valley, where the cambers helped her get that massive frame around the bends. It was again just a case of hoping she didn't break.

Hot Danish jumped best from gate 1, with Black Caviar a bit casually out. Luke hunted her up until she popped out and got up outside the leader, True Persuasion. Hot Danish was in the sweet seat, third on the fence, with Melito on our back. They had every chance.

In the end we had nothing to worry about. Nelly pulled Luke to the lead just before the turn, she put three lengths on them in a split second and came away to win by five, with Hot Danish second and Melito second-last.

It was seven from seven and the momentum and hype had escalated again. Already I commented in the post-race interview that I was running out of things to say, she was doing it so effortlessly.

'It's just scintillating what she does,' I said. 'Luke's got this theory the faster she goes the better she feels, but when I legged him on I just said, "I'm scared something's gonna fly off".'

I offered again that the great unknown was how she would go if something pressured her. We'd never had to find out, but now it was time to raise our sights to a situation where we might. Finally, it was time to take the most exciting horse I'd had and put her in a Group 1. She would go into the race sponsored by the bloke who'd tried to buy her, Nathan Tinkler, in the Patinack Stakes up the straight 1200 metres at Flemington on Emirates Stakes day.

It was also time to meet an opponent who'd been stirring up a lot of dust on our horizon. His name was Hay List.

....

I'd been watching Hay List from afar and I did think that, if any horse was going to really let us find out what we had on our hands in Black Caviar, it was him.

He had started out like Black Caviar himself, winning his first eight starts in Perth and later transferring to Gosford trainer John McNair. After a second at Randwick, he won the Group 3 Healy Stakes at Eagle Farm by five lengths. He really set tongues wagging then in Melbourne by winning the McEwen Stakes and the Group 1 Manikato Stakes at Moonee Valley, and the Group 2 Gilgai at Flemington. Now he would run against Black Caviar. People were salivating about our clash: the seven-from-seven Black Caviar, against the eleven-from-thirteen Hay List. It was the coming together of the two gun sprinters of Australia, at Flemington. It was pretty exciting stuff.

The questions, and some anxiety, had been bubbling away for me. I'd been asked if I was looking forward to meeting Hay List and my answer was 'no'. I did add, though, that I'd never been one to run away from a fight, so it was going to happen.

'We're undefeated. We've got to go forward and keep going forward,' I said, before adding: 'The more you win the closer you are to defeat'. It's nice to think back on those words today!

I'd be lying if I said I wasn't worried about Hay List, but I got a confidence boost from my Queensland jockey mate Chris Munce, who had ridden Hay List in his Brisbane win. He said while Hay List was very good, Black Caviar would be too good for him, even though he'd only seen her on TV. The bookies agreed. Black Caviar, with 56.5 kilograms at weight for age, would be marginally odds on. Hay List, with 58.5 kilograms, was $3.40.

But we had another problem to solve—the jockey. Luke had been suspended the previous week, so we had to find someone else for, hopefully, her first top-level win. The only other jockey who had ridden her was Jarrad Noske, but he had moved back to Perth.

Glen Boss, a great big-occasion jockey who'd done a fair bit of riding for me, was an option. But, while I love him as a rider, he also had that bit of theatrics about him, with his celebrations and reactions on the finishing line. This was Black Caviar's first Group 1, so I didn't want anything taking attention away from her. More importantly, her injury record meant she carried a 'handle with care' tag.

There was Linda Meech, who'd been apprenticed to me and was pretty much my No. 2 stable jockey behind Luke.

Here's one of my biggest regrets to this day—not giving Linda the chance to ride Black Caviar. She was an unbelievably loyal servant to the stable, and Neil Werrett was prepared to let her ride. But after a lot of angsting I decided not to. Hay List was on the horizon, I wondered how Linda would cope with the pressure, and I felt we'd be on a hiding to nothing.

In the end, the last person who wasn't Luke Nolen to ride Black Caviar in a race would be Ben Melham. He was only 22 and, like Nelly, hadn't won a Group 1, but I rated him. I thought his low, gentle, kind style would suit her. Still, when I legged him on for the big match-race, I reminded him: 'She's unsound, this filly, so when she wins, the last thing I want you doing is diving and leaning all over her. I know it'll be hard because it's your first Group 1, but I want no theatrics, no standing up in the irons and lairising.'

I said '*when* she wins', so I must have been confident. In fact, word was Hay List had hurt himself, putting his foot in a water trough or something like that. There were only five other opponents, headed by Blue Diamond winner Star Witness and All Silent, who had won the previous two editions of the Patinack and loved the Flemington straight.

Still, I was a bit toey that day, with this breakthrough win within touching distance. Among all of Black Caviar's wins, this was one of the most special—her first Group 1. Though it might seem modest considering what unfolded, I felt if she won that day she didn't have to get to the races ever again.

As it transpired, as so often, the mare made her rivals look second-rate, and my anxieties look silly. With the small field closer to the grandstand side than the flat, Black Caviar was up on the pace from the start, with Hay List keeping with her on her inside. But before long, those doubts about Hay List seemed to bear fruit. His jockey, Glyn Schofield, went for him at the 400 metres but he was already gone. As he dropped off, Star Witness came out from behind us and looked ready to pounce, but Black Caviar was cruising. Ben opened up a little on her past the 300 metres and she just pulled away. She won by four lengths.

'What a champion she is,' said Greg Miles. Again, she'd won in that effortless style. Again she'd looked like she wasn't moving compared to the others, who were going flat out. She won untouched in 1:07.96. She would have given the track record of 1:07.16 a nudge if shaken up, but that wasn't important.

It was a huge relief. Finally we'd claimed the Group 1 win to do justice to her talents. I was happy for young Ben, not to mention getting a chuckle out of the reaction he allowed himself. He didn't go mad, or stand up and take a bow. But he did allow himself one very reserved little wave to the crowd with his left hand upon hitting the line—like winning the lotto and celebrating with a cup of tea. You can also see on the video he's grinning like a Cheshire cat.

Star Witness got second, with Hay List second-last. There'd be more battles with him, at his peak, on the road ahead.

The buzz around Nelly went up a sizeable notch that day. Lee Freedman, who had seen Vain and trained Miss Andretti, said Black Caviar was the best sprinter he'd seen anywhere in the world. In the following days, another purchase offer would be knocked back—$5 million this time, from Gold Coast interests—while a fresh set of World Thoroughbred Rankings, from the France-based International Federation of Horseracing Authorities, would rate her the equal-best sprinter in the world, along with Hong Kong's Sacred Kingdom, with a mark of 122.

I was especially happy for Nelly's owners. After I'd blown their budget at the yearling sales, they now had a million-dollar winner. They'd been so patient, as they were through her career. Most people get to enjoy their horses having seven or eight starts per preparation. Nelly had had four preps and eight starts!

The owners would be great to deal with throughout Nelly's career. As they'd discover, having a champion brings a flipside, with lots of pressure from internal and external sources. Gary Wilkie once said that, as the story went on, he often found it hard to sleep. 'You realise it's the luckiest thing you're going to get in your life,' he told one newspaper. That in itself caused worry and stress—that something might go wrong and it might all end.

And the owners would have been getting advice from everywhere— friends, family, associates—on how to train the horse, where to run it, who to ride it, and so forth. But they never put any of that on me. Not once.

17

Black Caviar®

At this point, life at Booran Road, Caulfield, was pretty unbelievable. Forget about 'trainer Peter Moody'. I was Willy Wonka!

Going to work every day was pinch-yourself stuff. Fantasy land. In our main barn, boxes 1 to 8 were for fillies and mares, and in that row we had eight stakes-quality females. You just never dreamt of having that. We had Black Caviar, Typhoon Tracy, Set For Fame, who won a Group 2 at Caulfield that spring, and Avenue, who won seven stakes races. There was Willow Creek, who'd won a Group 2 in Sydney, Panipique, who won three Listed sprints, and Curtana, who won two. From the males, Anacheeva had just won the Caulfield Guineas. It was staggering. Tommy Smith, Lee Freedman and David Hayes might have had it in their time, but for me it was mind-blowing.

We were heading to our second premiership, and you just never imagined you could be this lucky. At the same time, it was part of the reason our celebrations for Black Caviar's first Group 1 were a bit quiet—dinner with the owners at a restaurant on Melbourne's Southbank, the first gathering we had had as a group. One, I couldn't wait to get to the stables the next day to see if she pulled up okay. Two, we had lots of other horses to look after.

While Nelly was special, and getting more special, we had to prepare all the others too. Black Caviar didn't win us that 2009–10 premiership. A lot of horses did. And it would annoy me to hear indirectly that other owners were complaining I was all about one horse and not showing enough attention to theirs. It wasn't the case.

That reaction was really disappointing. We weren't a one-man show. We were a big operation. But it was sad that you'd hear these negative comments from people: 'How could they be doing the right thing and caring for our horse with all the attention on Black Caviar?' We knew we'd really have to portray that we were winning 180 or 200 races a season, of which Black Caviar was winning three or four.

Still, that was a minor annoyance in the unbelievable scheme of things. We were now fully aware we had something pretty rare in box 1. Tony Haydon would go straight to Nelly first thing every morning to run his hands over her legs and check her out. He probably wouldn't have done that after her first couple of starts.

And the racing public had now clicked onto the fact they might be witnessing greatness. They weren't turning up in her colours or waving her flags yet, but that would soon happen.

The mare herself pulled up well from the Patinack, and it was time for another spell. The big show was about to really go boom the following autumn.

....

Black Caviar was thrashing everything she met but there were still some doubts being cast around: she still hadn't been away from home or done anything extraordinary; she'd won a Group 1 but Hay List wasn't right. She'd won eight from eight but had she really arrived? There was still a question mark.

The autumn of 2011 was the time to build on it. Things felt a bit less tense. Now she had won that Group 1, anything else would be a bonus. Thankfully for its trainer, a horse this good does allow a certain sense of freedom.

This would be Black Caviar's longest campaign yet. We'd kick off in the Flemington straight double—the Lightning and Newmarket. I was also mindful Neil Werrett was from Sydney and she hadn't raced there. I wanted to take her home to Brisbane, there were good races in Adelaide, there were Dubai and Ascot mid-year. Everything was on the table. Some wondered why I didn't try for the Lightning–Oakleigh Plate–Newmarket treble with her as I had done with Wanted. Mostly, I didn't want to push her too hard, and putting the Oakleigh Plate before the Newmarket would have forced her to carry two big handicap weights in the space of two weeks.

I ultimately settled on a plan of six Group 1s spread over three and a half months: the Lightning and Newmarket, the William Reid Stakes at Moonee Valley, the T.J. Smith Stakes at Randwick, and Brisbane's BTC Cup–Doomben 10,000 double.

Nelly had six weeks with Peter Clarke working on the water-walker and hanging out in a paddock, which she enjoyed. For mates she had a pony and a goat who lived on the farm. She'd mate up with anything really. She had a good nature like that.

Black Caviar returned to Caulfield in January 2011, even bigger than before. That ramped up the fear factor and, like always, we managed her very carefully. Had she broken down then and not raced again, she would be remembered now as a 'very good' type who won eight out of eight. She'd been labelled a champion but had only had a few runs in open company, one against a sub-par Hay List. This Lightning Stakes would be his chance to redeem himself, and I was very respectful of him.

Here's where the whirlwind really began.

When I got to Flemington that day, you knew things had changed. The VRC had handed out flags in Nelly's salmon-and-black colours to the crowd. There were more people around her race-day stall wanting a look and a photo. She'd zoomed towards the top of the ratings—not just the local ones, but the world ratings—and there was now this palpable buzz around her. No one would hear of her not claiming her second Group 1. She would start at $1.28, with Hay List at $5.50. That proved pretty spot on.

Nelly settled just off the pace for the 1000-metre event, with Hay List and Glyn Schofield on her outside. He moved up to pressure her about 350 metres out, and got within three-quarters of a length. But when it came time for him to fire up, you could see he was going flat out while she was just rolling. She just eased away, and beat him by three and a quarter lengths.

Now there was another new thing to behold—applause. Not after but *during* the race. Still just halfway down the straight, the crowd stood up and clapped Black Caviar. It was just incredible. It really hit me, gave me goosebumps and made the hairs on the back of my neck stand up. From that day on you heard this big surge of applause, and it was nearly overwhelming. Luke said he even heard it on occasion when he was riding her, and that, since he was usually able to look around a bit, he could see the crowd applauding when they were flying down the straight.

Like the crowd, I was able to just watch for a moment, observe and admire. I'd asked Luke to hold her together. When she got to the clock tower, 150 metres out, he hadn't asked her for anything, yet she was just motoring away from them and the others were all off the bridle. Even I felt it was pretty breathtaking to see a horse do that.

I was a bit lost for words in the post-race interview: 'It's . . . what do you say? Awesome.' Still, I was aware things had shifted to a new level, that we had a horse who looked like she was going to rewrite everything.

'I'm very proud to be an ambassador for racing,' I said. 'She's one helluva horse. Long may she stay sound and we can keep enjoying her here in Australia.'

There'd been growing calls for her to go overseas and be tested against the best from Europe. I wasn't dismissing the idea, but I had my own views too.

'They've got televisions in the rest of the world and they've got plenty of planes coming this way too,' I said. 'So if any of them want to come and have a crack, I'm sure they'll find a spot for them in a Group 1 here in Australia.'

It was a special day. Black Caviar had brought my 21st Group 1— a week after my other special girl Typhoon Tracy had delivered No. 20 in the Orr Stakes—and now Luke had one with her as well. Hay List had no excuses. And the crowd was amazing. It was this day that felt like Black Caviar's 'arrival'.

There was no doubt any more about the big mare up the end of our fillies' boxes. She had overtaken Tracy in our stable's pecking order. She had overtaken any horse I'd worked with.

We were dealing with a superstar.

....

The Black Caviar show and the demands that came with it were really building up. I wouldn't have swapped it for the world, of course, but there were a couple of frustrating bits.

One thing I noticed is that time was getting short. It was just starting to feel like there wasn't much of it!

I had to be mindful of other horses and clients but I was fielding a great deal of requests involving Nelly. She had started to transcend racing. I was getting requests for my time from a lot of non-racing media, magazines and so forth. I'd grown able to deal with the racing media well enough, but the non-racing kind was a bit of a test of patience. The thing was they hadn't really heard of me. I wasn't one of those household names like a Cummings, Smith or Freedman. So these guys would think I'd just arrived with this horse overnight, like Joe Janiak and Takeover Target. They didn't seem to know I'd won a Melbourne premiership and had been in the top four or five trainers in Australia for several seasons. I'd have to explain myself over and over, telling and retelling my story. It was 'Where are you from?' 'How did you arrive?' 'You've appeared on the scene with this horse . . .' I'd be like: 'Hang on—ten years ago I won the Derby with Amalfi!'

It was a lesson for me. Typhoon Tracy had prepared me but, in hindsight, what I'd been through with her was well short of the Black Caviar phenomenon. It was really trying at times but I knew I had to keep my cool and bite my lip. I realised I was becoming a bit of a poster boy for racing. With one loose word or intemperate comment, I'd suddenly have all these people thinking I was nark, or I'd got this good horse and it had gone to my head.

The other downside was that if it wasn't the media, or owners with noses out of joint, you'd also get the narks who would say: 'You're winning too many races. You've gotta be cheating.' People like my vets and horse chiropractor told me they were getting asked by people, including fellow trainers: 'What's he doing? What's he using?' I'd rather not name names but there were some prominent blokes, and various different people, who were putting it out there: 'This isn't right. This doesn't happen. You shouldn't have that many winners, or that many good horses . . .'

I wasn't an overnight sensation. We had been building to this level, with our winners rising by about 15 per cent each year. Still, it's the way the industry works, as other trainers have found on reaching the top. You're allowed to be good, but not *too* good.

The negativity was disappointing but I said to Chris Waller once, when he had copped some bad publicity and innuendo over a positive swab, that my favourite thing to say to anyone having a crack at me was: 'Yeah, I was a bit upset—till I took another look at the trainers' premiership'.

....

The pressure was building. You could feel it. Luke and I would say it was like being on a roller-coaster. It was exhilarating, but it was just absolutely hurtling down the hill.

With my phone ringing off the hook, to try to instill some order I started holding press conferences before Black Caviar's races, rather than have the press coming one by one. Lee Freedman did it in the lead-up to Makybe Diva's third Melbourne Cup, and it was a good idea.

First it was on Fridays but then we moved it to Thursdays, so it wasn't too close to the race. In conjunction with the Melbourne Racing Club, we arranged for the media to come to the stables, we gave them a viewing of Nelly, they could interview me or maybe Luke, we did it in one hit. There were still media who stuffed up and missed out, but at least I didn't feel bad telling them they had missed their opportunity.

The next step, the next test that sent it all up another notch again, was the $1 million Newmarket Handicap.

Of course, when superstars go into handicaps, they'll get a superstar's weight. We braced for Racing Victoria handicapper Greg Carpenter's decision. When it came down—58 kilograms—I had mixed feelings.

I wasn't gobsmacked but it was a big weight. She would have to set a weight-carrying record to win it. In the previous 50 years, 21 horses had carried 58 kilograms or more and only one had got up, the gelding Shaftesbury Avenue. Another great Bart Cummings horse, Maybe

Mahal, held the mares' weight-carrying record for winning the race since metrics came in. She had won five Group 1s but she'd only carried 56.5 kilograms to that 1978 victory. The only mare to win with more weight was Pendant, with the equivalent of 60.5 kilograms, in 1906!

Yes, Black Caviar looked special, but history was definitely against us. I did think at least she was a big horse who could probably carry a big weight, but sometimes I wondered if I was doing the right thing in running her, particular since Hay List had got 56.5 kilograms. After giving her 2 kilos in the Lightning, he'd be benefitting from a 3.5-kilogram swing against her.

I wondered if we shouldn't just stick to weight-for-age and set weights—which we would in fact do from then on. This certainly looked like a litmus test. It was a handicap, so everyone was invited, and weighted to their ability, so they would have their chance to beat her.

But I just felt this had always been lauded as Australia's greatest sprint race, and you didn't want Australia's greatest sprinter not winning Australia's greatest sprint race. So in we went.

Then we turned up and the pressure rose again.

The circus had really hit top gear. At Flemington it was unbelievable—people wearing her colours, or 'I heart BC' T-shirts. There were posters everywhere saying '10/10'. Again the club had provided fans with flags: Nelly's colours on one side and '10/10' on the other. And this was pre-race! I had been forewarned, but still when you turn up and winning is such a foregone conclusion, you feel uneasy. What happens if it doesn't come off? You'd look like a right dickhead, yet you've got nothing to do with it—the hype and the flags and so on.

At least it was worse for Luke than me. He looked around and saw all the '10/10' flags and said: 'God, I wish they wouldn't fucken do that! Surely they should put in a question mark.'

I guess it's superstition, tempting the gods or whatever. At least Black Caviar, as she always did, took all of that out of the equation.

It helped that Hay List had to be scratched, but there were other good ones left like Star Witness, Grand Duels and Hinchinbrook, who'd just been transferred to me from Sydney and had run third in the Oakleigh Plate.

But Black Caviar brained them again. Well, that might be understating it. History shows this was one of *the* great sprinting performances. It was certainly in her top two or three.

Drawing barrier 7 of 11, and at her shortest price yet of $1.18, she got away well enough to ensure clear running, preventing any risk of the only thing that might possibly beat her—getting boxed in. She eased to the front at the 400 metres, scooting clear of the Golden Slipper winner Crystal Lily and her 50 kilograms. The applause began at the 300-metre mark—which was pretty phenomenal—and she strolled away to win by four lengths. Greg Miles summed it up nicely: 'She's unparalleled: Black Caviar. Perfect.'

She clocked 1:07.36, just a fifth of a second outside that track record this time, and again she was untouched. It was also the fastest-ever edition of the race, which was first run in 1874. I also knew, because of weights, that the Newmarket would be her last handicap.

Hearing it now, my post-race interview sounds different. More than previously you can tell that mixed in with my happiness is a lot of relief.

'It's a special moment—there's been a big build-up, and it's great to put it behind us,' I said. 'I'd like to think we've kept our cool all week and I think that extends to the horse. The public perception is what's important. I know she's gonna give her all and the only thing that could bring her down is injury. I'd have been disappointed for the owners and everyone who'd come to see her if something had gone wrong.'

....

After the last race that day, things took another leap into the surreal, and it became clear that Black Caviar was touching the public in a very special way.

Someone from the Victoria Racing Club asked Luke and me if we could sign some autographs. They would run off a hundred copies of the photo finish, we could sign them, then everyone would go away happy with a little souvenir. It would take ten minutes. Maybe fifteen.

They set up a table just outside the members' area. Luke and I started signing . . . but soon we'd run out and they had to run off and print some more. I looked up now and again. The queue just kept growing.

And growing.

And growing.

We kept signing, and signing. Someone brought us a soft drink each. Then they brought us a stubby. The line kept getting longer.

Luke and I were gigging each other: 'What the hell are we doing? Two mongrel kids from the bush, who could barely write their own names when they left school, sitting here signing this photo for people!' We were thinking: 'How can this be happening to us?'

Again, it was pinch-yourself stuff. You'd never seen people lining up to get the autographs of a trainer and jockey before. But they wanted to take away a memento of how they'd seen Black Caviar. The Group 1 Australian Cup had been run that day too, won by Melbourne Cup winner Shocking, but it seemed that hardly registered.

It was very gratifying to hear people's stories, of where they'd come from to watch her race—Tassie, Broome, all over. It was Beatlemania type of stuff. And she'd still only had ten starts.

At one point a lot of Collingwood players were at our little table. Luke had to tell me they were AFL players, because I didn't know.

They were blokes who never had to line up for anything, but here they were, for a photo of this horse with our autographs on it.

We were there about two hours, with Luke in his riding gear the whole time, and we didn't get off the course until it was pretty dark.

I found myself thinking about that evening and other such happenings after I retired. Bart Cummings was a legend, a great man and trainer, but would he have sat there for hours signing autographs? Most probably he'd have quipped a one-liner and gone for dinner with his mates. Would T.J. Smith or Colin Hayes have promoted racing like that? I'd say not.

All I ever tried to do with Nelly was promote racing in a positive light. She was my opportunity to repay racing, for how good it was to me. By now, I realised I had a responsibility. That sounds fanciful but, as I've said, there was a touch of fantasy land about the way things were going. Black Caviar had become public property. Even Phar Lap, Kingston Town and Tulloch—there wasn't this kind of modern publicity and hype around them. There had been promotions for Octagonal, 'The Big O' and so forth. There had been facemasks in Makybe Diva's colours. But what we had on our hands was heading off the scale.

Furthermore, over the following few weeks that Newmarket win would be analysed in some great depth by the experts and would be held up as something historically amazing, almost unbelievable.

It was building. The phenomenon was building. And the pressure was too.

....

Just before the Newmarket we realised we had to take an extraordinary step for extraordinary times and do some outsourcing. When superstars and celebrities get big, one of the things they do is get a business manager to handle their affairs. We got one for our horse.

I remembered the hype around Makybe Diva as she went after her third Melbourne Cup, and it was looking like Black Caviar would go way past that.

The hysteria boomed with those Flemington wins, but I still had to concentrate on all the other horses. It might have seemed to some that Black Caviar was my only runner on Newmarket day, but I had fourteen others at Flemington. I won two other races, including Do Ra Mi's Group 2 Kewney Stakes, in which I had four starters. And let's not forget Exquisite Art winning for us at Echuca!

I had about 80 horses in work and 350 on the books. We were trying to plot a stallion-making path with Hinchinbrook, who came fifth in the Newmarket. And we had 50 potential Hinchinbrooks and Black Caviars in our system. Well, obviously not Black Caviars, but we still had to work on them.

I could handle enquiries about the horse, and our new press conferences reduced the media demands. But there were now other things to consider—merchandise and memorabilia. We needed someone we could palm things off to. So I said to Neil Werrett: 'This is going to get pretty big. You're going to have to put something in place like a management team for the horse.'

They hired Stephen Silk, who had previously been involved in marketing at Racing Victoria. It was certainly the first time I'd trained a horse with a 'commercial manager'. It was probably the first time any horse had one.

We soon wouldn't just be talking about a racehorse but the Black Caviar 'brand', like a mini-industry. There would be merchandise like caps and things sold to the public, and memorabilia auctioned for charity. Some unauthorised merchandise and fake memorabilia had already started appearing, like people making and selling copies of her silks with fake signatures from Luke and me on them. I had started a bit of the registration process with Intellectual Property Australia, but it was now handballed over to Stephen.

We put some structures in place, which felt odd, but was necessary. The name 'Black Caviar' and her salmon-and-black colours were trademarked along with a logo that would be printed on authorised products, and we appointed official merchandise and memorabilia manufacturers. This was important because authentic, signed Black Caviar items began being sold off for charity. A couple of sets of silks fetched around $30,000, one raising funds for the New Zealand earthquake of 2011, and another for the Very Special Kids foundation. The owners supported several charities in this way.

In time, there'd even be a line of Black Caviar equine products. A bit like Kate Moss bringing out some perfume, a Black Caviar brand of shampoo was released, as well as some hoof cream. There were also Black Caviar grooming kits, and even dolls of the horse for the kids.

One article in the *Australian*'s business section said the Black Caviar brand was similar in prestige to Ferrari or Gucci. But it also said it was all about winning. Once she lost, that mystique, aura and marketability would be gone in a flash. Thanks for the extra pressure! Fortunately, this horse was showing she could be relied on to uphold her end of the bargain.

....

It's funny to think of a Group 1 as a stepping stone, but that's kind of what the 2011 William Reid Stakes was, as I was spacing Nelly's runs. A $500,000 Friday night race at Moonee Valley in late March, it was two weeks after the Newmarket and two weeks before the $1 million T.J. Smith Stakes at Randwick.

I didn't think she'd have any trouble—back at weight for age, in a small field. Had I not also contributed Hinchinbrook and Master Harry, there would have only been five starters.

Maybe the best moment came before the race. As Luke took her onto the track, the crowd broke out in spontaneous applause. I broke out in goosebumps.

The race was less emotional. Nelly sat in mid-field this time, and three wide. There was a little alarm in Greg Miles' voice when Luke got busy chasing the leader Crystal Lily before the home turn. But within a flash she kicked clear, and won easing up by almost two lengths. It didn't tell us anything new, but other noteworthy things happened.

This was the start of the crazy odds. Nelly started $1.09, after getting the blows from $1.08. She would only start longer than $1.10 four more times in her last fourteen starts. While this put most punters out of contention, a lot would still back her just to say they had backed Black Caviar. The big-time professional punters would still get on, arguing it was better than bank interest as a dead-set certainty.

The other good thing was I had another kind of win—a Mercedes-Benz worth $130,000—in which I caught the Moonee Valley Racing Club a bit unawares.

As a promotional move, the club had organised a prize of a Benz for any trainer winning $1 million prizemoney in the night racing season, which runs from spring till autumn. Halfway through I'd won a few races but I was well off the million mark, and I think the club even dropped their insurance cover on someone winning the car.

But in the last few meetings I went whooshka, with a stack of winners. Fittingly, they included Miss Gai Flyer taking the Typhoon Tracy Stakes, and Tampiko winning a race called the Black Caviar 25 March Handicap, which advertised when Nelly would be appearing there. Golden Archer also won us a Listed race that night, and Lights Of Heaven had won a $200,000 Group 2 a couple of weeks earlier.

On the last night of the season I only needed Black Caviar to win, so I got the car. There was also a prize for a million-dollar night jockey, which Luke also got through Nelly's win. He had to make do with a TV set.

Trouble was, I had no use for a Merc. We contacted Mercedes-Benz to see if they wanted to maintain it for us, but they didn't. So I sold it and kept driving my Toyota Land Cruiser.

Then the Melbourne Racing Club got together with BMW, sponsor of their Caulfield Cup, and lent me a flash Beamer for a year. I guess it was another marketing move—the trainer of Black Caviar drives a BMW. It also took a pop at their rival Mercedes. Whatever the case, I was the winner.

Another chapter in my life as Willy Wonka!

18

Top of the World

Black Caviar had won eleven out of eleven. It was plain to see a lot of people were coming to the races just to see her, which was great, and something I or most people hadn't witnessed before. In fact, the night of the William Reid a woman was brought to the track in her hospital bed, just so she could see Nelly.

A few days later came confirmation of what we had all suspected for a while: she was the best horse in the world.

The latest World Thoroughbred Rankings (WTR) from France had come out and, based on her Newmarket win, Black Caviar had been given top rating of 130. It was some phenomenal achievement.

It was the first time an Australian horse had rated 130 or topped the WTR list since it started in 2002 (So You Think, then based in Ireland, was fifth on 126). It was the first time a sprinter had been No. 1. She was the highest-rated sprinter in history, and the equal top-rated mare ever, along with the France-based Goldikova, who had hit 130 in 2009. Even Zenyatta, the great American mare who I used to love watching on TV before she'd retired four months earlier, had peaked at 128. (She'd looked invincible, winning her first nineteen starts, before being beaten in her twentieth and last race—something to send a chill down the spine!)

Black Caviar was also ranked the world's best on the respected UK-based Timeform ratings, with 135. Only two mares had scored higher, with French filly Allez France in the early 1970s and England's Habibti in the early 1980s scoring 136. Since Timeform began measuring Australian horses in 1960, only Tulloch with 138, Kingston Town with 137, and Manikato with 136 had scored better.

All of this was nice, but now she faced another challenge. For the first time the Black Caviar show would go on the road—to Randwick for the T.J. Smith Stakes over 1200 metres, seeking to become the first Australian mare to win five successive Group 1s, and the first horse from this country to win her first twelve starts.

Facts and figures suggested she was the best but you've always got to keep your fingers crossed that they travel and settle in okay. Typhoon Tracy had gone to Sydney once and got sick, don't forget.

Nelly would also be running clockwise for the first time, and this seriously held some fears. Yes, she had run that way when broken in at Brett Cavanough's at Albury. And the Melbourne Racing Club was helpful in letting horses work the reverse way at Caulfield before a trip north. Either first or last thing in the morning, she'd gallop from the winning post to the 800-metre mark, quickening up from the 400 metres up the railway side. That home turn is tight, so if they can corner on their right leg it's a good sign. But while Nelly took to it like a duck to water, she still hadn't done it in race conditions.

There was another concern: Hay List. We'd be on his dungheap, and he could be tougher the Sydney way round. Two days after Black Caviar won the William Reid, he had won the Challenge Stakes at Warwick Farm. He was in form.

We took Nelly up by road and stayed at Paul Messara's stables on the home turn at Randwick, which was ideal—a small, secure stable where she was locked away out of the public eye, and where we could have security with her.

That was another first. We hadn't done that at Caulfield, since staff lived at the stables anyway. I didn't think anyone would want to hurt her, but having security would mean she could get peace and quiet; people wouldn't be coming over the fence and annoying her.

We now had a horse with her own commercial manager and a security detail. I just had to shake my head sometimes.

....

With people realising Black Caviar was extraordinary, some more in-depth analysis started. People were asking not how good she could be, but *why* she was so good.

The more obvious bits were the way she was built. A big shoulder for lung capacity, that huge rump where the power comes from, and that overstep. They combined to produce the most important qualities—her length of stride and her economical action, that Usain Bolt–like optical illusion where she seemed to be moving slower than her rivals, while powering away from them.

When you looked at the leg movement, the others were going a hundred mile an hour and she was just flowing. She was beautiful to watch. Incredible.

The other amazing thing was how she would be going along quick but then she would actually lower to the ground, drop by about six inches, and lengthen her stride. It was phenomenal.

In most races she would do the work from the 600 metres to the 400 metres to put the others away. Horses would travel with her till then, then she'd go into overdrive, pushing away but doing it under a hold. It was scary how she could do that.

Luke wasn't asking her to do that; it was purely that other commodity that made her so good—her amazing competitive instincts. Black Caviar would just break the others' hearts and tow Luke into the race, and he'd flow with her. It was the way she ran her races, as if she'd get halfway through and think, 'I'm sick of this', and then go *whoosh*.

That was how it looked. You'd think she was going too soon, for the average horse, but she used to just take the others off the bridle, then switch off for the last 200m and coast home.

I'd say of her 25 wins, her 600 to 400 sectional times would have been quicker far more times than her 400 to 200 or her last 200. In her Newmarket win, she ran that 600 to the 400 in 10.27 seconds, then finished in 10.65 and 11.75. That was one sectional the media picked up on (though better was still to come!)

I read where one analyst, Vince Accardi of the website *Daily Sectionals*, worked out that in the Newmarket—under 58 kilograms remember—she averaged better than 19 metres per second for three consecutive furlongs. Apparently, if horses can ever hit that speed, they can only do it for one furlong (or 200-metre section). Nelly had done it for three. Her effort that day was rated about 17.3 lengths faster than the average for 1200-metres races at Flemington. Takeover Target's best was 12.3 lengths better than average, suggesting she would have beaten him by five lengths.

How she was able to sustain that was her length of stride. This got measured as 8.33 metres, which meant she took 24 strides to cover 200 metres. Most horses take 30 strides.

We'd all stopped being amazed by what Black Caviar could do. But still everyone else—from average punter to expert analyst—used to shake their heads and say, 'We've just never seen this before'.

Luke always hated her being tagged with that old racing cliché of 'freak'. He thought it was disrespectful, undignified for a queen of the track, and made her sound like some sort of monster, to be caged and poked with a stick. He preferred to call her 'equine perfection'—the beautiful result of centuries of refining and improving the thoroughbred breed. I can't say I disagree.

Everyone was sort of waiting—waiting to see if she might ever be given a contest, if something would go wrong, if the bubble might pop. My horse Wanted had shown he might be able to push her, but he had been retired.

I was asked about Gai Waterhouse's super mare More Joyous, who won 21 races from 1100 metres to 2000 metres, but there was no way she'd have beaten Black Caviar in a sprint.

There was talk about Rocket Man, the Australian-bred who was setting records in Singapore and won a big sprint in Dubai, or JJ The Jet Plane, who had beaten him in Hong Kong. I would have backed Nelly—both of those horses were rated only 122 on the WTR—but they weren't on our radar anyway.

For the here and now, there was only one horse who showed any possibility of being competitive with Black Caviar, and that was Hay List.

....

The atmosphere was fantastic at Randwick the day of our third battle with Hay List. For me there was a bit of sentiment involved. I was going back to where it all started, to what felt like my home track after my formative years in Sydney. And I'd be going there with a racing phenomenon and tackling the event named after my earlier boss, T.J. Smith.

Through the day, lots of old blokes I'd worked with twenty-five years earlier would stop me for a chat. People I'd known from western New South Wales would say g'day over the fence. Kids came to Nelly's stall for photos, and she'd put her head over the fence and oblige them. There were strangers, fans, people I'd met along the way. It felt like a carnival, and it was stuff I'd feel again when I took her to Brisbane and Adelaide.

As for the race, there was no doubt in the markets, with Black Caviar $1.14 and Hay List and Crystal Lily next at $21 in the eleven-horse field. Still, I had concerns about how Nelly would get around the one turn, but it was comforting that I'd heard Darren Beadman talk about a part of the straight called Mulley's Gully, after former champion jockey Athol George Mulley. The track is famous for the Randwick Rise, a small but testing little hill soon after straightening. Mulley's Gully is a corridor about six horses wide where the rise isn't so steep. I told Luke that if Nelly wasn't handling the turn he shouldn't fight her. Let her flow and she'd probably end up in the best part of the straight.

Black Caviar dawdled a bit at the start but was soon third behind Hay List and Crystal Lily. But then came the moment the race is remembered for: Hay List exploded clear around the turn.

He opened a two-length lead on Crystal Lily, and Black Caviar was two lengths behind her. I have to admit, like a lot of people, I took a gasp when he booted away like that. It was the first time we had been behind him, and we were about to see how well he would hold onto the lead. I watched as Nelly got around the turn fairly, but then wobbled out a bit. But, as we'd hoped, she found Mulley's Gully.

Amongst the Newmarket analysis was a claim that, according to her sectionals, Nelly could give rivals a ten-length start at the 400 metres and still win. She wasn't quite going to have to do that this day, but 300 metres out she was still four lengths behind Hay List. Everyone was getting nervous.

But then, here she came, and it was a sight to behold.

Glyn Schofield, on Hay List, said later that while he normally didn't hear the crowd, this time he heard them start roaring. He said he didn't have to turn around and look—he knew what was coming. He also said he'd never been going so fast on a horse and have one go past him so easily.

On one of the few occasions ever, Luke gave her a little slap with the whip and our big girl went after Hay List. At the 200 metres she was still two lengths behind him. At the 120 metres, five seconds later, she hit the lead. She won by 2.8 lengths, in about half a second off the track record.

Black Caviar really was awesome that day.

Glyn told us later how he'd ridden around the world, including in Hong Kong against Silent Witness, then the top-rated sprinter on the planet. But he'd never seen anything like Black Caviar, who had now passed $3 million in earnings.

All up, it was a very heady day. I was pretty emotional, though I did disappoint certain 'punters'—mates who bet I'd shed a tear after the race. But I did enjoy the moment.

That night, there was a big party at Neil Werrett's on the north side of Sydney. I was happy for Neil with his home-town win, but also knackered with the pressure of it all. I had a couple of beers and sneaked off to my hotel to bed.

I said after the race Black Caviar was so relaxed you could probably run her over any trip. And I still wonder if I should have run her in the Group 1 All Aged Stakes over 1400 metres at that carnival. But I was desperate to take her to Queensland, and the owners were happy for me to do it. So we'd stick to the 1200 metres of the BTC Cup, before the 1350 metres of the Doomben 10,000.

....

I was very pleased that my home state would see Black Caviar. Adding to the fun, since the attention on her had reached some incredible heights, it became a cloak-and-dagger operation.

We were looking at flying her from Melbourne, for the experience on a plane. We might need to fly to England the following year. Plus Perth for the Winterbottom Stakes in November was a chance, as was the Hong Kong Sprint in December.

But the flights to Brisbane didn't work out so we had to float her up with our driver Peter Courtney. We had to lie a bit about this. After they had set off, we kept telling people she was still in Melbourne and she would be flown up closer to the race. This was because Peter was going to overnight in Dubbo and, as soon as people saw 'Moody Racing' on the truck, they'd ask questions. People used to always pull up at the lights and sing out to him: '*Is Black Caviar in that truck?*' Most likely he'd have some ordinary beast going to Stony Creek or somewhere.

As it was, he was refuelling somewhere when this old bloke came up to him. Peter thought he looked harmless enough so he confirmed that, yes, the great mare was inside. The old bloke asked if he could just touch the outside of the truck!

Once in Brisbane we had to play ducks and drakes some more. Things worked in our favour—for a bit.

My old employee Desleigh Forster was now training at Eagle Farm. Better still, she was the only one in these new stables they had built in the middle of the track. We could stable with Desleigh without having to stay off-course and walk Nelly around the streets, where our cover would be blown in two minutes.

I was also mates with Billy Schuck, the racecourse manager. I'd told him on the quiet we were bringing Black Caviar up, and he helped us. He and his team put security measures in place so no one could enter the middle of the track, and they did a terrific job. Apparently he had to tell some little white lies to his bosses too, which I was grateful for. The whole marketing for the Brisbane winter carnival was based on 'Come and see Black Caviar'. If news of her presence got out, the whole circus would be on again and we'd get no peace and quiet, which she needed after a long road trip.

Of course, we would have to work the horse. People would be standing right next to Black Caviar and would ask who this big brown mare was. We'd say it was Set For Fame, who was a similar colour. That covered us for a while as we told people Black Caviar would fly up later.

After three or four days, word got out. There were photographers stalking the course and someone identified Nelly, based on brands I suppose, and it was game over. Still, those few days were memorable—anonymity with the greatest horse in the world.

One of the funny things was Desleigh and I took Nelly and one of Desleigh's down to Nudgee Beach to stand them in sea water. We'd do that in Melbourne, at Mordialloc Beach. People would see the Moody Racing truck and work out she was there. This time, we were in Desleigh's car pulling a plain two-horse float. This middle-aged woman pulled up beside us at the lights and looked at me. She then started following us, and followed us the whole four or five miles to Nudgee Beach.

We pulled up and I did what I usually did—stripped down to my boxers and a T-shirt to go in the water with the horse. This woman got out of her car and came up to me, despite my state of undress. It turned out she wasn't a racing fan at all but had recognised me off the TV news.

She said: 'I saw you at the traffic lights. I'm very excited. You've got this world-famous horse. I was on my way home from work and I followed you in the hope . . . in the hope you might have this horse?'

I said, 'Yep, it's her'. The lady took a photo with her mobile phone, then I excused myself and took Nelly into the water. Next minute I've looked around and—you wouldn't believe it—this woman has stripped down to her undies and she's following us into the water!

It was hilarious. Here was this lady just overcome by it all. This is what the horse used to do to people.

....

There was another special moment in Brisbane. In fact, it was one of the two most meaningful moments I had in the whole Black Caviar story.

On a Friday lunchtime this lady rang and introduced herself. She said her son had just been diagnosed with inoperable brain cancer. The poor bloke was a cargo pilot and had been told he had a few weeks to live. His name was Andrew Porter and he was only 32. The lady said he loved the horses and was caught up in the whole Black Caviar saga, and asked if he could come have a look at her.

We had had a few requests up there. The staff from Eagle Farm would come and want a photo with her. I'd let them, as long as it was in Black Caviar's working hours, not her quiet time.

Our office would get inundated with emails and phone calls requesting a look at the horse. I couldn't say yes to everyone, but this was one occasion I wanted to help.

I'd arranged—on the quiet again—to take Nelly across the road to Doomben the following morning for a familiarisation gallop, so I said to the lady: 'I tell you what—if you can get Andrew here, he can come have the morning with me at trackwork'.

Next morning they turned up. Andrew was pretty sick and frail, but still walking around. I met his mum and his wife, Riannon, and a couple of other family members. He came to Doomben, watched Nelly have a walk around, gave her a pat, and we got some photos taken. Andrew was over the moon. There were some media there, but not in their droves like usual, and we didn't highlight Andrew's story.

That was extremely moving—to see the joy it gave Andrew, a young bloke whose life was about to end, having that moment with Nelly.

In my whole experience with Black Caviar, it felt special that I could share this moment with him.

As the morning went on and we gave the horse her gallop, the media cottoned on to Andrew's story. To the Brisbane Racing Club's credit they invited him back to the Doomben Committee Room and got him tickets for the big day in a week's time. He actually had a friendly bet with me that he'd still be alive to see her race.

He was there on race day and it was beautiful for him to experience it. He had a beer with us afterwards, in the owners' marquee.

To have that time at trackwork with Andrew, and the following Saturday at the races with him and his family—it was just very moving to realise how much Black Caviar meant to people. It brought me to tears. It nearly does still when I recount the story.

I got a phone call about eight months later from his family again, saying Andrew had passed away. His family reckoned that experience with Black Caviar had given him an extra four or five months, it had picked him up so much.

....

That day at Doomben, 14 May 2011, was fantastic. I made the comment that showcasing Nelly to the Australian racing public was a pain in the backside, since it was a bit like a travelling circus, with lots of things to tend to. But I said it was an honourable and pleasurable pain in the backside to have. It was my big thankyou to Queensland racing. Plus it was nice to stay with my mum, in her house behind Doomben.

I don't know if Doomben had seen a crowd that big before, and I know they haven't since. It was 1940s stuff, minus the hats. People were talking to me over the fence who hadn't been to the races for 50 years, or when they watched Bernborough win the 10,000 in 1946—that sort of thing.

Seeing how Black Caviar had gone clockwise in Sydney, I didn't have much anxiety going into the race, 'unlucky' thirteenth start or not. There were only eight starters, including Hay List again, who was short at $5.50 compared to our $1.14. Nelly was a fraction slow out from gate 4 but was soon in the box seat third, two lengths behind Hay List and Buffering. Luke popped her off the fence at the 600 metres; she was a bit tardy around the turn but again she gave Hay List a start and a solid beating. He stuck on a bit better than in Sydney, going down by two lengths.

With Glyn Schofield injured, the gelding had a different rider in Glen Boss, but he made the same comment—he'd never been travelling so fast and been passed so easily.

It was a party atmosphere after the race. This being my home state the owners pushed me out to lead Nelly in, which I was grateful for. Luke and I did our media and signed more autographs—all sorts of things thrust at us over the fence, even a cigarette paper some bloke asked me to sign.

Probably the most pressing question I was asked was whether, in two weeks' time, Black Caviar would handle the 1350 metres of the 10,000. I was keen to give her that first test beyond 1200 metres, and of course said she'd handle it comfortably.

....

While Nelly was doing it easily, her jockey and trainer had been catapulted to a level of fame that took some getting used to. It was mostly good but there was another side. There was always someone to annoy you.

After the Doomben win, I did what I used to do when living in Brisbane and headed down to the local racing pub, the Hamilton Hotel, hoping to catch up with old friends. It became hard work.

About 99 per cent of people were great. They'd say 'Well done', shake your hand, maybe even buy you a beer, and move on. But there was always a pest or two who kept bugging you. You'd try to say it nicely: 'Listen, thanks, but you've had your time' or 'I'm trying to catch up with friends. Please.' But as soon as you said anything like that they'd be: 'Oh, you're an arsehole then?' Some were full of piss but some weren't. They were just narks who wouldn't move on.

That really made me aware of what some other people go through—people who are full-time famous, not just for a few years. There'd been a spate of footballers in trouble for abusing people or pushing them away. I found myself grateful I was a bit older and more mature and could turn the other cheek and walk away. I could only imagine what these young footy players would get put through, and I could start to understand how those sorts of incidents happened. Of course that's nothing you envisage when you decide you want to train horses for a living but again, these were extraordinary times.

That night at the pub, like a few nights later on, it just became uncomfortable for me, and my friends. You couldn't get a roll going on your night out, couldn't have a decent conversation, you're always getting interrupted. In the end the easiest thing was for me to leave early.

I wouldn't swap it for anything, but I was learning that even having the best horse in the world was a double-edged sword.

The other thing was this ongoing issue of other owners of mine getting antsy. I'll admit it was getting harder for me to divide my time between Nelly and my other horses but, again, I had a great team in place. This team won us four Melbourne premierships, not just the trainer.

Still, a few owners wouldn't be convinced and took their horses away. While I lost nothing of great significance, in the years of Black Caviar I wasn't given a great many horses to train. The only horses coming in were those we bought ourselves, because people were a bit wary.

So, this sounds bizarre, but while the great Black Caviar was good for business in one regard, she was bad for business in another. I wasn't attracting new clients. What I was attracting was interest from people who weren't adding to my business, but were taking up my time.

On top of that, there was always the pressure.

As she kept winning, and perhaps the fear of an inevitable loss kept building, the pressure got bigger and bigger.

Aside from a million or two watching on TV, thousands of people were flocking to the races, to witness, to be a part of, what was becoming an unprecedented winning streak, hoping of course that this unbelievable fairytale wouldn't stop. I thought writer John Harms put it well: 'She's beautiful to watch. She can lift the spirit. And she is coming to mean so much to us.'

When she was in work, the pressure never stopped. My phone would ring off the hook all week right up till race day. I'd be on edge a bit and was probably smoking way too much. It was a real pressure-cooker situation, and building all the time. That's why there was never any big raucous celebration after her wins. More often than not I'd be glad to leave the track, go home and grab some fish and chips for dinner on the way.

The build-up started to tense up so much that, after each win, mentally I was just: 'Phew—thank fuck that's over'. I'd just get home, kick the boots off, have a shower, then flop on the couch and exhale.

On Sunday morning it'd all start again. The media would ring from 6.30 a.m., and it was on again, building and building till the next race. You only had that one night off, on Saturday nights. You did the media at the races, you signed all the things, and you were just utterly fucked.

In fact, there were one or two times where I found myself wishing Nelly would get beat. I might have been a bit touchy one day and I said to Sarah: 'You know what? I wish she'd just lose a race. Then she'd

just be a normal horse again and things would get back to normal!'
Thankfully, it only took me a few seconds to give myself a smack in
the head and move on.

I think Luke was much the same. But he didn't have to worry
about the hundred other horses at home next morning.

Of course, I'd always check on Nelly first thing Sunday morning,
by calling Tony Haydon. He was great with her. He lived and breathed
with her. But it wasn't until Monday that you could feel more relaxed.
On Sundays after a race she'd have a walk and a swim, and a good shot
of anti-inflammatories. So it wasn't till the next day that those wore
off and you'd see if anything bad emerged. Big things, you'd pick up
on the Sunday. But more minor things you'd have to address—soft-
tissue injuries or muscle tears—those usually wouldn't show up till
later. Mondays were always nervy.

The most common issue Nelly had was concussion trouble with
her big, flat feet. Because she was so heavy and she hit down hard,
the angles of her feet weren't great. She'd get a lot of bruising in her
heels that you needed to watch. We were forever messing about with
her shoes, trying different things to alleviate the concussion. Our
farrier, Matty Martin, did a good job but I'd often get other farriers
in too, to see if we could do things differently.

Nelly would also get heat in her knees and fetlocks and her stifles
and hocks behind, just due to her size. We'd give her cortisone, and an
intra-articular treatment—much like I'd learnt from Bill Mitchell—
called IRAP. They'd pull some blood out of her and use it to grow
blood cells, and inject it back into her knees and fetlocks mixed with
cortisone. The vets say this stimulates the horse's white blood cells to
produce anti-inflammatory agents, like enzymes. I'd call it a grease
and oil change. It wasn't after every run but a few times per preparation, when she started to feel things. Chiropractor Michael Bryant

was always working on her. Our vet, Peter Angus, was always around as well.

So, while we looked after all our horses, it did take a lot of maintenance to keep the Black Caviar machine humming. But what a machine she was.

....

The Doomben 10,000 had been won by some of the greats—Manikato, Maybe Mahal, Bernborough—though not General Nediym, who had run third after missing the start. I was very keen to add Black Caviar to the winners' list.

But a couple of days after her Brisbane debut, the big machine was giving the hint of a noise under the bonnet. I watched Nelly gallop and wasn't quite happy with her action. Her feet were playing up, and she had some heat in the knees and fetlocks. I phoned Peter Angus in Melbourne and asked him to fly up with his X-ray equipment. Michael Bryant, who knew her closely like Peter, flew up as well. While there was nothing huge, she had had five runs this preparation, which was a record for her, and she was feeling her legs a bit. We decided to spell her and look towards the spring.

The decision wasn't taken lightly. The BRC was eyeing another bonanza with a full house on 10,000 day. They were still extremely grateful to have had her the once.

Poor old Hay List would have had his chance to win the race, but had more bad luck, suffering colic and a leg infection. I felt for John McNair and his owners—especially when it seemed the horse might even die. Fortunately, he survived.

From a personal perspective, I copped some stick as well—from old western Queensland mates who'd planned to make just the one trip into Brisbane, to watch her second run. My mates gave me a gobful, but all in jest.

It had been a great preparation and, finally, it was mostly trouble-free. Over three months, Nelly had had five starts, won five Group 1s, saw off her only likely challenger in Hay List, astounded the world with her Newmarket win, and gone interstate and the other way around. But it was time to pack up the circus tent for a while.

She stayed in the warmer climes of Queensland for a spell and pre-training at Kevin Thomas' Washpool Lodge, where Amalfi had been all those years before. She would come back in the spring, fresher and fitter.

....

In the meantime, the stable celebrated two back-to-back successes. We won our second Melbourne premiership and—perhaps even more likely—Black Caviar succeeded Typhoon Tracy as Australia's Horse of the Year.

And I headed off for Royal Ascot again, though not with Black Caviar.

I thought I could finally win the Diamond Jubilee with Hinchinbrook, after two attempts with Magnus. I went to Newmarket again and waited for Luke Nolen to join me, but the day after he arrived Hinchinbrook strained a suspensory ligament. Luke and I watched the State of Origin together that morning, then he flew home again and Hinchinbrook was retired to stud.

Another item on my agenda was opening another satellite stable, this time in Sydney.

In Melbourne the stable was flying. While we had won our first premiership comfortably by 39 winners, in 2010–11 our total of 103.5 winners was 65.5 more than second-placed Mark Kavanagh.

I was a little reluctant about a satellite stable because it had stretched me a bit thin when I'd done it previously. But we now had a lot of carnival-quality horses, and a lot of horses full stop. It'd be useful to have my own place in Sydney to send them to.

We kicked it off early in 2012 with 10 boxes at Rosehill that Tim Martin had vacated. After a couple of years there, we'd move to Randwick and take up the stables of Jim Lee, who'd trained 1983 Caulfield Cup winner Hayai.

I at least had a good hand to run the operation in Clare Cunningham, who'd worked for us in Melbourne and now does TV work. She was only 21 but she was a great horsewoman, and very tough and resilient. She took on a lot of responsibility at a young age— I guess like I had done. We used to fight like cats and dogs, as you do, but she'd always stand up for herself and did a good job. That's why we enjoyed success up there, with 12 Sydney winners in 2013–14, and 18 the following year.

Clare was another of the many strong and capable women I've been associated with all my life—from my mum and sisters to Sarah, to people like Linda Meech, Desleigh Forster and Steph Little, who became my assistant trainer when Tony Haydon left to start training in 2013, to our priceless company secretary Marni Kelly. I've heard it said that I'm a bloke's bloke who surrounds himself with women. It's never mattered to me—male or female—as long as they can do the job, and I'd be the last person to doubt women's capacity to get things done. I'm now surrounded by three more strong and capable women in our daughters Cara, Breann and Celine. I'm a bit in the minority at home, but I love it.

....

In spring of 2011, things started getting ridiculous.

I was in my office at Caulfield when the phone rang. It was a PA for Prime Minister Julia Gillard. 'Shit,' I thought, 'this is pretty serious'.

It was crazier than I'd thought.

The woman said to keep it to myself, that it was going to be an 'off the radar' sort of thing, but she was asking about a quiet visit to meet Black Caviar.

Not for the prime minister—for the Queen of England!

It turned out Queen Elizabeth would be in Melbourne that October, and she would quite like to come to Booran Road, Caulfield, and see this wonder horse she had heard about. I said of course, and we said our goodbyes.

I sat there for a minute, stunned and looking about, probably blinking my eyes like they do in the cartoons.

I sang out to Sarah: 'Hey, love, the queen might be dropping in'.

It took a bit of digesting. I'm P.G. Moody from Wyandra, and Her Majesty's going to come by. We'd have to get out the good crockery!

About a month later, however, the woman rang again and said the queen's itinerary had changed. The Victorian government wanted her to take a ride on an old restored tram instead. I thought to myself: 'Here's a woman who loves racehorses. I bet I know what she wished she'd be doing instead.' Anyway, it didn't come off. She rode the tram—and it didn't stop at Caulfield.

The idea of a meeting hadn't died completely, however. When the queen did come out, the PM's PA contacted me again and said: 'We're having brunch with the queen at the Lodge on Sunday. Bart Cummings is coming. We were wondering if Black Caviar could come too?'

Now I had to laugh. Black Caviar was in the middle of her spring preparation. In fact, the brunch was on Sunday, 23 October, and she would race the day before in the Schweppes Stakes at Caulfield. You wouldn't take any horse for a 14-hour round trip to get a pat on the head in those circumstances, much less Black Caviar.

'I'm sorry,' I said, 'but I don't think you quite understand horses.

It's not really a simple matter of sticking her in the boot and driving up to Canberra for a brunch on Sunday morning.'

Not many people from Wyandra have said this either—but the queen would have to wait.

She would get her chance later though.

19

Race, Win, Repeat

It was a relief to step off the Black Caviar roller-coaster, but it was also fun to get back on. This spring would mirror her last: Group 2s in the Schillaci Stakes over 1000 metres on Caulfield Stakes day and the 1200-metre Schweppes Stakes on Cox Plate day, then a seventh Group 1 in the Patinack Farm Classic on the last day of the Flemington carnival. She would visit each of Melbourne's big tracks.

Had Black Caviar not resumed in a Group 2, she would have had a crack at Bernborough's Australian record of winning seven Group 1s in a row. That would come later, but you got used to such things happening anyway. From about start ten on, it seemed every time I saddled her, she was about to break some sort of record.

In any case, the frenzy went up another notch that spring. Our new Horse of the Year had been everywhere in the media. The ABC's *Australian Story* did an episode on her—the first they'd ever done on an animal. She was attempting her fourteenth straight win, which would equal the record of that benchmark for all other horses, Phar Lap.

There were more calls to take on the best from overseas. There was talk Rocket Man might be lured out from Singapore that spring, though that didn't eventuate. And there was also this horse in England called Frankel, who had won eight from eight, including three Group 1s, and who would challenge for her 'best horse in the world' tag. There was also the idea of a match race in Sydney between Black Caviar, Hay List and More Joyous, though we weren't that interested.

Black Caviar was now five and there were a couple of differences about her. She'd got even bigger, looking a bit like a broodmare, the big hulking thing. We gave her some time up on the water-walker to bring her weight down before she came into the stable. I felt she actually looked better than ever.

She'd also become more relaxed in her nature. That was good, because we were able to show her to the public a bit more after her races. People could give her a pat over the fence and things like that.

She still liked to keep moving. At the races, Donna Fisher would have to keep her moving most of the day. She'd stand still to get saddled up, but wouldn't much like it. Tony and I would go straight in there and get it on. She'd stand there and kick the wall to give us a hurry-up. She just wanted to get on with the job. You could call it white-line fever. She could have the odd ailment, maybe sore feet or whatever, but once she got to the races and heard the noise and knew why she was there, she was switched on. Any sort of pain she might have went out the window, and she was in racing mode.

That was her competitive instincts again. But she was also very smart. At Caulfield she'd be poking around with Donna and she'd stop at the same spot, once a day, and have a look around: 'This is my place. What's going on around here?' She'd stop for a minute then, when satisfied, she'd move on. At our press calls, she knew what had to be done. She'd come out for the photographers. Donna and I would hold her. She'd stand there and pose for about a minute, then she'd go, and you couldn't stop her: 'That's enough, boys. You've had your couple of minutes, I'm out of here.'

Did Black Caviar know she was special? Some people think a horse couldn't know, or that they assume this is what all horses go through. I disagree. I think she realised she was special. She wasn't silly. In the stables she didn't see press conferences happening for other horses, or the pats and adulation. She knew she was different.

She might have also wondered how it felt to finish behind other horses, as she went through wins fourteen, fifteen and sixteen in very straightforward fashion.

I had considered a different kind of preparation, possibly stepping up to 1400m, and the 1600m of the Myer Classic on Derby Day. In the end, though, I stuck to the shorter races.

In the Schillaci, Black Caviar started the shortest she'd ever been, at $1.07. We were confident, but not cocky. The build-up to another Black Caviar campaign had been pretty intense, another level up from last time, and as always I was looking forward to the race being over. That fear of her getting hurt was always there. And as trainer I only had a certain amount of control. It stopped when she stepped onto a track.

In fact, around this time I said to Luke: 'You know, if you ever take her onto the track and you're not happy with her, if you're scared her feet are playing up or something, scratch her. Don't run her.'

I thought I was doing the right thing, just letting Luke know I'd have his back. So I do get a laugh remembering how he blew right up, saying: 'Bloody hell—fancy putting that pressure on me!' Thankfully, it never came up.

With five months having passed since her last start, and with the AFL season finished, Black Caviar was all anyone seemingly wanted to know about. The press were going mad. One journo, I hoped not from the racing world, asked me for an interview before Black Caviar raced Phar Lap in the Caulfield Cup! I'm not sure if it was a wind-up. It was getting hard to tell.

It was around this time I gave this quote for a feature in the *Australian*: 'You know what I'd love to do? I'd like to win the lotto, buy a 5 per cent share in a racehorse and drive the trainer mad by ringing up every night to see how it's going. I'd be doing that while lying on a beach in far north Queensland eating prawns and drinking beer. I'd have my fourth wife, a 21-year-old six-foot blonde stroking my overgrown stomach, and I'd stay up there until I died from a massive heart attack with a cigarette in my mouth.'

Well . . . it was nice to get some release once in a while.

The crowd for her first-up run was huge—32,126—more than a third bigger than usual for Caulfield Stakes day. You watch the replay now, for a Group 2 on the support card, and you can sense the expectation as caller Greg Miles says before the start: 'Stand by—this is it!'

Thankfully, for Luke, me, and her fans, that was about as dramatic as it got. Black Caviar jumped fairly in the middle of the eight-horse field, settled mid-field, pulled Luke into it from the 600 metres, shot past leader Karuta Queen on the turn and won by four lengths.

'Fourteen straight, and she's up there with the greatest ever,' Miles says as she matches Phar Lap's record.

It was job done, another massive relief, with Nelly looking to me perhaps better than ever. In another sign of her status, Karuta Queen's jockey Tommy Berry and her owners came up after the race to say how happy they were to have run second to Black Caviar.

I had to settle for placings in the day's Group 1s. Lights Of Heaven came third in Descarado's Caulfield Stakes, King's Rose and Luen Yat Forever filled the minors in King Mufhasa's Toorak Handicap, and Huegill was third in Helmet's Caulfield Guineas.

Still, I was a relieved man as I headed for the hills, and the fish-and-chip shop on the way home.

....

There was never much superstition around Nelly. Someone started a story that Sarah only went to see her odd-numbered starts, but it wasn't true. If she happened to be there for more odds than evens it was just that she went when she could—when the demands of running three kids, who were big into Saturday sport, allowed. But one thing that did get picked up after that Schillaci win was 'the lucky coin'. While Black Caviar won $7.9 million in her career, there was one dollar that was particularly important.

It wasn't my doing. It was part-owner Col Madden. He'd noticed on race days that when I was just standing around, mulling things over or talking to the press, I had my hand in my pocket twirling a dollar coin. I wasn't that aware of it (maybe it was just something to do to stop myself smoking another cigarette!) but in any case, Col came up to me before Nelly's race one day sounding alarmed and said: 'Where's your coin?'

I asked what he meant and he said he'd always seen me with a coin. He quickly gave me another dollar, and from then on, for every one of her races he'd give me the coin and I'd give it back after the race. It happened during post-race interviews after the Schillaci, which was how it got out.

I'm not superstitious, so I don't imagine it helped. But it seemed to help Colin, so we kept it going.

....

From the Schillaci it was back to Moonee Valley. Again this was supposedly a lead-up race, to the Cox Plate, but it was just Black Caviar fever as she went after the fifteen straight wins of Bernborough and Carbine.

There had been more match-race talk. A week earlier, Frankel had won his ninth start and Melbourne Racing Club chairman Mike Symons had floated the idea of him racing Nelly at Caulfield the next autumn, perhaps over 1400 metres. These sorts of ideas were always swirling around, but I was more focused on the job at hand—the Schweppes Stakes.

Racing-wise, this did look a non-event, though that didn't put anyone off. It was the smallest field Black Caviar faced—only four starters. I'd have two of them, with Doubtful Jack also going round. Another starter was Scenic Blast, who'd won the King's Stand at Royal Ascot two years earlier and had been Horse of the Year before Typhoon Tracy.

Black Caviar was shorter again, at $1.05, but believe it or not there was still some cause for anxiety. As with one of her earlier races, it took the form of the fourth member of the quartet, Here De Angels.

I wasn't worried about him beating us but about his roguish behaviour in the barriers. He had been banned from racing in Victoria a year earlier and gone to New South Wales. That ban had been lifted and he was drawn in barrier 4, immediately outside Black Caviar.

Without exaggerating, I was seriously considering not running her. What if Here De Angels played up in the barriers, got his leg up and thrashed about, and Nelly's right next to him?

I rang Racing Victoria chief steward Terry Bailey and, in contrast with our bitter future, he was very helpful. He contacted Here De Angels' connections, and they agreed to leave a gap between him and our horse. It was unprecedented. Terry got criticised for it, but I was very grateful. In a sixteen-horse field it might've been harder, but in a four-horse field it was just common sense (I wish there was more of that around in a few years' time!). I'd have probably offered to start from barrier 6 had Here De Angels' connections not agreed.

It turned out it was the best Here De Angels behaved in the barriers for a long time, and he began like a rocket. So it worked to both our advantages.

Black Caviar also started well, and it was a procession. Doubtful Jack led with Black Caviar second. Luke let her go before the home turn and she coasted away. The six-length margin matched her second win as the biggest of her whole career, but again the owner of Doubtful Jack gave me a hug for the honour of running second to her.

It was a little sad to see a four-horse race, but then again, everyone was invited. Still, it was hit and giggle compared to some more serious stuff ahead.

....

The third and last start of this campaign came on a hot day at Flemington, and was just what Luke and I needed. While I'd had the honour of being part of the launch for Flemington's Melbourne Cup carnival, it had been a fairly bleak spring for trainer and jockey, Black Caviar aside. In fact, between Nelly's second and third runs I only had one winner, in a Stawell maiden!

We'd hoped for a Melbourne Cup start for Macedonian, but he needed to win the Lexus Stakes to qualify—and ran second. Black Caviar's owners had also kicked off another horse with me as trainer. Secret Indulgence, a filly who'd cost $300,000, came fifth at Ballarat and fourth at Mornington. As mentioned, buying yearlings is an unpredictable business.

As for the Group 1 Patinack Farm Classic, it was a little tougher than the Schweppes, with seven runners. Then again, four of them were mine, with Mid Summer Music to be ridden by Ben Melham, Curtana by Darren Beadman, and Panipique by Michael Walker.

There was talk that I'd bolstered the numbers to ensure the race would even go ahead, but that wasn't right. From my point of view, I had even heard that Group 1s would go ahead even if there was only one acceptor. (While this has never been put to the test, there was one with only three acceptors in the spring of 2016, when another great mare, Winx, scared all bar Black Heart Bart and He Or She away from the Caulfield Stakes). But I might have recommended the race to the owners of my other three for some easy prizemoney. There was $90,000 for running third. And since Group 1s paid to eighth, there was twenty grand for whoever managed to come last.

Black Caviar was $1.05. Bookmakers might have lamented a lack of betting in her races but she was drawing huge crowds who bet on the others.

The race unfolded as a lesson in tactics—the tactics of riding against Black Caviar. It might even have been a lesson for one of the greatest ever, Darren Beadman. He'd been riding in Hong Kong and maybe didn't have the first-hand experience of the mare that others had.

I said to my three other jockeys: 'You're there to try to win, but don't kid yourself and chase her from the 600 metres when she breaks their hearts. When she lets go at the 600, just don't. Hold them up and try to arrive on the line.'

Ben Melham carried it out perfectly on Mid Summer Music to get third (the very good Buffering was second). But Darren didn't wait on Curtana. He went for her about the 400 metres and she ended up fourth as Mid Summer Music went past her. As for Panipique at $201, she got the twenty grand.

Black Caviar bolted in by nearly three lengths. I wasn't getting blasé, but you did have to remind yourself these weren't donkeys she was beating. She was doing it routinely, and easily. 'They're all group horses behind her but once again she's toyed with them,' I said.

Luke said it was hard for him to grasp the size of her achievement: 'It's a humbling experience. Magnificent. But I'm probably not getting a great shot at it at the moment while the caravan's still rolling. I'll probably look back on it one day and feel good.'

Nelly had matched the successive-wins records of Bernborough and Carbine, not that I kept those things in my mind. (I was keen to better Zenyatta's nineteen straight though, as a modern-era mare whose career I'd followed.) Our girl had also breached the $4 million mark in prizemoney and matched the seven Group 1s of Makybe Diva and that great mare of the 1980s, Emancipation. The only mare now ahead of her for Group 1s was Sunline, with thirteen. And the only horse above Sunline was Kingston Town, with fourteen.

Again I was thanking my stars for Black Caviar, in an otherwise frustrating carnival. Forty-five minutes later we were beaten a lip in the day's other Group 1, the Emirates Stakes, when King's Rose lost to Chris Waller's Albert The Fat.

As for where to next with Black Caviar, we were thinking about taking the roadshow to Perth two weeks later for the 1200-metre Group 1 Winterbottom Stakes at Ascot. The West Australian authorities were eager to get Nelly for what would no doubt be one of their biggest days ever. I was quite keen to showcase her there, but I talked with the owners and we were concerned about the hard tracks in Perth, and that going there might overload Nelly's schedule.

This was because we were already thinking of the other course that shared the same name.

All roads were leading to Ascot, England.

....

When Black Caviar was at the stables, in late morning when everyone had gone and the paperwork was done, that was my quiet time when I could go have a look.

I'd take my phone to do my phone calls—there was always something to attend to—but I could give her a pat, run my hand down the legs and so on. I'd look at the other horses too, but I'd be lying if I said I didn't like taking a look over Nelly's door. Still, knowing she didn't like to be annoyed, you wouldn't overdo it.

Mind you, the number of people you knew suddenly dropping in to say g'day had grown quite large. Over the years we had her there would have been hundreds. Maybe thousands. Of course they wanted to see her. I mostly didn't mind. In fact, I'd feel a bit proud to show her off, certainly to people I felt I owed something to, who had helped me along the way.

When Nelly was 'off work' it was great to have her at home. It was nice to go out your back door and have a quiet moment and give her a cuddle. No crowds, no cameras, just me and Nelly.

The kids' mates would come over. They could hop on and have a little sit on her in the paddock, and Nelly was fine with it. Or one of the twins, Bree or Celine, could go down the bottom paddock of an evening and jump on her and ride her up the hill and put a rug on her.

It wasn't just Nelly, mind you. We'd keep eight or ten fillies at home. In fact I've kept a favourite photo of Black Caviar and Typhoon Tracy with their heads in the feed bin in what's essentially our backyard.

We don't advertise where we live or what we do, so you'd imagine lots of people driving by, for a day in the Dandenongs or a ride on the Puffing Billy steam train just up the road, would have loved to have known Black Caviar was standing just behind that fence they were driving past.

One day at home was a bit scary though. Thank Christ I wasn't around to see it.

Our farmer, Dennis Roberts, and our truck driver, Peter Courtney, were there doing something when they saw Nelly just take off in her paddock. She ran downhill flat chat and was coming towards the wire fence so all of a sudden she had to stop.

We'd had a bit of rain so the ground was damp, and the two blokes watched, horrified, as the one and only Black Caviar slammed the brakes on and slid . . . straight under the bottom of the fence!

If I had been there, I would have shat myself. Dennis and Peter apparently just closed their eyes. Amazingly, since only the good ones get hurt, Nelly squeezed under the fence, then just stood up and shook herself off. Dennis nervously went and got her and led her back to her paddock. Miraculously, she was good as gold.

You don't want that happening too often with the best horse in the world, let me tell you.

20

Pressure

I finished 2011 on a high with a winning treble at Caulfield on Boxing Day—Zoomania, There's Only One and Dayita. But I was just as excited to get back to the stables. Black Caviar had been brought back to town that day.

She looked great, in her condition and her size. She'd put on about 40 kilograms, tipping the scales at just over 600. When she let down, she let down big time. You'd take most of it off, but never all of it. She was that little bit bigger each preparation, which again meant the worries about the strains on her legs were always there.

The clamour from Britain to see this horse they had all heard about was growing louder. The end-of-year World Thoroughbred Rankings had come out, and Black Caviar had now gone from her 130 after the Newmarket to 132. She was the highest rated female in history—above even Goldikova, who had won fourteen Group 1s, which was unbelievable. Whetting appetites for a trip to England, though, was the news their unbeaten wonder horse, Frankel, had been given a 136, relegating Black Caviar to No. 2 in the world. As a result,

I was getting more phone calls from the British press about our mare, to add to everything else going on with the horse. Talk of a meeting between the two horses was warming up in the papers.

It still seemed like each time Nelly came back in she was getting better, as impossible as that sounded. Around this time, amid the pages of analysis that were going into her, I said the only way she could be beaten was if she hurt herself. No other horse around could touch her, and there was no way she could be boxed in, because her size meant she could bullock her way clear if needed.

But it was in this, her seventh preparation, I had my biggest scare yet.

People look back on how she went from the 1400 metres of the Orr Stakes to the 1000 metres of the Lightning as one of the more remarkable feats achieved by horse and trainer. But for half an hour or so before that shorter race, the trainer didn't feel too clever, I can assure you. I was horrified I might have ruined the greatest story on turf.

This was supposed to be the preparation where Black Caviar would step up to the 1400-metre Group 1 double at Caulfield: the Orr, and the Futurity two weeks later.

First up, in late January 2012, she made it seventeen out of seventeen in the Group 2 Australia Stakes over 1200 metres at Moonee Valley. It was a wonderful night with a massive salmon-and-black crowd. In fact, things got a bit crazy. The club had been expecting 8000 people, but about twice that many turned up. With long queues forming outside, since there wasn't enough staff on, and frustrations building up, the club finally decided to throw the gates open. There was drama about that in the following days. People who had paid to get in were understandably peeved. But this was the kind of pandemonium this horse could cause.

Channel 7 was showing the Australian Open tennis, but halfway through the semifinal between Novak Djokovic and Andy Murray, they crossed live to Nelly's race. That sort of thing was now par for the course.

She went round in a field of six and gapped them, winning by more than four lengths, in a super 1:09.44. Had Luke given her a squeeze no doubt she'd have broken Miss Andretti's track record of 1:09.29.

The only thing new was her odds: $1.02—her record short price. Good thing I've never been much into punting.

I was running out of things to say, but I was mindful not to take it for granted. You only had to look around to be reminded we were living a pretty wild dream. We all thought the hysteria for Makybe Diva's third Melbourne Cup was pretty amazing. By now, that's what it was like every time Black Caviar raced.

'It's just great for our industry,' I said after the race. 'We're usually getting a kicking about something if we're on the front page of a newspaper, but this really puts us on the front page for the right reasons. And it's great to be part of it.'

Luke was always good for a quip, on this occasion it came when asked about the crowd. 'We should be getting a percentage of the gate, shouldn't we?' he said in his interview. 'Mind you, a percentage of nothing is nothing.'

More seriously he added: 'Look, it's a wonderful privilege to be on the back of Black Caviar. I thank God every day.' It was great to see him enjoying his part in the story.

I was desperate for that first go at 1400 metres at Caulfield a fortnight later, and the longer trip provided a talking point—briefly.

'You want to back one of those to run her down in an extra 200 metres?' I said to my interviewer. Not surprisingly, no one was putting their hand up.

....

Apart from the media at home and in Europe, race clubs were also calling all the time, trying to entice Black Caviar.

England, France, Ireland, the United States, Singapore, Japan, Hong Kong—everywhere wanted her. Dubai had drawn my interest, with two big sprints on Dubai World Cup night in March. They were mostly interesting as they might have been a good stopover on the way to Ascot.

Nelly's owners had always been great at not putting any pressure on about her racing plans. The only thing they did say was that, if she did go overseas, they would be keen on Ascot. We decided we'd be going that coming June.

To run out that testing 1200 metres up the hill at Ascot, any Australian horse should be proven over 1400 metres on our flat tracks. This was one reason I was so keen on the Orr Stakes as Black Caviar's eighth Group 1.

The longer trip held no fears, though some people tried hard to find reasons for doubt. In the end though, it was handed to her on a platter.

The Melbourne Racing Club learnt from Moonee Valley's mistakes. It was free entry to see Black Caviar, so it was another dizzying day. The racebook was printed with a special fold-out poster of her, with an autograph page on the back. I spent much of the day, while going to and from the saddling stalls, stopping to sign for people. These days were great—actually unforgettable—and it was nice to hear people's stories. But I was just flat out. I had eleven other starters at Caulfield that day, plus one in Sydney, two in Adelaide and another in Bendigo.

Black Caviar was $1.05 against seven others, one of which was our stable's Doubtful Jack. Jason Benbow might have stuffed up on him. He should have led and gone at a good pace. Instead, he settled third and the bolters Danzylum and Midas Touch got in front and slowed them right up. Black Caviar settled fourth, waiting for a sprint home.

It was bizarre. How on earth were they going to outsprint the fastest horse in the world? Their only hope would have been making it a flat out 1400 metres and finding her out at the end. But it was a jog, and she cantered in by three and a quarter lengths, a full four seconds outside the track record. Second was Southern Speed, the previous spring's Caulfield Cup winner, who had won impressively over this course and distance.

'It's unbelievable. It's mind-boggling. I know people doubt the opposition but they're good horses,' I said. 'What she does to good horses is unbelievable.'

I was a little emotional. Partly I felt blessed to be associated with this horse. She had drawn another overflowing crowd, decked out in salmon and black. It was amazing what she was doing for racing. A few people could have little whinges about the depth of the opposition, which was annoying. These were decent horses, the best of the rest. Some might have highlighted the fact horses like Kingston Town and Makybe Diva won from sprints to two miles. But sometimes you'd stop and pull back from the eye of the cyclone and just think about what Black Caviar was doing for the sport—that people, thousands of people, were coming just to see her, just to cheer for her, even though they hardly ever backed her. There aren't many horses who have done that. Maybe Phar Lap. And now Nelly.

Even rival trainer David Hayes turned up that day wearing a salmon-and-black tie. One lady told me she had left her flooded house in Grafton to come down to see Black Caviar. Others came from north Queensland, Tasmania—all over. One lady made the trip from Benalla. That wasn't far, but for Luke it was special. It was his mum, on a rare trip to town to see one of the highlights of her son's career.

They put up a big board on the way out of the track that said 'Thank You Black Caviar', and thousands of people signed it. One of them wrote that he'd flown all the way from Chicago just to see her. Incredible.

There was also a bit of emotion in my voice through contemplating something that hadn't come up much. 'I suppose the end is closer than the beginning,' I said.

....

After such a light run in the Orr, on the Monday it was as if she hadn't even raced. So a little idea I'd had at the back of my mind came to the fore. After a chat with the owners, it was decided we'd go for a very un-Black Caviar–like three runs in three weeks, with a 400 metre drop to the Lightning wedged in before the 1400 metres of the Futurity.

I look back on this prep with some very mixed feelings.

At least I can say the decision on the Lightning wasn't made out of greed. Yes, I'd been training her with 1400 metres in mind, but the style of the Orr Stakes meant she'd need extra work on the following Saturday anyway, in preparation for the Futurity. Had the Orr been tougher, I wouldn't have considered the Lightning. But I thought: 'Why not have her work down the Flemington straight, which she loves, for three-quarters of a million dollars?'

Everyone made a big deal about the drop in distance. Horses had dropped 400 metres before, but they rarely do it in a week and win. One article said in the previous four years it had been tried 120 times, and only one horse had won—at Kangaroo Island.

Nelly didn't need any work at all that week. She was just cantered and led off a pony. I wouldn't say I had no fears about the drop in distance, but I felt there was one horse in the world who could do it, and she was it. So I was feeling okay.

Then I got to Flemington and shat myself.

We hadn't seen our old sparring partner Hay List for a while. He'd got really sick after that BTC Cup and apparently nearly died. He had come back but hadn't raced yet, though he'd won a Randwick barrier trial the day Black Caviar won first-up at Moonee Valley.

But when I saw him on the day of our gamble with the Lightning Stakes, I couldn't take my eyes off him. He just looked pumped, absolutely magnificent, the best I'd ever seen him, and I felt my blood run cold. It would be like Muhammad Ali coming up against George Foreman again after giving him a belting, but this time George is a million times more fit, more muscled, and more scary looking than ever before.

Adding to my panic, I didn't see Hay List's trainer John McNair all day. I'd become friendly with him through our horses' rivalry, and we'd usually have a chat. But this day I'm sure he was dodging me. It was like they had gone right into battle mode, and that scared the shit out of me too.

Another huge crowd had come to see Nelly match Zenyatta's nineteen straight, but while I was watching them parade and the crowd was going mad, I just had one thought: 'Fuck! You idiot! You've trained her for 1400, you were just using this as a track gallop, and here's this monstrous hulk that's arrived and never looked better. He's the one horse in Australia, maybe the world, that was the only possibility of beating her, and he's arrived at 120 per cent.'

In the minutes before the race, I wished I hadn't taken her. It was the most daunted I ever felt with her, thinking today could be the day she goes eighteen-and-one. Those moments when I'd thought of the upsides of her getting beaten, I certainly wasn't thinking them now. All the prestige of a perfect record? What if we turn up to Royal Ascot with this horse from Down Under who'd *almost* had an unbeaten career? I was feeling sick.

Luke tried to calm me down, saying: 'We'll be right, we'll be right'. I said: 'Listen, Hay List is pumped'. Luke said: 'It's fine. We'll cruise along and nab him late.'

I felt I had to leave no doubt. I said: 'Mate, he's fucken pumped. You grind him into the turf or this bloke's a chance of beating us today.' I seriously thought it.

The bookies were finally taking some bets against Black Caviar, with some punters feeling the drop in distance was too much even for her. Maybe they'd seen Hay List too. She was a relatively easy $1.10, with Hay List $12. Had the bookies known how I was feeling, she would have certainly been longer.

Horse trainers are sporting figures who don't really get into direct combat with each other, but before this race it definitely felt like I was in a fight.

I said to Luke again: 'You hit the ground running and grind this bastard into the ground'. Hay List had led us up the last two times we'd met, at Doomben and Randwick, and he had kicked away on us. I thought if he led and kicked away today and that 1400-metre run had taken the edge off Nelly, she might just struggle to run him down.

This day was when the pressure felt bigger than any other day, outside Ascot.

....

Black Caviar jumped well from barrier 5, slightly better than Hay List in 7. Glyn Schofield hunted him up to the front at the 800 metres, with Buffering sharing the lead on Nelly's inside. The three of them went at it like that for about two furlongs, then Buffering started to feel the pinch.

Passing the 400 the white blinkers of Hay List were still pushing up level with us. Luke started to let Nelly step it up a gear, but as Glyn got busy on Hay List, he started to respond as well. It seemed he wasn't going away. Luke later told me Hay List had him worried for about a furlong. As they passed the 300, I too was starting to fear the worst and was swallowing hard.

Fifty metres later, she'd broken his heart.

Let go under hands and heels from Luke, with maybe a sight of the whip, Black Caviar just pulled away. The relief was just enormous. To think we'd come so far, over nineteen starts, with this folk hero of a horse and then got the shock of our lives. But our girl had done it again.

As she passed the post one and three-quarter lengths in front of Hay List, the crowd showed appreciation for both horses and stood up to applaud. Buffering got third, with Foxwedge fourth.

Luke summed it up well: 'She touched me today. The chips were down . . . but today she showed how much courage she's got.'

It wasn't any training feat. It was all the horse. The greatness of the win was shown in the times. Finally pushed out to a great extent, though still not hit with the whip, Black Caviar set 55.53 seconds, just .03 seconds outside the 'untouchable' track record that had been held by Special since 1988. A lot of people also gasped at the sectionals. In that furlong where she usually went hardest, from the 600 metres to the 400 metres, she'd clocked 9.98 seconds. Everyone had been amazed when she covered that stretch in 10.27 seconds in the Newmarket. You just weren't supposed to set sub-10 second furlongs. It just didn't happen. No one had heard of it before or since, and it'll be a very long time till we see it again, if ever.

Hay List was a great horse. He was just unfortunate to race in an era where he ran into a phenomenon. I was pleased for him and his connections a few weeks later when he won the Newmarket. (When Foxwedge then beat him in the William Reid, it meant Black Caviar had beaten the winners of all fifteen Group 1 sprints in Australia— a nice stat for anyone doubting her opposition).

For me, the relief after the Lightning was enormous. More than ever, I couldn't wait to get home, flop on the couch and exhale. And, after what I'd felt was a bit of a great escape, the plans were about to change.

....

I'd pretty much made up my mind after '55.53' flashed up at Flemington that the Futurity was out. I would have liked to have paid back the Melbourne Racing Club for how good they had been to me over the years and take Black Caviar back to Caulfield, but I'd asked her to do so much.

After a couple of days at the stables this was confirmed. She was knackered. The Lightning drained her more than I thought it would. To run that 55, and run it all the way, it was the hardest race she'd had. She felt it, mentally and physically, more than any race outside the one coming up at Ascot four months later.

The decision to bypass the Futurity—which was front- and back-page news in Melbourne's *Herald Sun* newspaper—would mean that the Orr Stakes was the only run she ever had beyond 1200 metres. That remains a bit of a regret, but not a huge one. For one thing, you can't be greedy. For another, her career just never really panned out that way.

I had entertained some thoughts of putting her over longer distances. As I said, when she was three I thought about the 2040-metre Cox Plate, and the 1600-metre Thousand Guineas, but those ideas went out the window when she hurt herself at the start of her fourth race, the Danehill Stakes. I also gave some thought to the 1600 metres of the Myer Classic at Flemington on Derby Day when she was four or five, but then the fact she had a history of injuries probably stopped ideas of longer distances taking hold. I would've been worried that the workload I would have to put into her to get her ready for a

1600-metre trip or longer might run the risk of having her break down again.

For the record, I know she would have coped with 1600 metres with no worries at all. Probably 2000 metres would have had some questions about it, though you wouldn't have bet against her.

In any case, while people ask, 'Why didn't you?', I'd also say, 'Why would you?' She was the best sprinter in the world. When you've got a horse who's the best in the world at something, why make her do something else? I know I'm pretty satisfied with what Black Caviar did in her career, put it that way!

....

After two weeks at home Nelly had a couple more weeks on the water-walker and in the paddock at Peter Clarke's. Then, with Dubai now out, we would need another stepping stone to Ascot.

There was the possibility of the Sydney autumn. The Brisbane Racing Club had made a video using some of Queensland's biggest sport stars pleading for her to come back. But now it would be Adelaide's turn.

Racing wasn't doing too well over there, and I knew, as did the South Australian Jockey Club, that an appearance by Black Caviar would provide a huge financial boost. In the end, they got two.

The two 1200-metre Group 1 races at Morphettville fell in a good timeslot. Ten weeks after the Lightning, she would go back to fillies and mares competition for the Robert Sangster Stakes, before the open-company Goodwood two weeks later.

It was a boon for South Australian racing, and mostly good fun. But, looking back, this is probably where the trouble started that would rear its head in England. In hindsight, I probably should have just given her the one Adelaide run.

It was maybe a bad omen for some, but just funny for others, what happened to Peter Courtney when he took Black Caviar over in our truck. Heading out of Stawell he got booked for speeding, doing 70 kilometres per hour between the 60 and 80 signs. Again, the copper saw 'Moody Racing' on the truck and when he found out who was inside, he just wanted to talk to Peter about Black Caviar. He still pinched him though. Fancy getting done for speeding when you've got Black Caviar in the truck!

In Adelaide, where we stabled with my mate Philip Stokes, the hysteria was as strong if not stronger than ever.

The day before the race we took Nelly for a swim and a press call at the Morphettville track. I was expecting a good local media turnout, but word must have spread like wildfire. Before long there were about a thousand people flocked around the swimming pool.

They came from everywhere to watch her have a swim. There were cars pulling up in the middle of the road next to the course, people were emerging from behind the stripping sheds, seemingly jumping out of the proverbial trees and crawling out of drains to see her. There were media all around, a helicopter overhead. It was like the pope had come out.

Afterwards, with the stables off-course, police closed a bit of street so she could safely walk home, then reopened it once she was inside. Again, Nelly had a security detail to make sure she was left alone.

Black Caviar mania had also been given another kick-along due to the deeds of her relatives. Two-year-old half-brother All Too Hard had won his first three starts. And Nelly's half-sister, by Redoute's Choice, sold for an equal-record $2.6 million at the Sydney Easter yearling sales. I had bid at the auction, but was knocked out pretty early.

The build-up in Adelaide was immense, dwarfing even the AFL derby that weekend between the Crows and Port Power.

And race day was just phenomenal. Adelaide wasn't going to miss its chance. People were shoulder to shoulder and just going berserk, excited like it was a massive party—held in salmon and black. There were officially 30,000 people there. (I reckon it was a fair bit more, but Morphettville was only licensed to hold 30,000. Similarly, Doomben had said the crowd there was 22,000, but it was probably more like 40,000.)

I was appreciative that the SAJC roped off our end of the day stalls, so people couldn't get too close. But all day as Nelly and Donna Fisher strolled around, a huge cheer went up whenever people saw the horse. Even when I legged Luke aboard, the crowd erupted. Again—the amazing way she affected people. The other interesting thing was that, with Channel 7 showing her race and Channel 9 broadcasting that day's Sydney Cup meeting, it was the first time in Australia racing had been on two free-to-air channels at the same time. You just lost count of the remarkable things that happened due to Black Caviar.

As for the race itself, win No. 20 and Group 1 No. 10 was a procession. There were ten other, mostly local, horses, with Black Caviar $1.05. From barrier 3, at weight for age, I knew she wasn't going to get beat. After sitting one-out-one-back, she strolled in by four-and-a-half lengths.

Black Caviar had now won more races than Zenyatta, and beaten the Australasian record of nineteen straight by Gloaming and Desert Gold. I was over the moon, and delighted for what she'd done for Adelaide racing.

....

It seemed Black Caviar had pulled up okay when she arrived home next morning. But when I think back, though she was well, she wasn't exactly thriving; not bouncing out of her skin. It was May now too, and she had started growing her winter coat.

In hindsight, I probably erred in giving her a second Adelaide run. But I thought that, unlike say Brisbane, racing in Adelaide could really use a lift. The year before they'd got 3000 people to Sangster Stakes day. When we'd been there, they got at least ten times that.

The hype was possibly even bigger second time around. To illustrate the Black Caviar effect, that day's AFL game at Football Park between Adelaide and reigning premier Geelong was brought forward half an hour to give the crowd, and no doubt the players, time to get to Morphettville for the 4.20 p.m. Goodwood. Heightening everybody's mood, the Crows got up.

The partying crowd again gave a huge cheer when the gates opened. Nelly jumped in front from barrier 8, and after briefly sharing the lead she got sick of that and pulled ahead past the 600 metres. The crowd started roaring as Luke let her cruise around the turn five or six wide. He didn't move on her as she pulled away, winning from Mark Kavanagh's We're Gonna Rock.

The time was nothing special, as with her first Adelaide win, and nor was the length-and-a-quarter margin. In fact, the margin was a thorny issue at that time.

For a while bookies, trying to get some wagering going on Black Caviar's races, would take bets not on whether she'd win, but by how far. Margin betting—nicknamed 'Black Caviar exotics'—has now been widely banned. But at this time, the odd smart-arse suggested Luke could have plotted her margin for wagering. It pissed us both off, and was probably even libellous. Little wonder Luke snapped a bit when asked if the margin had gone to plan.

'No, there was no plan. I'm not a punter. Just as long as she wins.'

That was a minor sour note, but we weren't going to flatten her. Asked about margins I said: 'No one has ever given us more money for winning by bigger spaces'. I had in fact joked to Luke that, if he hit her with the whip, I'd do the same to him.

With another one down, I also called it the best 21st I'd been to.

And with that, it was off to see the world. The Diamond Jubilee Stakes was only seven weeks away. We were also considering a second English race, the July Cup at Newmarket.

But there were more dark days ahead, starting with the one after the Goodwood.

21

The Road to Royal Ascot

After three trips to England I knew that, to pull off a successful coup going over there, you needed everything to go right. One mishap could scupper the whole plan, as we'd seen when Hinchinbrook did a tendon.

But with Black Caviar's trip to England, one thing didn't go wrong. A whole lot of them did.

The venture has gone down in Australian sporting folklore. People know what happened in the race. What most don't know are the dramas that led up to it.

We had to keep some things in-house. Yes, we kept saying she was right, but with stakes this high and pressure this great, you've got to keep some things to yourself. We didn't want extra attention and pressure on top of the truckload we already had. We didn't want the idea that Nelly was struggling to be associated with her. And I didn't want to worry Luke and the owners.

It's testament again to the amazing qualities of the horse that she even got to race at Ascot, let alone beat some of Europe's best sprinters there.

Some were critical that she only fell in by a head. Some, in England particularly, questioned how great she was. Many, unfortunately, focused on Luke's ride, his dropping of his hands near the post, which then required a summoning for that last desperate lunge.

I've kept my cards close to my chest, till now. But when you factor in what Black Caviar really went through before still coming away with the prize, whatever regard you've got for her now should be a hundred times greater.

....

Trouble didn't wait long to emerge. The day after the Goodwood, Michael Bryant discovered Nelly had torn a muscle. She had a 4-centimetre tear up high behind around her hip, in the equivalent of a human quadriceps.

It's an unusual injury for a horse. It was a bit hard to believe, because of the easy run she had had, but not when you remembered this was Black Caviar: a fast, heavy unit prone to things like muscle tears. There was a tear here or there popping up for most of her career. We only had three weeks till her flight, so we got busy, with Michael using everything he had—massage, ultrasound, laser.

Nelly also came over a bit stale. Maybe she was just sick of all the treatment, all the bother, because she generally liked being left alone. She had had the three runs in late January–early February including the quick back-up to the Lightning, then a little freshen-up before going to Adelaide and back twice in a fortnight by road.

I started second-guessing myself, and kicking myself. Sitting on a volcano this precious, you always do. It's the downside of having a great horse. With the clarity of several years of hindsight, I shouldn't have run her in the Goodwood. She should have just had one run in Adelaide. And I should have stuck with my Melbourne plan of just the Orr and the Futurity. Memorable though it was, she wouldn't have had that hard Lightning run, which took a toll. And even if she had only done the Orr and Futurity, she still should have run only once in Adelaide.

After Adelaide I should have spelled her for a week or so to change things up. Instead, we kept her in the stables, and Melbourne was cold and wet. I was trying to keep her work up, because I'd learnt you want to load a fit horse onto that plane. You don't want to have to do too much in England, in case they travel badly and lose weight on the way over, which is pretty common.

The result was that, when Black Caviar boarded the plane at Melbourne Airport late on the night of 5 June 2012, she was way below her best. Yes, she had a level of racing fitness, but she was flat, mentally stale. Looking back, she was buggered.

The muscle tear had improved but still required treatment, and it was annoying her. Nelly had started growing a winter coat, of thick, wiry hair. That's not so uncommon in the cold months, but she shouldn't have had it. Horses don't really grow them if they're doing well and thriving.

Remember the famous body suit she travelled in? It caused some excitement when she wore it at her last press conference at Caulfield. Yes, the lover of sports science in me was hoping the tight spandex would be good for circulation, like people wearing pressure stockings on planes. But the greater benefit was that with the suit on, people couldn't see she was actually off in the coat and looking pretty shabby.

So why persevere? I was second-guessing myself a lot. I wondered if I was becoming over-protective. In hindsight, I know I wasn't. Nelly was out on her feet. But I took input from Michael Bryant, Peter Angus and Tony Haydon, and we decided that, while she was off her top, she was still right to make the trip. We were backing the horse, possibly hoping she would thrive better in the English summer, but mostly backing her incredible capacity to get the job done. And there was so much expectation. It seemed the whole country was dying to see her go and take 'em on at Ascot.

Nelly's saving grace was that her demeanour suggested she'd travel well and cope with the trip, which she did.

....

Black Caviar was always being compared to Phar Lap. They were both equine national heroes, yes, but from a racing sense, I never really got it. It was unfair on both. They were different. Their eras were different. Racing conditions were different. It was pointless.

But here was one similarity—the grand overseas adventure. As everyone knows, Phar Lap went to America to race in 1932, winning then dying there. We've all seen the scratchy old footage of Phar Lap being lifted onto the ship by crane in Sydney Harbour, but there was little other documentation of the adventure remaining.

So the owners, Nelly's commercial manager Stephen Silk and I thought we'd make sure this trip was well recorded. We signed a deal with a TV production company who had close access the whole way through. That's why there's so much good footage of her being loaded onto the plane on a cold, wet Melbourne night, and of her work at Newmarket leading up to the race.

She travelled with Tony Haydon, as foreman, and my trackwork rider, Paddy Bell, to ride her work. The interest was at fever pitch—not just from Australians or the English, but also halfway in between.

Nelly's plane stopped in Singapore then went to Abu Dhabi, where the boys really got the sense of how her story had travelled the globe. After the plane touched down this orange Lamborghini drove up, on the tarmac! Out stepped this bloke who was a sheikh, or the son of one or something. In any event, Tony learnt that he owned the airport. He was into horses too, and had got wind of who was on the plane. He was pretty excited.

The guy's minders asked Tony if he could meet the great mare herself. Tony said: 'That'd be fine, but I'm dying for a smoke'.

That was a problem, since they were on an airport tarmac. But the bloke whistled up another car, and Tony got driven around in that while he had a smoke, while the bigwig went onto the plane with Paddy and got some selfies and a pat with this horse from Australia he'd heard so much about.

Finally, smokes smoked and pats patted, the trip resumed.

....

If I had thought Black Caviar in England would be lower key than Australia, I was very mistaken. I had been held up by a day, so I arrived the day after Ascot's major press conference. That was one less duty but I soon learnt there was, shall we say, a fair bit of hype around the unbeaten horse from Australia.

I'd pick up a newspaper and there was Black Caviar. It was amazing enough she was on the back page. The Euros soccer tournament was in full swing, with England participating. Wimbledon and the London Olympics were about to happen. And the unbeaten Frankel was about to supposedly be the other headline act at Royal Ascot. Yet here was Black Caviar dominating, with barely a mention of Frankel.

But Nelly was on the front pages too, taking space from the hullabaloo about Queen Elizabeth's Diamond Jubilee (the reason the race name from that year on changed from the Golden Jubilee). One paper said there hadn't been this much media interest in a foreign horse in twenty years.

Black Caviar was on TV. She was on billboards. There was even a London cab, owned by a fan, which was painted pink with black dots!

It felt like a pleasure to escape to Newmarket. Still, wherever we'd take the horse that week, there'd be a photographer or a TV camera sticking out of a hedge somewhere. It was phenomenal.

While all the owners travelled over, Sarah decided she was better off at home. There were the girls and their school schedule to look after, but also she tipped—correctly—there would be a bit going on in England and I probably didn't need the distraction of my family there as well.

Brett Cavanough had come with me, which was good. Not only were we old mates from the bush, but he is an excellent horseman and I might have needed his input. Michael Bryant, who I had also become close to, rounded out our three-man party, and would continue to work on the horse. We were a good mix. Brett's a light-hearted, funny sort of bastard who can defuse any stressful situation, or tell you if you're being a dickhead. I'm also pretty like-minded with Michael, who's got a real dry wit.

So it felt like a bit of a boys' trip away. In fact, on race day, as we were donning our top hats and tails, it felt like a wedding party—right down to the fact we wouldn't see the 'bride' until we got to the venue, since Nelly had gone down with Tony and Paddy earlier that day.

Peter Angus was over too, with his family, so it'd be good to have him if needed. We had also got special permission for Glen Darrington to make the trip. Keeping everything as normal as possible for her, Glen would fit her barrier blanket behind the gates, then go in and sit on the rail beside her to keep her calm. They don't really use barrier attendants much in England, or even clerks of the course to assist fractious horses. Plus they'd hardly seen a barrier blanket before, so Glen had to show that to them to get their approval. I was grateful the authorities didn't have a problem with Glen being involved.

This time, that flat where I'd had my nude lockout would be swapped for a house that Brett, Michael and I rented. But the man who had saved me and clothed me that time, Phil Harlow, would help out as our driver.

Black Caviar had travelled well and settled in at the stable of trainer Jane Chappel-Hyam, the Australian-born daughter of former Opposition Leader Andrew Peacock.

Jane, who I'd see when she brought horses to the Melbourne spring carnival, was a great host, and even provided a mate for Nelly since she had no other horses near her, an old gelding called Saloon. She didn't really need companionship, but we were trying to keep it similar to home, and the two of them got on well.

Having missed that press conference on the Thursday, we did a press call just with Nelly on the Friday, again covered up in her compression suit. I stirred the pot a little by saying it felt odd to have to prove Black Caviar to the world by going to England and racing inferior horses for inferior prizemoney than we had in Australia, but despite that banter I was of course pretty keyed up for the mission.

Nelly had a trot, canter and swim on the Saturday. She seemed okay fitness wise, though she was lighter than for most of her starts. When Luke saw her, he said that, instead of looking like Serena Williams as usual, she looked more like her sister, Venus. In any case, regardless of her physical condition, I still had my concerns about her mentally.

....

I'd be on edge most of that week, but on the Sunday there was a chance to relax with some mates and a couple of beers. And it was capped by a very special moment.

One of those mates was the well-connected Angus Gold, racing manager for Sheikh Hamdan's Shadwell Stud operation. This being Newmarket, everyone in racing was around. Angus asked if I'd like to go see the wonder horse, Frankel, who was nearby at trainer Sir Henry Cecil's place. I said I'd love to.

Angus' secretary rang Cecil's secretary, but she said: 'I don't think that will be possible. Henry doesn't let anyone into the stables.'

I was disappointed, but that was that, and I had a couple more beers.

But about 7.30 p.m. Angus got a phone call. It was Henry Cecil. He said: 'Bring Peter down and he can have a look at Frankel. But there's one condition . . .'

'What's that?'

'I want to come have a look at Black Caviar, too.'

I almost ran down there! It was phenomenal. To see Frankel and have a good look at him up close was fantastic. Here's this amazing horse, who's top World Thoroughbred Ranking rating of 140 has never been beaten, and who in two days' time would be going around at Ascot. I've had some handy ones myself but it did feel special to be giving him a pat.

Then Henry came to ours and had a look at Nelly. It was unfortunate he didn't see her at her top. He admired her for the horse she was, for her great girth and hindquarter, but even he commented that she didn't look at her best.

Still, it was quite remarkable—me viewing his champion and him viewing mine. Here's me and Sir Henry Cecil, one of the greatest trainers in history, spending half an hour in the quiet, otherwise deserted stable, with Black Caviar. I'd met Henry, who sadly passed away a year later aged 70, when there with Magnus, but to come back with this world-renowned horse was brilliant. To see this man appreciate Black Caviar—I was quite moved by it.

It was like when Don Bradman met Babe Ruth, except the horses didn't meet. Of course there was still this clamour for that to happen, and in fact the Qatari sponsors of the Sussex Stakes, over 1600 metres at Goodwood in August, had said they'd boost prizemoney from £300,000 to a million pounds if the two horses went in it.

To settle the score on any match-race ideas once and for all, it was never going to happen.

I did wonder about it occasionally. My opinion now is, great horse though Frankel was, over 1400 metres Nelly would have pushed him. Over 1600 metres, I don't know. That would have been unchartered territory for her. But I also thought: 'Why should we race him over a mile over there? Why couldn't he race her in Australia over 1400 metres?'

Sir Henry dismissed the match-race idea as 'stupid' when we were there. However, a month earlier in the papers he said a meeting of the two might be 'good for racing', so the thought obviously crossed his mind too.

When we met, though, we didn't mention it. I think we were both just grateful to have two of the best horses in history. Why be greedy and ask for more? Why have a match race? Why, for that matter, compare Black Caviar with Phar Lap? Just appreciate and enjoy.

Another idea that popped up was breeding Frankel and Black Caviar together to produce the fabled 'superhorse'. It wasn't given much thought though. In fact, some experts did an analysis on the two bloodlines and it wasn't a mating that rated very highly, for one reason or another. Of course it might have worked—it's an inexact science—but the data on the bloodlines suggested it wouldn't have been a simple case of super stallion, super mare, super foal.

....

Two days after our meeting, Frankel kicked off the Royal Ascot carnival in the Queen Anne Stakes, the Group 1 that, oddly for Australians, is race one on day one. Brett, Michael and I felt like a break, so we put on our morning suits and Phil drove us down.

It was amazing. What Frankel did to that field, winning by eleven lengths, was as explosive a win as I'd seen.

And for we three louts from Australia, it was a great day. It was fantastic to go to the races under no pressure whatsoever!

We also got a prime spot. If you look at a photo of the finish, you'll see Frankel hitting the line, daylight second, and in the background right beside the winning post, three blokes in top hats and tails. It's me, Brett and Michael—like a group of kids getting close to the action.

No one was looking at us, of course. In fact, we joked that, had we wanted to be some ugly Aussies on tour, we could have pulled our flies down and hung our knobs out and absolutely no one would have noticed, because they'd all be watching the wonder horse! The idea sounded tempting until someone said people would probably notice in the photos in the next day's papers.

We were carrying on like kids in a lolly shop—having a great day out and watching Frankel.

....

That release was welcome because, with four days till our race, I was still far from happy with Black Caviar.

We'd had to keep working on that muscle she'd torn. Behind closed doors, Michael was massaging her, using ultrasound and laser, and we had to ice her after she did anything. The muscle had improved, but was still really annoying her.

Nelly was still off in the coat and wiry. Even when a horse is growing a winter coat, they can look healthy through it. But she didn't. She was a long way off glistening.

That Tuesday morning, she'd also had her first proper sprint, over 800 metres up the Newmarket stretch they call the Limekilns with Luke aboard. Unfortunately that went a bit wrong. She had her 'boyfriend' Saloon out in front of her under Paddy Bell and wanted to get up there with him; Luke didn't want to fight her and risk hurting her, and the result was she worked harder than I'd wanted, especially given her condition. Luke would later say she perhaps had one good gallop in her that week, and she spent it on the Tuesday.

It wasn't a huge setback, but it was enough—enough to heighten my already full book of anxieties. And on top of all that, after the gallop her fetlocks were a little tender.

At Ascot that day I met with her owners. A few had planned holidays around Black Caviar having two runs in England, so I thought I'd give them a heads up. I didn't want to worry them, so I just said, while I wasn't unhappy, we'd only get one run in England.

In my own heart I was still undecided whether Black Caviar would even get that. And the next morning, as if we needed it, things took a new and major turn for the worse.

22

Rough Diamond

On the Wednesday Black Caviar had a light trot and canter, before more work from Michael on that muscle. That was the last day we could give her any injections before the race, and we decided on cortisone shots for her fetlocks. We got a local vet for the routine task of injecting the cortisone, and then we could finally leave her alone for a few hours.

After the injections, you need to put cotton wool and bandages around the fetlocks to guard against infection or soreness, and the vet's young assistant lad did this. Tony or Paddy would usually do it, but whatever. It was no big deal.

Well, it shouldn't have been. But when I went back in the afternoon I couldn't believe what I found. The lad had put the bandages on too tight. He'd also used too little cotton wool. As a result, the tendons in both of Nelly's forelegs had blown up with inflammation.

On top of her sore fetlocks, her feet, which were always problematic, her torn muscle, and the fact she was worn out, now she also had what's called bandage bows. It's not quite the more serious bowed tendon, which will usually end a horse's career. But it's what happens when a tendon gets bound too tightly, leaving it with a minor bow and swelling. You then run the risk that, if you work the horse too hard, it will get a bowed tendon.

Had the bandages been on for another hour, it would have been goodbye Ascot. As it was, it was a bloody disaster.

It was action stations.

Brett remembers how I came flying into the house, where he was having a nap, yelling out to get ice, buckets and money. We might need to buy some treatments.

With Tony, Paddy and Michael in London for the day, Brett and I bolted back to the stable, and this race began. It was too close to Saturday to legally give her anti-inflammatories, so it was just standing her in buckets of ice and water, then putting poultices on her, trying to get the heat and swelling out of these tendons. Tony, Paddy and Michael came back and joined in, and we worked feverishly, till late at night, to ice her.

We went back Thursday morning with our fingers crossed, but the swelling was still there. We started up our production line of ice and poultices again, to try to bring it down. She still needed to do something, but we made sure it was just a very light trot, then continued the treatment into the afternoon.

We had to take up most of the day with this, the time Nelly was used to as *her* time, when she could be left alone. We had to do all this with her fetlocks, and Michael had to keep working on that muscle. Individually, these weren't things that would automatically make you scratch a horse, but it was annoying the shit out of her. She just wasn't in a good way, and the toughest race of her life was two days away.

By Friday morning, thankfully, we had got the tendons to go down. But Nelly was buggered. It had been a rough and abnormal week for her—certainly a very disrupted preparation, and something she just wasn't used to.

Her trainer was in an equally bad way—still in grave doubt as to whether she should run. After 21 wins, through the Black Caviar phenomenon that had built over three years, with a lot of careful management, this was supposed to be the highlight. The racing world would be watching, not just Australia. And it felt like we just weren't meant to be there, that it wasn't meant to happen.

I just wanted to spend that day before the race alone with her. I told the boys to have a break. They went to London while I looked after Nelly myself.

In the afternoon I took her for a walk and a pick of grass. The media were still onto us. There was one bloke in a cherry picker taking photos, and the phone kept ringing. I just kept saying, 'Yeah, happy with her, happy with her', but in these few hours with her I was doing some real soul-searching. She was a very intelligent girl. She could tell you a lot with her eyes. The rest was body talk—just me watching how she moved. I've said before it can be a lonely job, being a horse trainer. That day it was illustrated more starkly than ever.

This wasn't just any six-furlong sprint. It was possibly the toughest six-furlong sprint in the world. With a run uphill to the winning post, you had to be a good 1400-metre horse to run it out strongly. No mare had won it for 27 years.

Time was ticking away, but, like a puzzle you can't solve or like many of the biggest decisions of your life, the answer wasn't coming easily. So I turned to the horse person whose judgement I'd valued more than anyone's for the past twenty years. I rang Sarah in Melbourne.

Her answer was blunt and to the point. 'You haven't asked my advice with her before, so you probably don't need to now. You'll make up your mind.' On top of that, she wasn't what you'd call keen to embrace the pressure of making a call as momentous as whether

Black Caviar should race at Royal Ascot. So it wasn't enormously helpful, but she was right, especially since she was ten thousand miles away. I'd have to make the decision myself.

I put Nelly to bed no clearer on whether she would run. The decision would have to wait till race day.

....

I might have hoped I'd wake up and the answer would be staring me in the face. Instead, all I had was the huge knot in my stomach I'd had for three days.

We got up about 3 a.m. and threw Paddy Bell on her for a trot. Luke, lucky bastard, was in London with his family. I hadn't let him in on the drama. I didn't want it to cloud his mind or influence his ride if she did race.

Paddy trotted her up and we had a conference. Me, Tony, Paddy, Michael and Brett. We still weren't happy with her. But we had to make the call.

'Bugger it,' I said. 'We're having a go.'

I'd back this amazing animal to carry the day, as she had all her life. Mick reminded me that, apart from the speed everyone saw, she was mentally the toughest horse he'd known in forty years in the business. She was, clearly, a long way off her top, but I'd back those competitive instincts, that white-line fever she had come business time. She was loaded onto the truck and Tony and Paddy went with her to Ascot.

That didn't mean it was plain sailing for me. Brett, Michael and I had a few beers at the house while getting into our suits. I was smoking like a chimney. Eventually it was time to get in the car and leave, and we had a couple more settling beers on the trip. I was as nervous as hell. Brett told me later he could see I was spent, that I had a flat battery. He felt that, after all this time with this world-famous mare, I was staring defeat in the face.

At one point we came to a fork in the road, where you had to go right to Ascot or left to London. The latter sounded pretty attractive. 'How about we just go into town?' I said. 'Tony can saddle her up.' Brett didn't exactly hose down the idea. There's no doubt we wouldn't have gone through with it (probably!) but in any case it brought a timely boot up the arse from Mick Bryant: 'Are you fucken kidding? Pull your head in.'

We continued on to the biggest race meeting of my life, feeling nervous anticipation and pure dread.

....

There were at least a lot of good vibes on course. It was a full house, with salmon and black everywhere—blokes' ties, women's hats, on little flags in the crowd. It was great to see lots of Aussie flags too. It was like you might see at Wimbledon, only much bigger.

There were loads of Australian tour groups, one led by former jockey and TV commentator Simon Marshall. He later said it was the worst he had seen Black Caviar in the mounting yard—dull in the coat, agitated, giving the odd kick at anyone who got too near, which wasn't like her.

I went and saw the horse. At least nothing else had gone wrong. I met up with the owners, but didn't say too much. Then I caught up with Luke, and he and I, Brett, Michael and Tony took a walk up the straight, just to appreciate how undulating it was, before the first race. The great Irish trainer Aidan O'Brien was out there with his jockeys too. After a while the police came along on their horses. I wondered if we'd done something wrong, but they said: 'You'll have to clear off the track. The queen's about to come down.' I pointed at

Aidan's mob and said: 'What about those Irish bastards? Wouldn't they be more danger to the queen than us?' The coppers had a laugh.

We ducked under the rail at the 400-metre mark and found ourselves in a tent, having a beer with someone (though Luke wasn't, of course) as the queen's procession went by. We went back on the track and back to the enclosure, still with two hours to get through before our race, the third of six for the day.

Finally, it came time to put the saddle on my big mare, this time for the biggest race of her life. It was game on, and it felt different than ever before. As a trainer I used to feel like stepping onto the racecourse for the day felt a bit like a footballer stepping over the white line. Maybe it's the frustrated footballer in me, but I did approach it like going into battle, against all the opposition, and trying to make plans for all the variables in front of you. I did view walking onto Flemington or Caulfield for the afternoon's competition a bit like an Artie Beetson running onto Lang Park, or a Wayne Bennett going into the coach's box.

This time brought a new element. It felt a bit like this was our Olympics, that we were representing Australia on the world stage. Of course, with winning at anything depending so heavily on preparation, I only wished horse and trainer were in better shape for it.

The fourteen horses paraded. Luke got on, and Tony and Paddy led her through the tunnel out onto the course. I walked alongside and walked out with her onto the track. I remembered what I'd said to Luke before about pulling her out if ever she wasn't right, but I didn't dare say anything like that now, even though she was in the worst shape of any of her 25 races. Luke did tell me later she felt a little rough going down to the gates.

Finally, 1200 metres down the undulating mile-long straight, the field started to load. Glen Darrington fitted Nelly's barrier blanket, then took her into the outside gate and sat on the side rail keeping her calm. Brett, Michael and I took up the spots we'd occupied on the Tuesday, on the flat side near the winning post. On the big screen they crossed to Federation Square in Melbourne, where a few thousand people had gone to watch in the freezing cold at 1 a.m., which was amazing to see.

And then it was time for all those harrowing questions to be answered. Black Caviar started a relatively long £1.16, ahead of French mare Moonlight Cloud at £6.00.

The gates opened, there was a huge cheer, and I saw Nelly start okay from the outside. Godolphin's horse Soul, an Australian who had been many classes below Black Caviar at home, took the lead under Frankie Dettori. Nelly settled third a length behind, with the bolter Bogart between her and Soul.

From very early on I started to feel uneasy. You could tell she just didn't travel up as strongly as usual. She would normally be powering into the race, keen to go, with Luke high in the saddle sitting against her. But here he was leaning forward, having to nudge her along. He told me later it was here, early on, he felt there was trouble, because she hadn't dragged him into the race.

At the 600 metres, she was still a length off Soul. Everyone was waiting for that part where she flattens out, bounds clear and puts the race to bed. But instead she was off the bridle 500 metres out. She'd got to the lead, but Luke had to shake her up to do so, and that zip wasn't there. At the 400, I was breathing hard, and I said to Brett: 'Fuck, we're in trouble here'.

Nelly dug deep, and pushed ahead, but she only ever got a length clear. And Luke had to give her a few flicks with the whip. She had the inside horses beaten, but I knew her tank was empty.

Then, on her outside, came Moonlight Cloud—who'd been cleverly taken across from barrier 5 by Thierry Jarnet to be the widest runner—and her fellow French horse Restiadargent, a £41 chance. We were really in trouble now.

Still, we expected Nelly to get home like we were used to. But then, with 50 metres to go, came the part everyone unfortunately remembers. Luke felt she would run through the line. It was what she normally did. And he tried to be kind to her. Perhaps not quite aware of how fast Moonlight Cloud and Restiadargent were coming, or assuming she'd naturally hold them out, he stopped riding. He rested his hands on her neck, for half-a-dozen strides.

He'd done it in her past dozen starts, but this day, instead of coasting to the line, she just stopped. Powered down. Everyone later talked about the uphill finish. Even Dettori said to Luke as the horses were pulling up: 'You've got to ride them right out here!'

It wasn't about the hill. The reason Black Caviar stopped was that she was buggered. In any case, as I was watching it unfold in graphic detail, from just 40 metres of open grass away, it was definitely a horror moment. I nearly coughed my heart out of my mouth.

As we all know now, Luke shook her up again. On the replay you can tell it's only three strides. It seemed like bloody ages. Moonlight Cloud was flying, but only Black Caviar could have got the job done from there. She couldn't lengthen stride again, but she just got her head up and kept it there.

A hush fell over the place as the judge called for the photo. I found out later some of the owners, who were in different spots, had thought she had lost, while some thought she had held on. Neil Werrett was past the post and had a rotten angle through his binoculars, and was convinced she'd got beaten.

On the inside of the track, I knew she'd won. You can see me on the replay by the winning post. I'm not moving much. Maybe I was a bit numb? Inside, I was going like the clappers. We still had to wait for the photo, and though I knew she'd lasted, in racing you always think the unthinkable. Finally, number 11 went up, and I could breathe again. Black Caviar had beaten Moonlight Cloud by a head, with Restiadargent a neck away.

The boys were whooping it up, Brett, Paddy, Tony and Michael. I was a bit dazed, just washed over by this wave of relief. Finally this was broken, in unusual fashion, when Luke brought the horse back. I've walked alongside and said something intelligent like 'Holy fuck, what'd you do there mate?' Lukey leaned down, grabbed me round the neck, and planted a kiss on my cheek.

'We still won, mate,' he said. He did later confide that he had shat himself there for a minute, but basically he hit the nail on the head. We had gone to the other side of the world, and against a ton of adversity Black Caviar had won Europe's biggest sprint. That was what mattered.

But after Luke gave Black Caviar a lap of honour in front of the crowd, the inquisition started.

It was understandable, I suppose. It was a huge, dramatic moment that almost cost her the race. But bloody hell it was annoying, and disappointing, that it seemed like that's *all* anyone wanted to talk about—Lukey *almost* stuffing it up. He told me later he had thought of Shane Dye's infamous 'wide' ride on Veandercross when second in the 1992 Caulfield Cup, and knew that, like then, there would be questions asked. He wanted to get out in front of the issue, and from the post-race get-go he stuck his hand up and admitted his mistake. He thought that might nip it in the bud. Alas, he was very wrong.

I had people asking me about it straight away, and the questions about Luke went on and on. I felt like throttling them. One bloke blurted out: 'Is Luke's job in jeopardy over that?' I felt like smacking him in the head. The fastest horse in the world has just won a Group 1 on your home turf, and you just want to talk about the jockey?

It was very nice of Aidan O'Brien to come and have a word. He knew everyone was talking about Luke. He said to us that it was a great victory, that the achievement of winning Europe's best sprint shouldn't be underestimated, and that in time the win would be seen for the triumph it was.

I was mindful to very publically show my support for Luke, who I knew would be feeling a bit sheepish, and to focus on the greatness of Black Caviar. You can tell on the videos I was pretty emotional.

'You've only got to win by a quarter of an inch. We came to win and we got the job done,' I said. 'We never expect dominance. We've never asked her for dominance. She gets the job done. We're more concerned about her next run than we are about today. We're extremely proud of her. She's 22 out of 22. It's never been about margins, or dominance.

'I'm an extremely proud Aussie. Words can't describe the feeling, just to be here and take it all in, it's an unbelievable feeling.'

All that was true. I still have to pinch myself to remember that I was a part of it. And then came the most surreal moment of all.

After we unsaddled, Nelly was buggered but agitated, so Paddy, Tony and myself were walking her around the enclosure, which was pretty crowded with people. We stood her with the owners for a photo, then Paddy and I walked her around behind the owners and bang—all of a sudden Queen Elizabeth was standing right in front of us.

We shook hands and had a little chat. I can't remember what I said, but you could see she was genuinely interested in the horse and very keen to see her.

We're standing there, Black Caviar with Queen Elizabeth only a metre in front of her. Then Paddy says in his Kiwi accent: 'Would you like to give her a pat?' We both tugged the horse forward and she was that buggered that she just kind of slumped towards the queen. I was scared she'd collapse on top of her for a second, which would have been bad. Fortunately, she stayed up, and the queen was very appreciative of being able to pat this horse she'd heard so much about (especially having missed out in Melbourne the previous year!).

We had the presentation. The queen gave the trophy to the lady who had named the now world-famous Black Caviar, Pam Hawkes. Pam held it above her head like she'd won Wimbledon. The queen gave Luke and me our silver snuff-box trophies, which was nice (although neither of us is still entirely sure what a snuff box is) and then we all stood there for photos. It was very special.

....

After the presentations it was time for the media. And boy, didn't that go on for a while—all made worse by the continuing obsession with Luke's ride. Again, instead of basking, we found ourselves getting agitated. 'She still fucken won, you know!' I felt like barking back.

We went from press conference to TV interview, to another TV interview. At one point a bit of the Aussie lout factor came out in the royal enclosure. While Luke was waiting around, some Aussie fan passed him a stubby over the fence. He was quite enjoying it, until one of the attendants said to me: 'Peter, can you please speak to the jockey about holding the stubby?'

Luke says that all these years later, he still can't watch a video of that race, because it makes him cringe too much. At the same time, he says he was glad in a way that he copped the bagging rather than Black Caviar for just falling in, which says what kind of bloke he is. For the record, he reckons if he had pushed her flat out, and not dropped his hands, she still would have won by only about half a length.

Luke and I were caught up in the post-race media duties for more than two hours, which meant we missed the other races. Aside from that, Frankie Dettori still bags Luke because he couldn't get around to doing what you're supposed to do after riding a Group 1 winner at Royal Ascot—shout the jockeys' room a round of champagne.

I finally got clear of everything and went to have a look at Nelly, but by the time I got there Tony and Paddy had already taken her home.

So Brett, Michael and I, and Phil our driver, went to the car park where I could finally have a beer. After one or two we decided to go home. But it was at this point that our car broke down. So we settled in.

One lady we met had a chauffeur. She said: 'James will pop me back into London then he can pop back out here and drive you up to Newmarket if you wish?'

We were fine where we were, just me and two good mates, dressed in the various warming gear that had been lent to us, and letting down in my favourite way, with beer and bungers. It was nice to be able to enjoy it, at last.

And standing there, watching the sun go down over Royal Ascot and taking it all in, charging a glass with Brett, thinking back to when we were kids in Charleville, how he'd got me a job with his grandfather when I was eleven, and thinking of how far I'd come, it was all pretty surreal. We're not overly sentimental but we did feel blessed, smacked on the arse by a rainbow, thinking about where we'd come from and where we were at the time. It wasn't lost on either of us.

In fact, it was terrific to have Brett and Michael Bryant there to share the experience, share the pain and adulation.

We finally got the car fixed and left after 11 p.m. We found a pizza place in the main street of Newmarket, had a couple of beers and then flopped into bed.

....

I was up at dawn to see Nelly. The news wasn't good. Not only would she not run again in England, it seemed that time was up completely.

Peter Angus and Michael Bryant went over her, and a scan showed an old enemy had reappeared: she'd reopened that hole in her suspensory ligament that had first happened after her fifth start. She was also just dead in the eye. Everything screamed that she had had enough.

I rang Neil Werrett and told him. We agreed we would wait till we all got home, then call the other owners together and tell them.

And that would be it. The greatest show since Phar Lap would come to an end.

Brett, Michael and myself left her at Newmarket with Tony and Paddy, and got away as we'd planned. We caught a train to Paris for some very welcome R&R.

I was still a bit dazed and worn out. We dropped our bags at our hotel and took a walk and bingo—we happened upon the Louvre art museum. We went in to see the *Mona Lisa*, but I'm slightly embarrassed to say we never found it. I had no idea what was going on, really. We went back to the hotel and found a little bar and, after all the build-up, tension, triumph and frustration of the past few weeks, we proceeded to have a bloody good drink.

Next morning, we took an hour-long trip north to the racing hub of Chantilly. We had arranged this beforehand, but we didn't know then the significance of the first place we'd be visiting. It was the stable of Frenchman Fred Head—the trainer of Moonlight Cloud!

I felt a bit sheepish, walking into the den of the horse we'd just nutted two days earlier. All the stable lads were there, and we heard this muttering amongst them in French. But then they realised who we were and who our horse was, and they were coming up congratulating us and doffing their caps, which was nice.

We went into Fred's office with him and, for the first time, we watched the race again. Let me tell you, it was a lot easier to watch knowing the result.

Despite Fred's pain at the time, Moonlight Cloud ended up a champion herself, which is fitting for the horse that got closer to Black Caviar than any other. She won eleven out of eighteen, including seven Group 1s.

We went to the stables of Alain De Ruypeye, who'd trained Americain to win the Melbourne Cup, and the magnificent stables of the Aga Khan. It was a nice, relaxing couple of days before flying home—to start my life after Black Caviar.

....

In the meantime, the incredible Black Caviar story got another incredible twist, an unwanted one this time that in fact nearly ended it all.

While in quarantine at Newmarket, she was standing in a paddock when this swarm of bees flew in and attacked her. Tony saw the whole thing, and said it was just horrible. The bees were attacking her head and stinging her all over the place. She had bee stings from the tip of her nose to her tail. She was screaming in pain, and it looked like she was having an anaphylactic reaction, puffing up all over the place. Tony had never seen anything like it. There hasn't been that much said about it, but it was serious. It really was.

Tony told me later he was in a mad panic and thought Black Caviar could die. Her throat could have swollen up and she could have choked. She was also throwing herself around that much she could have broken a leg. It's horrifying to think, but had Tony been down the road getting a sandwich or something, it's a very big chance Black Caviar could have died in quarantine.

Thankfully, as Tony was there hosing her—which was all he could think of to do—he asked someone to call the vet, who came and quickly gave Nelly a shot, and in time the allergic reaction calmed down. But it was just bizarre, and almost lethal. You hear about horses suffering snake and spider bites, but I'd never heard of this. They say bad fortune only happens to the good horses, but how the hell did the bees know this was the great Black Caviar?

....

Back in Melbourne, I had started moving on, and was getting ready to announce Black Caviar would be retired and everyone could look forward to seeing her babies. But when I went to see her at the Werribee quarantine station the day she arrived home, she amazed me again. I couldn't believe it was the same horse.

Her coat had turned, she'd picked right up, she was brighter in the eye. I asked Peter Angus to scan her legs, and he was astounded. I can only conclude that apart from being freakishly fast, she must have had freakish healing capabilities too. Her whole career, these soft-tissue injuries would come, and then go again a lot quicker than in other horses.

When Neil Werrett and Gary Wilkie got home, we decided we would keep going. We wouldn't rush her into the spring, but we'd give her a nice slow build-up towards the autumn. If she still wanted to be there, we'd be off and running again.

Skip forward a few months and there was this amazing horse, pulling Donna around the yard, and bursting out of her skin like never before. We gave her a jump-out at Caulfield, then an exhibition gallop there one day.

Nelly really proved to us she wanted to be there. There'd be more to the Black Caviar show after all.

23

Better than Special

I'm so thankful Royal Ascot wasn't the end of the Black Caviar story.

She would have finished with 22 out of 22 and, with twelve Group 1s, she would have sat fifth on the Australian list, having passed Manikato's eleven.

But it still would have been a disappointing way for this amazing horse to go out—injured, scraping in for her narrowest win, and with all talk focusing on Luke's ride and not the unbelievable effort of the horse. So for Black Caviar to come back and do what she did in her last three runs was very satisfying. More than that, start 23 was just amazing. After a much-needed long break she was raring to go. But she surprised even me.

As the horse chased her third Lightning Stakes, Racing Victoria decided to permanently name it after her—the Black Caviar Lightning—which was nice. Again, there weren't many rivals sticking their hands up. Seven others entered, including our stable's Moment of Change and Golden Archer.

I was probably more nervous for this run than any of them. Nelly had had seven months off. I was hoping she'd stay in one piece, and vindicate our decision to keep going. I got all that and more, as did her fans. Thousands turned up at Flemington with their salmon-and-black flags and banners, as keen to see her return as I was.

Starting at $1.10, Nelly jumped well from barrier 2, cruised to the front and was in control a long way out. Luke gave her a squeeze at the 300 metres and she kicked clear. He wasn't going to drop his hands this day, so he shook her up at the 150 metres.

'It's the Black Caviar of old, all right,' said Greg Miles as she coasted home. She in fact eased up in the last 25 metres, which made what happened next all the more stunning.

The year before Black Caviar had won in 55.53, a tick outside Special's fabled 55.50. Now, her third win was posted at 55.42! It was stunning, possibly her best performance. And she could have gone a good bit faster.

Rounding out the day, Moment Of Change was second for Linda Meech two and a half lengths back, with Golden Archer and Daniel Stackhouse completing a Moody Racing trifecta.

I was a bit emotional after this one. After I had thought it was all over, it felt so good to have her back. We had been on a hiding to nothing, and she's won and broken a 25-year-old track record. I said I might have been too close to previously appreciate how good Black Caviar was, but I definitely felt it that day.

It was a wonderful atmosphere as Luke brought her back to scale, and I made a point of mentioning the owners in the post-race interview. They'd been so great throughout, but I don't think they got the accolades they deserved, maybe because it's hard for the media to talk about a group of eight owners, rather than just one.

It's a weird thing, being a racehorse owner. Can you imagine Tiger Woods having to pay to get onto a golf course? These owners had the best horse in the world, and still had to keep sticking their hands in their pockets—nomination fees, acceptance fees, trainer's fees, transport fees.

And they went out of their way to showcase Black Caviar to the Australian public. Imagine having a horse that good and having to share her with every bastard? If it was me, I'd want to hide her in my sock drawer.

Name another horse people had access to like Black Caviar. And the free promotion she did for racing—the crowds she drew, the publicity. Yet the owners were still paying a daily rate to have her housed and fed. Those bills are normal in racing, though it seems odd that even superstars have to pay their way. For the access to Black Caviar that the owners allowed, realising she belonged to both them and the whole country, I reckon they deserved to be in the Racing Hall of Fame before the horse or anyone.

....

We had been thinking about returning to Neil Werrett's home town of Sydney with Black Caviar, then maybe Brisbane.

The Newmarket Handicap was coming up, but she would have had to carry the grandstand. Showing the horse's extraordinary status, handicapper Greg Carpenter actually contacted us to confirm she wouldn't be entered before he did the weights. Had she been in it, it would have altered the weights set-up massively. Instead I ran Moment Of Change, who led for Luke but was just collared by Shamexpress. Unfortunately I wasn't at the races. I was in hospital instead for a few days with septicaemia, due to an infection in my leg.

Five weeks after the Lightning, Black Caviar chased a second William Reid Stakes at Moonee Valley, trying to equal Kingston Town's Australian record of fourteen Group 1s.

After what she'd shown at Flemington, I was pretty relaxed. I even got a few hours' kip during the day, which I normally couldn't do if she was racing. There were six other starters, one of them mine in the speedy Karuta Queen. She had come to me after being bought by the bloke who'd wanted half of Black Caviar four years earlier, John Singleton. Nelly was the second-shortest price of her career at $1.03 and gave Luke another armchair ride.

It was a beautiful night, another huge crowd, and they started applauding and going wild at about the 400-metre mark. Luke had parked Black Caviar third on the outside and she dragged him into it before the bend, then skipped away. Karuta Queen, though $51, got us the quinella four lengths back.

Nelly looked fantastic. Or, as Greg Miles said, like 'brutal power wrapped in an elegant machine'. But I guess it was hard to remember all her greatest days. She gave us so many.

I was also proud she had matched Kingston Town's Group 1 tally. Three weeks later, in April, we'd make our second attempt on the race named after the King's trainer and my old boss, T.J. Smith, as we sought to break that record.

....

It was the full Black Caviar circus for start 25 at Randwick—a huge build-up, the media in a frenzy. Though there were two other big Group 1s that day, the Australian Derby and the Sires Produce Stakes, the club scheduled Black Caviar's race as the last of nine to ensure a full house throughout, rather than an emptying out had her race been earlier.

Even now, there were some tiresome things said in the press: how she had been so carefully managed; how she hadn't had a hard run her whole life. If only they really knew how hard she'd done it, not just at Ascot but throughout her career.

Even New South Wales Premier Barry O'Farrell pulled out the silly stick. He said the only thing better than a Black Caviar win would be if Sydney became the place where she finally lost, tipping the John O'Shea–Jimmy Cassidy combination might upset her with rival mare Sea Siren.

In reality, I was a little worried. People reckoned it was the best field Black Caviar had met. Hence she started at a long-since unheard of \$1.14, ahead of another Bel Esprit horse Bel Sprinter, an easy last-start winner of the Galaxy, at \$13, and Sea Siren at \$31. On the next line at \$41 it was hello again to Hay List. Unfortunately his best days were over, and he was only three runs from retiring. But at \$51 was Joe Pride's Rain Affair, who was tipped to go at a million mile an hour and put Black Caviar to the test.

My main issue wasn't the field. Nelly had drawn barrier 1, and the inside was off that day, with most winners coming down the centre. I chatted to former jockey and analyst Ron Dufficy and he said to make sure we weren't on the fence. That led to something that still gives me a tickle watching the replay today—Brenton Avdulla's 'look'.

Black Caviar settled third behind Rain Affair, while Avdulla brought Howmuchdoyouloveme across from barrier 7 to sit at the leader's rump, outside Nelly. He might have had ideas of boxing her in, and probably thought he was doing a good job of it. But after 300 metres Luke just popped her around Avdulla's heels in a split second, as you can do with great horses. Avdulla then takes a look on his inside to make sure Nelly's still boxed up, but you can almost hear him say: 'Shit—where is she?' It was 'now you see me, now you don't', and Nelly was now in clear running.

Hay List moved up on Black Caviar's outside 600 metres out, but was gone soon after straightening, which just left it to Nelly to run down Rain Affair. Using Mulley's Gully again, Black Caviar quickened for a couple of strides, gobbled up the leader and put the race away, bolting in by three lengths from Epaulette, who also finished on.

'She's truly in a league of her own,' said caller Mark Shean. And she truly was. Fifteen Group 1s—more than Kingston Town, or any horse to race in Australia, and now just one behind the world flat-racing record of sixteen held by American galloper John Henry.

That could give us something to aim at, but for now it was time to savour another unforgettable day in her magical story at my old home track of Randwick, which was full of fans in party mode who didn't seem to want to leave.

I'd said post-race that she was going as well as ever. My interviewer said it looked like she'd be racing for another season, and I said: 'Wouldn't that be a dream!'

It turned out that it was.

24

End of an Era

Twenty-five starts, twenty-five wins. This amazing thoroughbred had taken us all—trainer, jockey, staff, owners and the Australian public—on an incredible ride, and to many surreal, otherworldly situations.

There was still talk of a return to Brisbane, and then—who knew? It was a terrific run in Sydney.

But it's funny—I had a bit of a feeling that day. I looked at her, in awe, after the race and thought: 'I wonder if you're gonna keep going, old girl?'

On her way home she had a couple of nights at Peter Clarke's and he gave her a good going over. She came back to Caulfield on the Tuesday, and I got Michael Bryant to check her. We found a few issues again—slight inflammation in her suspensory ligament, and a couple more muscle tears.

It's hard to articulate, beyond saying I just had a gut feeling. Her injuries weren't career threatening. We could have treated her, and she healed quickly. Looking back years later, I've no doubt she could have got through another couple of campaigns. But that Tuesday at

Caulfield, I think I just knew. Black Caviar had done enough. She had done everything asked, and so much more. I rang Neil Werrett and said the owners should come to the stables as soon as possible.

At midday on Wednesday everyone got to the stables. I don't think the owners expected what I was going to say. She had just won again, and I didn't say what Michael had found. I got Nelly out of her box and she got the odd pat. Tony Haydon was there, but he ran and hid. I think he knew what was happening.

I got Michael to explain to the owners the issues she was carrying. He gave a bit of history, which was helpful in just giving an overview of all the problems she'd carried.

I think I said: 'She's got to spell. We could bring her back again, but do we need to?'

It was then that Colin Madden said: 'What would you do?'

I took a little breath and said: 'Well . . . I'd retire her'.

And as soon as I said the word 'retire', that was it. Tears started running down my cheeks.

It was very moving, very emotional. I said, 'I think twenty-five's a pretty good number', and then after that, it wasn't mentioned again. Most of us had tears in our eyes and a lump in the throat. We were all quiet. It wasn't put to a vote. Everyone sort of nodded, silently, in agreement.

Pam Hawkes was the first to come over and give me a hug. Then we all embraced, still not really saying anything. We gave Nelly a cuddle and a pat, and that was it. It was a nice scene, really, just me and the eight owners—Michael had sneaked off—in the front section of our stables, reflecting on it all. Again, plaudits to the owners for the grace and dignity with which they took it. No one questioned it, or suggested we push on.

It's funny to think I'd got through every amazing stage in her career but it wasn't until the curtain came down that I finally blubbed.

I think it was just the relief of it all. We'd got through it. We'd survived for about the last 23 runs, and there were question marks on pretty much all of them, either before or afterwards. It was also very special to come back after the climax of Ascot and win three more, especially with that record in the Lightning.

We'd survived.

There was sadness, but I knew it had to end at some point. In fact, it was a unique situation, emotionally. It wasn't like a death in the family, because she wasn't dead. There was sadness, but not too much, because we knew we had had so many great times.

But it was a very moving moment. In fact, for me, it was the equal most special moment in her career, along with seeing her with Andrew Porter in Brisbane.

Finally, the silence was broken when I said our biggest problem was going to be announcing it. A few owners wanted to tell family members, but I knew it would spread like wildfire. I called a press conference for 3 p.m. First, the owners and I went to lunch at a local pub.

The press started ringing but I told them they would have to wait. We all got back to the stables about 2.45, and the media had gathered. We pulled Nelly out, let everyone have a look at her, and then Neil took the rostrum and announced her retirement, which was broadcast live on TV and radio.

The press duties took about an hour and a half and it was about 5 p.m. when I saw the owners off, and Nelly was put away for the evening.

Then, with no one else around, I went and sat in my office and googled 'Black Caviar'. My phone had been going berserk, so I switched it off and sat there in the peace and quiet, with a beer and a smoke, and watched all 25 of her wins, one after another.

It was the first time I'd watched them all. And that was pretty surreal, too, to sit there and think: 'Shit—that's pretty big, to do all that'.

Things went through my mind: growing up with horses, my dad, old Frank Cavanough, what Sarah and I had built. All of those things.

And, to be honest, I'll always feel proud of how I did my job with her: the patience that was required; the handling of the extraordinary pressure. I once heard a line: 'Anyone can train a good horse. Not many can train a great one.' Watching the replays it felt nice, well unbelievable really, to have helped guide Black Caviar through her career.

Eventually I switched my phone back on and listened to about 30 or 40 messages, which were great.

And that was that. I went home and set the alarm for 3.05 the next morning, got up and went to work.

On the Saturday we showed her to the public one last time, with a farewell at Caulfield. It was free entry and a big crowd of about 10,000 cheered and clapped as Luke trotted her up and down, which was very moving again. They were again cheering the best horse in the world. With Frankel retired, she'd returned to the top of the World Thoroughbred Rankings, on 130, and the Timeform charts with 136. She'd been the world's best sprinter four years in a row, and was about to collect her third straight Australian Horse of the Year award.

Then Black Caviar left the track and went off into the sunset, winner of $7,953,000 in prizemoney, fifteen Group 1s and seven Group 2s, leaving the rest of us to think how lucky we'd been to know her, or even to contemplate our place in history because of her.

To think—25 out of 25. Horses can have off days. Mares especially can go off on you. They can get in season and not want to perform. And sprinters, apart from Usain Bolt, don't often stay at the top for so long. Younger, sharper rivals will usually come up. You'll also see horses with great ability, and horses with great heart, but not often together like in this horse. There was also Nelly's amazing competitiveness and ability to push through the pain barrier.

Black Caviar showed up 25 times—not seven or ten or fifteen—and raced beautifully each and every time.

Unbelievable.

Still owned by the same eight people, Nelly started a stud career. Again, the megabucks offers had come from some of the world's biggest breeding houses to buy her as a broodmare, but they were rejected. To time of writing, she's had three foals—a filly by Exceed And Excel called Oscietra, a colt by Sebring, and a filly by Snitzel. The last one was valued at about $5 million, but Neil Werrett and the rest of Black Caviar's owners say, typically, the foals are not for sale.

Where it all starts. Me with two of my old favourites Luke Nolen and Moment Of Change at early morning track work at Caulfield. *(Getty Images)*

One of those moments that changed my life: Amalfi scores his incredibly gutsy win in the 2001 Victoria Derby. *(Fairfax Photos)*

I was now a Group 1-winning trainer, and it just felt surreal. Here's Damien Oliver, owner Ron Wanless and me proudly holding our trophies. The icing on the cake was that my mum Jan, in the all-yellow, could be there with me. *(Fairfax Photos)*

I had to wait two years till my second Group 1, also at Flemington on Derby Day. Ancient Song, one of those tried mares I trained for my very loyal owner and dear friend Stuey Ramsey, gets up in the Salinger Stakes for Scotty Seamer. *(Getty Images)*

Magnus ploughs through the pouring rain to win the Galaxy at Warwick Farm with Damien Oliver aboard. The stallion was a special horse for me for a few reasons. He brought my first trip to England, and the fact his mum, Scandinavia, was Black Caviar's grandmother helped persuade me to buy that amazing filly at the yearling sales. *(Fairfax Photos)*

The beautiful Typhoon Tracy wins the 2010 Futurity Stakes in a superstar stretch of four Group 1 wins in a row, all with Luke aboard. Unlike many other tough-looking champion mares, 'Cyclone' was a real supermodel. *(Getty Images)*

Wanted and Luke Nolen lead all the way to win the Newmarket in 2010 at a dark and gloomy Flemington. Just moments later the heavens opened, with an extraordinary hailstorm wiping out racing for the rest of that Super Saturday. *(Getty Images)*

Nelly, where it all began: Win No. 1 of 25, in the Cromwell Handicap for two-year-olds at Flemington on 18 April 2009, with baby-faced Jarrad Noske on top. *(Getty Images)*

Black Caviar's Newmarket in March 2011, made it a perfect ten out of ten. It also really set the pandemonium going, being analysed as one of the most astounding sprinting performances ever seen, and catapulting her to the ranking of best horse in the world. I had to pinch myself every day. *(Getty Images)*

My super mares Typhoon Tracy (left) and Black Caviar nuzzle up at my Caulfield stables. A trainer could wait a lifetime to get one this good, let alone two. (Fairfax Photos)

A small sample of the kind of fervour Black Caviar created. After about her first nine or ten wins, it was like Makybe Diva's third Melbourne Cup pretty much every time she raced. *(Getty Images)*

All set for the big show: At Royal Ascot, getting ready for Black Caviar's Diamond Jubilee Stakes. Don't let the smile fool you. I was churning up inside.

My first meeting with English 'royalty'. Giving the mighty Frankel a pat at Newmarket in the week he and Black Caviar won at Ascot.

Phew! Having gone ten thousand miles and battled enormous adversity, Nelly hangs on to win the Diamond Jubilee at Royal Ascot from the flying Moonlight Cloud. I'm one of those figures under a top hat in the background looking very still, possibly mortified! As I said later, they don't pay you any more if you win by six lengths than if you win by a quarter of an inch. *(Getty Images)*

A sweet moment indeed. Accepting my trainer's trophy of a snuff box from Queen Elizabeth, as part-owner Kerrin Wilkie looks on. The snuff box now holds pride of place at the bar in my man room. One day I'll work out what it's for! *(Getty Images)*

Though I'd thought she'd be retired after Ascot, there were more sensational deeds ahead for Black Caviar. Here she breaks Special's Flemington 1000-metre record, long considered 'untouchable', in winning her third edition of the race now named in her honour, the Lightning Stakes, in 2013. *(Getty Images)*

High-fiving the Black Caviar faithful after win no. 24, the William Reid Stakes at Moonee Valley. The crowds always turned on a great atmosphere for Nelly's races, and it was a thrill to be part of it. *(Getty Images)*

Announcing Nelly's retirement at a packed press conference at the stables, alongside owner Neil Werrett, whose $100,000 budget I blew by more than double when I bought her. Black Caviar's owners were magnificent throughout her career. *(Getty Images)*

One of the horses I was most proud of my work with, Manighar. He showed you can train a turn-of-foot into these dour, grinding, European stayers with a burst of three Group 1 wins in succession, starting with this courageous Australian Cup triumph over Southern Speed at Flemington, with Luke aboard. *(Getty Images)*

You can't be afraid to look like a goose now and again, especially if it's for a good cause. Here I am getting a shave for charity promotion Movember from a hairdresser who was probably well out of my league, France Khamees (right). My bemused stayer Brambles looks on, along with his strapper Rami Myala. Rami and I would later be in the news for somewhat more serious reasons. *(Getty Images)*

Contrasting the nitty gritty of the pre-dawn world of trackwork, it's all sunshine and silks here on race day at Flemington. For me, stepping onto the track for an afternoon's 'battle' felt like being a footballer and walking onto Lang Park for a footy match. Here I'm with two of the most talented riders I had through my stable as apprentices, Regan Bayliss and Linda Meech. *(Getty Images)*

Dissident, my third Australian Horse of the Year after Typhoon Tracy and Black Caviar, wins his last start, the All Aged Stakes at Randwick under the powerful jockey who suited him best, Jimmy Cassidy. It's a point of pride that these three horses all retired after Group 1 wins. And this one by Dissident hopefully also made up for my dogs tearing apart Jimmy's fancy snakeskin boots when he stuck them under our gate one day. *(Getty Images)*

Dark days. Addressing the media outside the cobalt hearing which led me to walk away from training. I'd just been cleared of deliberately cheating, but found guilty of a lesser charge for which I'd get the six-month ban that prompted my early retirement. I could have appealed, and subsequent events suggest I'd have got off, but as this photo shows, the strain was taking a toll and I'd had enough. *(Getty Images)*

Me and my old adversary, Racing Victoria chief steward Terry Bailey, having a word at Flemington a few days before my guilty verdict came down. *(Getty Images)*

Shut the gate. Closing the door on my life as a horse trainer, after announcing my retirement to the media . . . *(Getty Images)*

. . . but first, there was one more pleasure to attend to, celebrating Group 1 win No. 53 on my last night of training, with Flamberge and my family: (L to R) Sarah, Breann, Cara and Celine. (*Getty Images*)

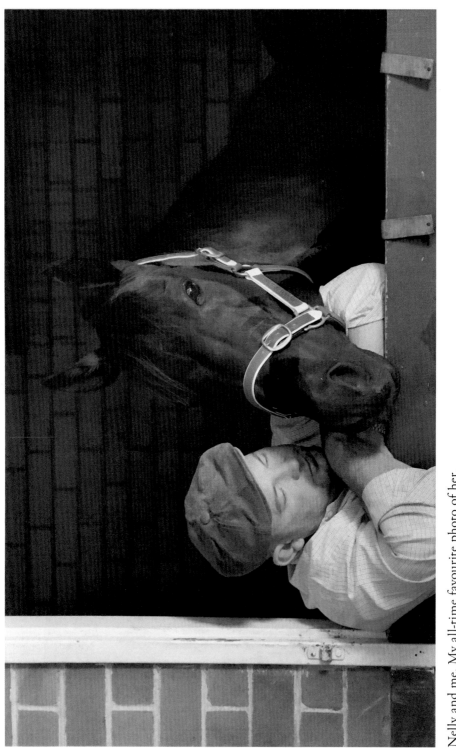

Nelly and me. My all-time favourite photo of her.

25

Making Manighar

Of course, life goes on.

And Moody Racing had a very big life outside Black Caviar.

In the four years Black Caviar raced, we won our four premierships. Weeks after her Ascot win, we celebrated the third, our 91 winners a comfortable 40 ahead of my mate Mick Price in second. We made it four in 2012–13 with 69 winners, to David Hayes' 51.

I was delighted for Luke Nolen to win his first three Melbourne premierships in these years, though he just missed his quartet when third in 2012–13.

In the year to February 2012 we won nine Group 1s, eight from Black Caviar. The other was Lights Of Heaven's win in the Schweppes Oaks at Morphettville in March 2011. She had become part of that great row of fillies and mares we had. It was also great that she rekindled memories of my first Group 1, as she had been bred by Amalfi's part-owner Judy Wanless.

By Zabeel out of I'm In Heaven, a mare I'd trained, Lights Of Heaven wasn't big but was well put together. Luke bonded particularly

well with her. In fact, the pair performed a fair Black Caviar impersonation when Lights Of Heaven won her first four starts, the last her
three-length Schweppes Oaks win. She recorded four more Group 2
and 3 wins and a gutsy third in Dunaden's 2012 Caulfield Cup, and
retired in 2013 having won $1.5 million.

But probably the horse I was most proud about was Manighar—
a good example of something cricket coach John Buchanan might
say: if it ain't broke, break it and fix it again.

Manighar had started out a very good long-distance horse in
France for Luca Cumani, winning six of twelve from 2400 metres to
3000 metres. Bought by the OTI syndicate of Terry Henderson and
ex-cricketer Simon O'Donnell, he performed well in two spring trips
to Australia in 2010 and 2011, finishing not far off the placegetters
in the Caulfield and Melbourne cups each time.

The owners almost gave me Manighar in 2010, but I was still
happy a year later to see the grey gelding walk into our stable, where
we dubbed him Luca. He had looked a very tough stayer but I thought
there could be a different horse underneath.

At first Manighar seemed very one-paced, very dour, very English.
Some English people might say that's just what stayers are like, but
you can train some zip into them, teach them to accelerate. I've also
seen Australian horses go to England and they train that turn of foot
out of them, and make them more English.

I tried to teach Manighar how to quicken. We stayed short and
sharp. He did a lot of pace work but we never galloped him more
than 400 or 600 metres. At first, he was quite slow, but the more we
did with him, the sharper he got.

In the autumn of 2012 we resumed him over 1600 metres in the
Group 3 Carlyon Cup at Caulfield. As Black Caviar stepped up to
1400 metres for the only time in the Orr Stakes that day, this was
the first time Manighar had dropped below 2400 metres. We also

knew he'd get in well under the set-weights-and-penalties conditions, because, while honest, he hadn't actually won for over two years. He had carried some very big weights in Europe, but dropped to 56 kilograms this day.

I told the owners their six-year-old had developed a turn of foot, and we were actually quite confident at the $8. He won comfortably, by almost two lengths.

The grey finished a fair third over 1800 metres at Group 2 two weeks later, and we thought we might have some fun with him that autumn. We didn't think he'd win three Group 1s in a row though!

First was the Australian Cup, over 2000 metres at Flemington, where the market was headed by Americain. I'd asked Americain's part-owner Gerry Ryan if I could train him when he stayed in Australia too—thinking that, a bit like Manighar, he would win from 1400 metres and up—but he went to David Hayes. It ended up good for me, because Luke gave Manighar the perfect ride up off the pace, he and Southern Speed fought a battle up the straight, and Manighar fought back after being headed to win by a nose. Americain was third.

This gelding who never won had now won two from three. To win a million-dollar race like the Australian Cup, my thirtieth Group 1— it doesn't get any better than that, I thought. But there was more.

We took Manighar to Sydney for the Ranvet Stakes over 2000 metres at Rosehill. He was second-favourite behind the gun horse of the time, Shoot Out, but we were confident. It took him all day to win it, after being challenged by Rangirangdoo and Shoot Out in the straight, but Manighar was a tough bastard and he got home by a head.

Next up, in the rich $2.2 million BMW over 2400 metres, Manighar was dominant. Again Americain was favourite, at $2.40, with our bloke $4, but he beat him by a length and a half. And yes I did feel proud when caller Mark Sheen finished the race with 'Hasn't Moody turned him around!'

Manighar was the first horse ever to win the Australian Cup–Ranvet Stakes–BMW treble, and I thought he was unlucky not to add two more Group 1s after that. With Luke riding Black Caviar in Adelaide, we put Damien Oliver on for the Queen Elizabeth Stakes over 2000 metres at Randwick. Nash Rawiller pulled their pants down that day, being allowed to canter in front on More Joyous and win a sprint home. Damien lost us that race. He should have used Manighar's toughness to pressure the leader, but instead handed the race to her, and was second two and a half lengths away.

Manighar then started a $1.75 favourite in the 2000-metre Doomben Cup, jumping from barrier 1 for Luke, with Lights Of Heaven an $8 chance from barrier 6 under Damien.

Rawiller was our nemesis again. On Anthony Freedman's Marwingo he carved Manighar in half, crossing in front of him passing the winning post the first time. Manighar had to be reefed back and, though we had hoped he would be up on the pace, he was still third-last of the twelve at the 500 metres. He came home well for third, 2.2 lengths back, as Marwingo beat Lights Of Heaven.

I felt Manighar was badly robbed and, while I've never been one to do things conventionally, this was right up there: protest, from the trainer of the third horse, against the winner, alleging interference at the 1700-metre mark!

I had hoped Luke would protest, but he didn't. That bewildered me.

Okay, I wasn't hugely confident, but I did think Manighar should have won. Besides, Lights Of Heaven would be promoted to first if my protest got up. The stewards heard me out, but concluded it was a combination of Nash's overzealousness and Luke not holding his ground. It was a bold protest, but I've seen more like it since, some of them successful.

So Manighar probably should have won five Group 1s that preparation, though he still might not have won Horse of the Year, since Black Caviar won six. I was top Group 1 trainer for the season, with ten.

We had high hopes for Manighar that spring, but things took a downward turn. He ran twice at Group 1, but was beaten a lip in the Makybe Diva Stakes by Southern Speed, then bled internally when sixth in the Underwood Stakes.

Manighar was susceptible through his career to internal bleeding (as opposed to bleeding from the nostrils). We managed it for a while but it started taking too much of a toll. He had ten more starts in 2013 for one second before being retired. He was still part-owned by an Englishman, the Honourable Earl Mack, who lived in America and took him back there for a showjumping career. He was quite good at it too, I heard.

Manighar was a lovely horse who won $3.6 million. He could have won a lot more, too, had we got him a season earlier. I'm not criticising Luca Cumani, but Manighar appreciated being trained shorter and sharper.

....

Despite Manighar's Doomben Cup, that 2012 winter carnival was very memorable.

At Brisbane's biggest meeting of the year we took the jewel in the crown, the Stradbroke Handicap, with Mid Summer Music, claimed another Group 1 with Brambles in the Queensland Derby, and Lights Of Heaven won the Brisbane Cup, which had been downgraded to Group 2 only a few years earlier.

I had bought Brambles from New Zealand for $100,000 and he cemented my affinity with the offspring of the sire Savabeel. Like Manighar, he raced in the OTI colours, though I kept a managing share. Also like Manighar, there was a bit of 'if only' about him. He won six and was placed in six out of only twenty starts. Unfortunately there was a big two years off in the middle of that.

Brambles was a late developer who missed his two-year-old season, so we sent him to Clare Cunningham in Sydney, hoping he would be ready for the AJC Derby. That didn't happen, but he went to Brisbane and went bang.

He won the Group 3 Rough Habit Stakes (2000 metres) with Brad Rawiller on him, since Luke was in Adelaide with Black Caviar. We stuck with Brad for continuity, and he led throughout to win the Grand Prix (2200 metres), also at Doomben, by three lengths, with Luke second on our other runner Vatuvei. I thought either could win the Queensland Derby but it was Brambles who led and won, with Vatuvei fifth.

That was a different kind of thrill. I'd trained Group 1 winners. And I'd bred one. (That moderate filly Ron and Judy Wanless gave me along with Amalfi, More Diamonds, ended up owned by my mum. I arranged to send her to be covered by Zabeel, at Sir Patrick Hogan's famous Cambridge Stud in New Zealand, and the result was 2010 Sydney Cup winner Jessicabeel.) But now I had my first Group 1 as an owner. Showing again what fragile creatures we deal with, Brambles got travel sickness on his way back to Sydney—a kind of pleurisy of the lungs. We'd been salivating about the Caulfield Cup—a front-runner at a front-runner's paradise—but he missed the spring. We were gutted.

Worse came in the autumn when Brambles bowed a tendon, hence his two years off. He went to Peter Clarke and the water-walker, but Peter was very doubtful. As a last throw of the dice, we tried trotting trainer Leigh Everson at Longwarry, near our place. Leigh brought Brambles along carefully with long, slow work pulling a gig to help his tendons, and we finally got him back in the winter of 2014.

At his fifth run back, the now six-year-old gelding was second at Caulfield, before a win over 1700 metres at Flemington, and a good third in Lucia Valentina's Turnbull Stakes. (He was actually promoted to second when Lidari, also trained by me, was disqualified, in a fairly momentous event for my career!)

It was on to the Caulfield Cup, two years delayed, and Brambles went terrific, finishing fourth to Admire Rakti. I had reservations about him at 3200 metres, but we simply had to run him in the Melbourne Cup after that Caulfield run. Alas, he failed to stay, as did Lidari.

Then disaster returned, when Brambles rebowed his tendon in trackwork and had to be retired.

It still pains me today. Seeing the way he had come back in 2014, we had really wanted him in the spring a year earlier. That would have been his time. He was a very good, though unfulfilled, galloper. But history's littered with them.

....

Contrasting Brambles, Mid Summer Music was a mare I thought would do very little but achieved a lot.

A plain little chestnut by the unheralded Oamaru Force, she was bought off the farm for just $5000. She became my version of the Takeover Target story, winning $1.4 million.

Mid Summer Music was a slow developer and, when she won her debut at Warracknabeal as a four-year-old, I told her ten owners they'd had a big birthday. I even suggested that now she'd won a race, she should start breeding. Just as well her rider Linda Meech said I might be wrong.

Mid Summer Music won eight of her next thirteen races, ending with two Group 3s on soft tracks at Caulfield. She was then a neck second in the Group 2 Let's Elope Stakes over 1400 metres at

Flemington behind Cox Plate winner Pinker Pinker. After a third to Black Caviar in the Patinack Classic, she was spelled with the 2012 winter in mind.

Her first four runs back were patchy, so she was a $31 long shot in the big eighteen-horse field for the Stradbroke. A wet track would help, though. She won two out of three on heavy, seven of ten on soft, and only two of eighteen on good.

Why are some horses wet trackers? It's a mixture of their physical make-up and inner confidence. No horses go faster in the wet. Others go slower because they lose their confidence. It's a bit like people running downhill. Some go a million mile an hour, while others edge their way down. In the wet, horses' hoofs land and they slip. Horses with shorter, choppier actions tend to get through the wet better than a big flowing horse with longer strides who might slip more.

Though there was rain on Stradbroke eve, I told a sportsman's luncheon that while Lights Of Heaven would win the Brisbane Cup (I actually said she could win it with hobbles on!), and Brambles or Vatuvei would win the Derby, it probably wouldn't be wet enough for Mid Summer Music in the Stradbroke.

But on a soft 5, she proved me wrong again. Luke rode her perfectly, settling mid-field then sneaking up to seventh on the turn. He presented her at just the right time, moved up on the inside, eased around the heels of leader Buffering and beat him by almost two lengths.

With Lights Of Heaven and Brambles also winning, it was a beautiful note to sign off on before flying out to Royal Ascot a few days later. It was a nice contrast, between the best horse in the world in Black Caviar, and a battler made good in Mid Summer Music.

She won one more from eight starts before being retired. Her first foal, a colt by Black Caviar's half-brother All Too Hard, sold for $225,000 at the 2016 Magic Millions sales.

Horses like Mid Summer Music are enormously satisfying for a trainer. She didn't have a pedigree, or a lot of expectation, but she was all racehorse.

....

After Mid Summer Music came success with a different kind of sprinter. Moment Of Change looked good from day one and didn't handle the wet. He certainly earned a place in my heart. It wasn't just because he won three Group 1s and $1.6 million (though that doesn't hurt!). The old gelding simply was, and still is, just a lovely animal.

We called him Slade, because his managing owner was a good client of mine in Rob Slade of Slade Bloodstock, who bought him at the Perth Yearling Sales for $50,000. And talk about early ability: on debut at Murtoa he shat in by ten lengths in near-record time.

Moment Of Change won his next start at Sandown almost as easily, spelled and returned for the autumn, when he ran two Group 2 placings in Sydney. We put a noseroll on him—my favourite bit of gear to improve concentration—and, despite top weight of 60 kilograms, he won a 1400-metre race at Caulfield by two lengths as favourite.

In his four-year-old spring of 2012, Moment Of Change really blossomed. He won and ran third in Listed class, both at Warwick Farm, then we stepped him up to Group 1 for the Rupert Clarke Stakes over 1400 metres at Caulfield. He was favourite at $4.40, had a nice light weight of 52.5 kilograms, but had the outside gate at 15. But Luke Nolen just parked him outside the leader and he brained them, hitting the lead on straightening and fighting off We're Gonna Rock.

He then injured himself, but came back in the autumn good enough to be beaten by only Black Caviar in the Lightning Stakes. With Nelly not contesting the Newmarket Handicap, we thought Moment Of Change could win that. But, as favourite, he was just collared by Danny O'Brien's Shamexpress.

After a frustrating 2013 spring, the following autumn Moment Of Change finally got some more laurels. Following a narrow second in the Australia Stakes at Moonee Valley, he went into the Orr Stakes at Caulfield and brought the stable our fourth win in that Group 1, after Typhoon Tracy's two and Black Caviar's one. A short favourite in a six-horse field, Moment Of Change sat a couple of lengths in front for Luke and held out the fast-finishing Eurozone by a lip.

Two weeks later Moment Of Change contested the Group 1 Futurity over the same course, for the same result, only better. Second favourite behind Gai Waterhouse's Bull Point, he led, kicked two lengths clear at the 200 metres, and held them off again to score by a half-length from Sertorious, with Bull Point fourth.

He failed under 58 kilograms in the Newmarket, then came back in the spring but was an uncharacteristic last of eleven in the Memsie Stakes. We found out that was because he'd bled internally. Like Manighar, Moment Of Change became susceptible to this late in his career and it was hard to get him right.

But he was a lovely old horse, a real gentleman. That's why when he retired in 2015, I asked the owners if I could keep him. He lives in my backyard on the farm, and I love hopping on and going for a ride on him from time to time.

26

Moving On

After Black Caviar and Typhoon Tracy, you'd have to be lucky to get another one anywhere near as good. But after their four straight Horse of the Year titles up to 2012–13, I was fortunate enough to get another one in 2014–15 with another super horse.

Dissident was no battler. He was regally bred, by Sebring—who I love as a sire—out of Diana's Secret. Her dad Anabaa was forging a reputation as a broodmare sire, and had sired my Caulfield Guineas winner Anacheeva.

While Dissident showed great ability from the outset, there was some early drama. I bought him at the 2012 Magic Millions sales on the Gold Coast for what must be my lucky price—$210,000, the same as Black Caviar. While her owners were wonderful right back to the matter of that blown yearling sale budget, I'd strike trouble with some different interests this time.

Most of the partnership who bought him said they would retain the majority shareholding in him of 70 to 80 per cent. As a trainer whose business is training and trading horses, *not* owning them, you think: 'Great—I've only got to sell 20 per cent of the horse, not 100 per cent'.

Gradually, all bar one of the partners pulled out and left me holding the baby, which was pretty ordinary. I had to pay up for the horse myself, then scramble to put a syndicate together.

Approaching Dissident's spring two-year-old campaign, I still didn't have any owners for this magnificent, well-bred colt. Fortunately, some of my stable clients finally took a fair holding in him. Owen Egan, a good client though another I'd often argue with, came on board, as did several others. That's why the owners' list reads like a bag of all sorts, with no fewer than seventeen people and groups.

So it was rewarding that Dissident turned out so good. Those who pulled out would have had a lot more fun had they stayed in. And it was good luck for several of our stable's loyal clients. I had to retain a managing share of about 10 per cent, but fortunately again, racing in my white-and-blue colours, Dissident became the second Group 1 winner I owned. Better still, he won five of them.

Nicknamed 'Surf', for reasons mysterious, he was beautiful to look at, which is why I was keen to buy him. He lived up to it with some good trial form, then two weeks before Black Caviar's record Lightning Stakes of 2013, Dissident debuted in the Blue Diamond Preview at Caulfield.

We also had the favourite Thermal Current, who Luke rode, and we thought Dissident might find the 1000 metres too short. But he stormed home to win by a long neck under Vlad Duric, with Thermal Current third.

After a third in the 1100 metres Blue Diamond Prelude with Luke aboard, we had to pay a late entry fee of $50,000 for the Blue Diamond, where Vlad got back on because Luke stuck with Thermal Current. We put blinkers on to keep him focused, and while he recouped only

$20,000 for running seventh, it had still been worth a shot. He was a very good prospect, if a little immature.

That spring we sent him to Clare Cunningham in Sydney for the season's first three-year-old Group 1, the Golden Rose over 1400 metres. He ran well for second in both lead-up races, but was unlucky in the Golden Rose when second again, to the fast-finishing Zoostar.

Here's how the choice of jockey can be crucial. Dissident was a strong, good-sized colt who needed a dominant rider. Tim Clark had ridden him for those three seconds and, while a lovely rider, he probably wasn't right for this horse.

There are dominant jockeys, then there are your more gentle types who just float along with the horse. Sometimes colts need a rider like a big brother who'll stand over them and give them a boot up the arse and make them travel into a race. That's why Dissident went well under the strength of Jimmy Cassidy later on. In Melbourne, someone like Brad Rawiller is that kind of dominating rider. Luke's a bit in between the two styles of grace and dominance.

That's why I hate being asked 'Who's the best jockey you've seen?' It takes all types to suit all different types of horses.

....

After a fair sixth against older horses in the George Main Stakes at Randwick, Dissident ran an okay fourth in Long John's Caulfield Guineas. Dissident hadn't won in seven starts since his debut, but Guineas third-placegetter Shamus Award soon won the Cox Plate, so the form wasn't bad.

The colt then had a spell at our farm, sharing a paddock with some other colts and geldings. Some might keep their star colts isolated, but this can turn them into precious prima donnas, like Lidari. They need to be in there competing for a spot at the trough, again like being surrounded by uncompromising big brothers, even if they might get the odd kick.

Dissident returned to Sydney for his three-year-old autumn and, under Jimmy Cassidy, he thrived. First up in the Listed Eskimo Prince Stakes over 1200 metres at Rosehill, Jimmy made him travel hard and strong, up on the pace and with his mind on the job. He got beaten two lengths into second by the favourite, classy New Zealander El Roca. But then over the 1400 metres of the Group 2 Hobartville Stakes, Jimmy gave him the same treatment and he won by a head from Atlante.

We felt good about returning to Group 1 next start for the 1600-metre Randwick Guineas, though Dissident wasn't much fancied at $11. Barrier 12 of 14 wasn't ideal, but the favourite El Roca had 13.

Dissident really showed his toughness. Jimmy got him across to be second on the fence at the first bend, but didn't let the leader Romantic Touch get across him. El Roca settled third on Dissident's outside. Cassidy pushed our bloke into the lead 800 metres out, and he was still there rounding the turn.

Over the rise, as they all drifted off the inside, El Roca pushed up and looked all over a winner, actually hitting the front 150 metres out. But, as the two horses settled in for another torrid battle, Dissident regained the lead inside the 100 metres and won by a head.

It was a great, gutsy effort—reminiscent of Typhoon Tracy's first Group 1 after she'd been headed in the Coolmore Classic. It was great to get a Group 1 with Dissident too, after his frustrating second in the Golden Rose.

He then found 2000 metres was too long at that stage when sixth in Criterion's Rosehill Guineas, then showed he didn't like heavy going when twelfth in Sacred Falls' Doncaster.

Dissident spelled in the warmer Queensland winter, and came back an imposing four-year-old stallion. We weren't sure if he would go to the Cox Plate, Caulfield Cup or where, but we wanted him in Sydney first, with Moment Of Change in Melbourne. But with the tracks wet in Sydney, we brought him home and both horses contested the first Group 1 of the 2014–15 season, the Memsie Stakes.

While that was the race where Moment Of Change bled and came last with Luke aboard, Dissident showed his class under Ben Melham. At $12, he boomed out of the gates, sat third and put it away in the straight, winning by more than two lengths.

He stepped up to 1600 metres as $2.70 favourite in another Group 1, the Makybe Diva Stakes at Flemington, where we stuck with Ben Melham. Dwayne Dunn on $11 shot Messene exploded out of the gates and Dissident, though caught wide early, went with him. The pair broke about six lengths clear of the rest at the 800 metres, with Dissident still serving it up to the leader.

On the turn the field had caught up, and it looked like our boy would have an enormous job to hold out the challengers, after that early pace. He hit the lead at the 400 metres, but Caulfield Cup–winner Fawkner ranged up and looked like racing past him at any stage from the 300 metres onwards. Dissident just wouldn't let him, and won by half a head. By crikey, it was a tough win.

We were heading confidently to the Cox Plate, but we needed a 'gap run'. Dissident almost won that too, dropping to 1400 metres in the Group 1 Rupert Clarke Stakes and going under by a lip to Darren Weir's Trust In A Gust.

I wanted a 2000-metre race as his last run before the Cox, so I ran him in the Caulfield Stakes, with Ben on again. A $4 favourite, he had a beautiful run in second, loomed up to lead at the 350 metres, then weakened to come sixth, to Fawkner. We were gutted that he just hadn't run the trip, but we soon had our answer. He came back with blood in his nostrils, which means an automatic three-month ban.

It was a bit freakish, and a lot frustrating. We had had Moment Of Change bleed internally a couple of months before. Dissident hadn't bled before, and never would again. There was nothing to be read into it. These things happen. He might have had a virus or something, but it was out of left field.

In the autumn of 2015, Dissident had a fresh new set of colours. Gone were the Moody white and blues, and in came the red with yellow stars of the Shanghai-based China Horse Club, who'd landed in Australia in a big way and bought into the horse. Breeding operation Newgate Farm had also bought a majority of him. Some of the original owners sold out, me included.

It would have been nice to get his new owners a win first up, but I felt Ben Melham rode a bit too cute in the 1200-metre Australia Stakes at Moonee Valley, letting him settle back in fifth spot. He ran third, but at odds on and beaten by two moderate horses in Mourinho and It Is Written, he probably should have won.

We didn't have to wait long though. Dissident was still favourite, though not odds on, when I chased my fifth Orr Stakes at his next start. This time Ben had him up on the pace, and the horse responded as you'd expect, hitting the front at the 150-metre mark and powering home by a length and a half.

As Typhoon Tracy and Moment Of Change had done, Dissident attempted to complete the Orr–Futurity double, but turned in a plain ordinary run. At $1.45 in an eight-horse field, he travelled well, hit the lead 300 out, but weakened to third, two lengths behind Sauvito. Horses can baffle you. He just had an off day.

....

During this autumn the girls' side of the barn also put their hand up, in more ways than one.

Mossman mare Plucky Belle won the Coolmore Classic (1500 metres) at Rosehill. She was superbly, and patiently, prepared at our Randwick stable by Clare Cunningham, and beautifully ridden by Linda Meech to arrive on the line, nosing out odds-on pop First Seal as a $16 chance. It was great that Linda finally won a Group 1. She was such a loyal servant and trusted adviser for the stable, and I'd felt bad for not putting her on for Black Caviar's first top-level win.

It was a feel-good win in another way, as Plucky Belle was bred by Phillip Esplin at Twin Palms Stud, who'd been a great supporter of mine. Sadly, Phillip passed away in 2011, but Plucky Belle was raced by his wife, Michele, their sons, Hamish and Patrick, and daughter, Elise.

Another filly who shone was Pasadena Girl. She was a little thing who didn't overly grab me as a yearling. In fact, she was passed in. I got her for $25,000 and syndicated her to twenty owners, including eight who had raced Mid Summer Music.

Pasadena Girl won her first two starts at Flemington for Vlad Duric—the first at a ridiculous $61, the second at a more realistic $3.40. She was then fourth in the Group 1 Sires Produce Stakes (1400 metres) at Randwick, where I felt she could have won if Vlad had been more forceful.

I made a tough call and got gun Sydney rider Hugh Bowman for the Group 1 Champagne Stakes (1600 metres) where she was a $2.80 favourite. Hugh rode her superbly and she got up by half a length.

I was happy for the owners, especially the eight who had had Mid Summer Music. Their two horses had cost just $30,000, but were both Group 1 winners who reaped just under $2 million! I love those stories.

Alas, even Hugh Bowman had an off day the next spring when an indecisive ride cost Pasadena Girl any chance as $4 favourite in the Group 1 Thousand Guineas at Caulfield, where she finished fourth. After failing to stay in Jameka's VRC Oaks over 2500 metres, she came back in the autumn of 2016.

I thought she was a great chance in the Group 2 Kewney Stakes at Flemington, with Glen Boss up, but incredibly, he didn't get a ride at all. When the gates flew open, Pasadena Girl, fancied at $8, just stood there. It was dumbfounding. And everyone missed it. I kept looking for her, but after about 400 metres I said to the bloke next to me: 'Mine's not there! Mine's not there!'

She took no part. And, on that bizarre note, it was Pasadena Girl's last start with me as her trainer.

....

At least Pasadena Girl had won that Group 1 the previous autumn, on a huge day at Randwick. Hi World also won us the Group 3 Sir Frank Packer Plate under Kerrin McEvoy. And Dissident won his fifth Group 1, and my fiftieth, in the All Aged Stakes.

With a stud career beckoning, we had had to decide after his Futurity flop whether to push on with the four-year-old. Thanks to Dissident and Jimmy Cassidy, the All Aged Stakes was the right choice.

The 1400-metre feature drew a bloody good field, featuring Chautauqua, Wandjina and Lucky Hussler, so Dissident was a generous $10. (He could score for his backers at a good price, though those who took the shorts might have been peeved once or twice, not that I worried about odds.)

Wandjina led and Cassidy had Dissident well into the race on his girth, and moved him up to take the lead topping the rise. Wandjina fought back strongly but after a stirring battle up the straight, and thanks to the power of J. Cassidy, our boy got up by a head, with the future world's-best-sprinter Chautauqua third.

The owners and I decided that was a fine way to end a fine career. Dissident retired to Newgate Stud in the Hunter Valley a winner of seven from 21, and was crowned 2015 Horse of the Year. It was our fifth such award in six years (as we became embroiled in battles elsewhere, it was a pick-me-up we needed).

Dissident won five Group 1s, four in one season. But what I'm most proud of is his retirement meant my three best horses bowed out after Group 1 wins: Typhoon Tracy, the Orr Stakes; Black Caviar, the T.J. Smith; and Dissident, the All Aged.

Not many people can say that. In fact, out of everything I've done as a trainer, that's probably my greatest achievement. I'd like to think it shows I'm not a greedy person, and I always put the horse first. Not people—not the public or the owners who might have wanted some more—but the horse.

My three best retired at the top of their game, after Group 1 wins. Funnily enough, so would I.

27

Darkest Day

Two years earlier, it seemed I was the toast of the racing scene. We had won at Royal Ascot with Black Caviar. I had met the Queen. I had retired the great mare as the best horse in the world, emotional scenes at a packed press conference and a big farewell at Caulfield closing one of the most fantastic chapters in racing. I was on top of the world.

But late on this winter's night, in July 2015, you could have found me in very different circumstances. I was alone in my white four-wheel drive. It was parked by the side of Wellington Road, near my home. I was sitting inside it by myself, and I was in tears.

I was just completely bewildered. Very distressed. At my wits' end. 'What have I *done* to you people?'

....

I was kind of glad I was on my own. I wouldn't have wanted people to see me having a sook. But I was gone, worn down. I was crushed.

It had been six months since my life was changed utterly, though I didn't suspect it at the time, by a single positive swab out of my stable. What I had thought was a puzzling, innocuous anomaly had festered into an enormous and scarcely believable ordeal. It really did feel like a nightmare. Wherever I turned there was something else lashing out to bite me. You just keep falling over and having to pick yourself up again.

But on this night, by the side of the road in my car, getting up again seemed an extremely hard thing to do. I felt shell-shocked, disappointed, betrayed. The emotional toll, on myself and my family, had got the better of me.

One minute, it felt like I was the bee's knees, or Willy Wonka. Now it felt like everything Sarah and I had worked so hard to build up over twenty years was being taken away from us, wrongly and unjustly, and I was powerless to stop it.

I'd had an incredibly clean record throughout my career. I'd been successful because of hard work, by me and many other people, because of innovation, because of the astute placement of our horses, wherever that might have taken us. Yet now I'd been accused of cheating, of using a nothing drug—which had no benefits anyway—on just one of our 400 or so horses, to try to improve its performance.

I have never cheated. I can't stand cheating in any form. It's something instilled in me from when I was a boy, by my mother mostly, to do things properly, cleanly, with honesty and with hard work. So to be accused of cheating is something that cuts and hurts me very deeply, to say nothing of making me pretty bloody angry when you know it simply isn't true.

This night in my car came after I'd been told by stewards, not that I'd been charged with cheating (that had come a couple of weeks earlier), but worse still, that I'd have to show cause why I shouldn't be banned even *before* my hearing, while the stewards were getting their prosecution together. It was extraordinary. I just couldn't believe it.

But while by then I felt like I'd already been through the wringer, this darkest chapter of my life still had eight more months to run.

Ultimately it would lead to the end of my training story. I'd walk away in disgust, chased out of the career I loved. I was relieved at least to be cleared of cheating. But in the end—especially considering some events afterwards—it still seems so pointless, so disappointing, so dumbfounding and, yes, very hurtful.

28

Cobalt Blues

As 2015 dawned, the stable was still going well, though there was a now massive rival around in Darren Weir. He had knocked us off for the 2013–14 Melbourne premiership, with 86 winners to our 64. We put some more pressure on him the following season, but he still pipped us by seven. Still, we clocked up triple figures for winners, city and bush, for the twelfth successive season, and in the end got to 200 for the third time, having also done it in 2011–12 (a personal best of 210 winners) and in 2012–13. We'd had at least 190 winners for six straight seasons.

Overall, I didn't have a worry in the world really. I went to the Magic Millions sales on the Gold Coast, then the next day, 13 January, in my Caulfield office, I began the task of finding owners for the fifteen or so horses I'd bought.

But after I knocked off and started driving home, I got another one of those phone calls that turn your life around, this time catastrophically.

It was Racing Victoria steward Dion Villella, saying the stewards needed me at the stables. I probably rolled my eyes, wondering what annoying bit of detail this might be.

'I've been there all day,' I said. 'Can't we do it tomorrow?'

He said: 'We've got an irregularity in one of your swabs'.

I blithely guessed it was ibuprofen, which had been cropping up a bit around the country. House Of Hingis, out of our Sydney stable, had been found to have the painkiller in her system in two swabs in late 2014, but it was a fairly minor issue.

'I'm guessing it's ibuprofen,' I said. 'We had this problem in Sydney and we can't explain it. Is tomorrow okay?'

He said: 'We need you back at the stables now. It's not ibuprofen. It's cobalt.'

....

Cobalt?

I was gobsmacked. I turned back to the stables mystified, my mind running a hundred mile an hour wondering what or who it could have been.

The racing industry had just heard about Darren Smith, the Newcastle trainer who'd been charged over cobalt positives for eighteen of his horses. Victorian father–son training team Lee and Shannon Hope had been charged after three of their horses tested positive to it too, and ten trotting trainers had been banned for it in New South Wales. Still, cobalt wasn't part of our regime, so I was baffled.

When I returned to the stables, three stewards were there interviewing my staff. They went through our whole regimen—our feed room, vet books, treatment sheets. Everything was documented.

I was anxious to learn more. They sat me down and commenced a formal interview process, which they recorded. And they revealed the root of the problem: Lidari. After running second in October

2014 in the Turnbull Stakes—where we'd also had Brambles coming third—Lidari tested positive to cobalt. I was dumbfounded.

The interview was lengthy, and felt like a police investigation: 'Who does this?' 'Who does that?' 'Who feeds this horse?' 'What are that horse's treatments?' I tried to be as forthright as I could, but I was searching my own mind as to how this might have happened.

The stewards were there past 6 p.m., and said they would put out a press release about the positive. I arranged for something to go to our clients before that hit the news, saying we were baffled and were looking into it.

It was weird, and disconcerting. Still, I thought I'd get a slap on the wrists and it would soon pass.

....

I've learnt a little more about cobalt now than I knew then.

It started getting noticed in American harness racing in early 2013, when detected in a lot of samples. Harness Racing NSW began testing for it in September 2013, saying horses couldn't have more than 200 micrograms of it per litre of urine. They had to set acceptable thresholds because cobalt occurs naturally in all animals. It's present in vitamin B12, and so it's found in humans as well.

Racing Victoria stewards set the same 200-microgram threshold in April 2014. Nobody took any notice, including me. Cobalt just wasn't a factor.

I wasn't that bothered about Lidari's positive. I knew we hadn't deliberately given him cobalt. What's more, I was perplexed about the sudden interest, because it hadn't been proven that cobalt could make horses go faster. Granted, there are side-effects with over-consumption, but I just can't see why you'd give cobalt to a horse deliberately. Research suggests it boosts red blood cells, which helps endurance. But if that's the case, you must have to feed it to them by the shovelful.

Lidari came from France through the Terry Henderson–Simon O'Donnell OTI team in early 2013 as a possible Cups horse. Before that Turnbull Stakes, he had won two of twelve for me, including the Group 2 Blamey Stakes at Flemington, as well as three placings. The start before the Turnbull, he had run a fair fourth in the Group 1 Underwood Stakes at Caulfield. The start after, he ran sixth in the Caulfield Cup. His Turnbull effort wasn't any big performance spike.

Most of all, he was just a prick of a horse. European stallions often get this piggish mentality from being locked up from the day they are born and spoilt rotten. You can fix some, but others will continue being a pig, and that was Lidari. So it's fair to say I didn't like him. I didn't know he'd become the bane of my existence.

....

As for racing officialdom, I'd always got along okay with those running our sport, including the stewards. Largely, they did their job and myself and other trainers did ours. However, through the few years leading up to Lidari's swab, I had felt that the waters were becoming a bit murky.

Around the time I was building towards my first Melbourne premiership in 2009–10, it was clear my horses were getting drug tested more and more. I approached Des Gleeson, then Racing Victoria's (RV) chief steward, soon before he retired in mid-2008, to ask if I had a problem. I also asked RV's chief vets John McCaffrey and Paul O'Callaghan. The gist of their responses was that no, I didn't have a problem, but since ours was becoming one of the leading stables they had to keep an eye on things, to make sure there was a level playing-field.

That was okay. My stable's records showed they had no cause for concern. We were training plenty of winners, had lots of horses, and most were being swabbed.

I did have one thing crop up in May 2011. After winning at Pakenham, our gelding Lethal Arrow tested positive to oripavine, an opioid related to poppy seeds, which had accidentally appeared in my oat silos. I pleaded guilty to a charge of presenting the horse at the races with a prohibited substance in its system. The horse was disqualified, but the Racing Appeals and Disciplinary (RAD) Board took no further action, as it couldn't be determined whether the horse had ingested contaminated feed or had the substance deliberately administered.

Unfortunately, this perception arose that I was getting a free hit because of Black Caviar, who had won fourteen races by then. That was disappointing, and it hurt. Even some of my mates had a dig, light hearted, but with a noticeable serious undertone. Again my vets Peter Angus and Dave Shepherd got asked by rival trainers: 'What's he using?'

We were 'using' hard work, hard feed and good horses. Some people couldn't accept that, especially the older generation of trainers, which might be a price of success at a relatively young age. They were probably thinking they couldn't have had our rate of success without a dodgy advantage.

Simply, we were just good at our jobs. Our success stemmed largely from the placement of our horses. Jeff O'Connor was terrific at it. I was terrific at training them, our jockeys were doing a terrific job, and everything gelled. But still there was this suspicion and innuendo.

It's the mentality of our industry, as other successful trainers have found: John Size, Chris Waller, Darren Weir. I had the same perception of some successful people myself, till I had to put up with the same rumours.

No one ever thinks the worst of someone who runs fourth or fifth in the premiership, even if they're batting above their average. The thing is, I was never batting above my average. My strike rate was always consistent, at around 17 to 22 per cent. It only declined in the last few months of my career, when this inquiry was weighing on my mind, and on some clients' minds.

....

As time went by there was a stark change in the atmosphere we in the industry were operating in, and being overseen in.

Gleeson retired and was replaced by Terry Bailey, a man I'd known for more than twenty years since we were both juniors in our respective fields, and who I'd come to have quite a bit to do with. RV instituted its Compliance Assurance Team, and its Integrity Services division, the latter headed by former police detective Dayle Brown, with a couple of other former policemen from Victoria's Purana Taskforce brought on board as well.

Under Bailey, the old regime was pensioned off very quickly. The older stewards with a lot of experience were gone. In came a heap of younger stewards, while the integrity department was full of ex-police.

All this brought a massive change, which I felt was quite sad. The mindset of officials towards trainers used to be: 'We're here to police the industry', which is how it should be. Now, it had become: 'You're all cheats, and we're gonna catch you'.

As with a lot of things, I was one of the few trainers to express concern about this. No doubt that gave more fuel to trainers who suspected I was cheating. If only they knew how much my horses were being tested! But there's also no doubt my comments ended up biting me on the arse.

You can understand someone like Bailey coming into a job and wanting to put his stamp on it. But the exasperating thing is there just wasn't any great need for a crackdown. It wasn't like there'd been some huge damning revelations about the gallops like we'd see around the same time with the *Four Corners* TV report on greyhound racing.

We suddenly had this big police presence in the integrity department, and it became a flagship. Previously it had rocked along and done its job. Now, it had to come with bells and whistles.

Previously, the mindsets on both sides of the fence had been that we're all humans, all here for the good of the game, and you could all knock off at day's end and have a beer and a yarn. But when this new regime came in you could sense their mentality was 'us against them'.

There was a frostiness that came in, which I felt was sad for the industry. You didn't want to be walking around on eggshells. It seemed trainers were being pinged for little things more and more. Things like getting fined $50 or $100 for declaring a rider late. Trainers don't do that on purpose. If it becomes a habit, punish them, but mostly it should just be: 'You've done the wrong thing, pull your head in', and get on with life.

But everything became dotting your *i*s and crossing your *t*s. There was no room for the human element. You couldn't make a mistake. The assumption now was trainers didn't 'make mistakes'. They were cheating.

....

I've always been fairly outspoken. I don't see why we trainers should just lie down and cop everything pushed onto us, like new rules. If asked, or if I object, I'll make my feelings known. Sometimes it's just ideas to challenge the status quo. I once made the papers for saying that if colts and geldings weren't allowed to run in Oaks races, then why should fillies be allowed into Derbies?

Other times it's been more serious, but I've also never been scared of a fight, perhaps to my detriment.

Late in the Des Gleeson years I clashed with some other, mostly older, trainers when the stewards ramped up race-day blood testing of horses. Gallopers were getting tested willy-nilly, sometimes as they were about to go into the enclosure. I felt it was over the top, because it ran the risk of upsetting a horse before it was supposed to race. Yet Lee Freedman, David Hayes, John Hawkes and Danny O'Brien came out backing it, basically saying the industry had to get to the bottom of everything, weed out wrongdoers, etc. etc.

I didn't agree with this kind of testing and said so. On top of that I also called the other four 'the White Knights'. It made the back pages. 'I'm not sure how they would like a two-year-old to have a needle produced in front of it with two 14-stone blokes hanging off its ears as it's ready to compete in a Blue Diamond and think that wouldn't affect its performance,' I said.

I was pretty disappointed. I felt those other blokes were having a go at those coming through the ranks, me included. The older three—Freedman, Hayes and Hawkes—must have forgotten most of us younger people had worked around or beside them on our way up, and we knew they weren't quite as pure as they wanted to be perceived.

At the same time another rule came in that horses had to be on course three hours before a race. The stewards felt some people were using illegal drenches, such as bicarbonate of soda, and this rule would stop them doing it at home as close as possible to the race. Some trainers had been caught doing that, and were deservedly punished.

Again I asked: 'Why? Why penalise everyone, not just those causing suspicion?' The three-hour rule might have also affected me more than other trainers, since I travelled a lot. It meant you'd have to set off for some far-off meetings before you even knew the track rating.

While my intention was to help trainers and horses, it might have looked like me bagging people who said we should clean up the industry. I actually made some calls to those other trainers and apologised, to a degree, for the 'White Knights' line, but I still told them I didn't agree with them, or with this testing.

As we became the biggest stable in town, I still wouldn't be shy of making my feelings known, and journalists probably knew that when they rang me for a quote. While this helped put that target on my back, I truly did feel a responsibility to my fellow trainers. Many contacted me—and still do—about various things, because they felt I had more clout, or could be heard in the media, whereas their voices wouldn't be heard because they had smaller operations.

There were some fall-outs along the way. I'd always had a good relationship with Danny, though we stopped talking from around this time on.

The night Lidari's positive made the news, one of O'Brien's owners, Jeff Dimery, attacked me on social media about being a possible cheat. He had attacked me before. This time Dimery sounded positively gleeful, crowing that they'd caught the filthy cheating bastard at long last.

....

Under Bailey, the testing of my horses kept ramping up, far more than under Gleeson. That had its upside—they were testing everything and finding nothing—but it did feel they were testing me more than others. Granted, I had more runners than most, but still I'd ask other trainers at Caulfield and the stewards were undoubtedly at my place more.

Then in 2013 came another development that took me very much by surprise.

I got a call from a bloke called Michael Healy. He said he'd been taken to lunch at a Chinese restaurant by Terry Bailey and Dayle Brown, and they had asked him to do a job, for which he would be paid secretly. They had asked him to get employment in my stable— and spy on me for them.

Healy was supposed to watch everything—the feed, what time my vets came around, and all else besides, then report back to them each night.

This felt like a real stab at my integrity. When I thought about it, I just felt that to have such an air of suspicion and paranoia around was dismaying and, really, just a sad state of affairs for the industry. But also, the way they went about it might have been comical if not so serious. What Bailey and Brown didn't know, and hadn't checked, was the bloke they chose to spy on me had been a nearly 30 years! Michael and I used to work together at Tommy Smith's in the 1980s.

Oops.

Michael rang and told me straight away, and said—like I probably did—that he couldn't believe they would ask someone to do that.

I was pretty upset about it all, but after I calmed down I said: 'Take the job! You'll be getting paid my me and by them.' I knew he'd been doing it tough. He'd been on workers' compensation after getting injured as a barrier attendant. I had nothing to hide, so I thought Michael could at least earn a quid, but he had already rejected them. They had also said he could spy on another stable after three months at mine, but I topped the list.

What had we come to? Again, the mentality was everyone was cheating, and we just need more and trickier ways to catch them. Obviously, it was a very disappointing thing to have thrown at you. Again it felt like I was being accused of being a cheat, of having everything I'd worked so hard to achieve and build up cast into doubt and suspicion. But still, I kept this particular development under my hat.

....

About a year after that in the autumn of 2014 came something just as ridiculous and, I felt, pretty dismaying. The stewards demanded a set of keys to the stables of every trainer at Caulfield and Flemington.

Again, I just thought it was wrong, and said so in the media. I was stunned that the Australian Trainers' Association hadn't objected, stood up for its members, and instead just went along with it. I resigned from the ATA board.

I didn't see why I should just lie down and hand over the keys to my stable. The stewards already had enormous access. They could come to my stable any time and do what they wanted, which they did often. They legally had access to my car and house if they wanted. They had the means, or the desire, to plant spies in stables. Getting the keys was ridiculous.

Again I asked 'Why?' And again people—fellow trainers, authorities—would all say: 'Oh Moody's got something to hide'. That was maddening. Can you really not comment on anything like this without it ending in an accusation of cheating?

Our stable had been scrutinised so much. Stewards would frequently come and test every horse—anything from 80 to 110 of them, for what I didn't know. The out-of-competition testing was also extraordinary. I still had nothing to hide but, unavoidably, it was annoying. The stewards knew our operation inside out. They had all our records. They knew we didn't cheat.

My take on the keys issue was the stewards would have too much power. I didn't trust them. Even the police don't have those powers over the public. Why should the stewards have such a level of power over trainers, 99 per cent of whom are hardworking, honest men and women? Here was a team of stewards I didn't know personally. Why should I trust them with my livelihood? Why should they have a set of keys to get in any time they wanted? How was I to know what they'd be doing with my horses?

The stewards feared that if they had to knock and wait at the door, there would be people inside hiding things, which again is a disappointing attitude. In any case, our stable wasn't Pentridge Prison.

If they couldn't get through the gate, they could jump a fence or get through a side gate or a back gate. The stables were never locked up 24/7 anyhow, because 25 staff lived on the premises.

Upset as I was, I called my fellow trainers spineless yellow bastards in the press, saying they liked to whinge but never had the balls to actually stand up and do anything.

You had trainers saying: 'I've got nothing to hide. They can have the keys to my place.' But those people weren't aware the stewards tried to put a spy in my stable. I just didn't trust them. How did I know they hadn't actually succeeded in planting a spy in my stable before or after trying Michael Healy?

In the end, I had to hand my keys over. And then, the stewards said all of us would have to hand our keys over on the Friday, and then they'd address concerns with us the following Tuesday. I said in the media this was like shutting the gate after the horse had bolted.

I still don't agree with it, but I got zero support from my fellow trainers.

....

News of my opposition to the keys edict broke during the Sydney Easter yearling sales of 2014. Racing Victoria chairman Robert Roulston and CEO Bernard Saundry approached me there and suggested I pull my head in, that I couldn't make such outrageous statements.

I told them about the spy issue, saying it was one reason I didn't trust the stewards.

When that had happened, the only person I had told was David Moodie. A breeder and owner, at the time he was probably our biggest individual client. He had a promising three-year-old with us—Flamberge. He was also an RV board member, and would become chairman in May 2015. I'd always had a good relationship with David but, when I'd told him about the spy plan, he doubted me.

Now, a year on, Roulston and Saundry also doubted me. They asked Moodie, then they went to Bailey, and Bailey denied it to them. When they told me this, I said: 'I can have the bloke, Michael Healy, on the front steps of Racing Victoria and prove it to you'. When they went back to Bailey with this, he admitted that the spy idea had been discussed and was a possibility. Moodie told me he'd suggested to Bailey he should apologise to me, whereupon Bailey had gone off his head.

Saundry later rang me and said: 'We've sorted it out. There's no issue going forward.'

I said: 'I haven't got the issue. You have, because your chief steward lied to you. I didn't lie to you. Remember that.'

Again, though, I chose not to go public with the spy issue.

But still, here was Bailey, who had been caught out lying by his own employers, and, at the end of that week, I was supposed to hand his organisation my keys. It didn't worry me because of anything we were doing. It was just that there was this thing called the integrity department and, for good reason, I just didn't trust it.

29

Testing Time

Fast forward nine months, to my investigation at the stables over Lidari. I sensed very early on that the stewards didn't want to work out how this had happened. In line with that ever-deteriorating 'stewards-versus-trainers' atmosphere, I felt their mentality very clearly: 'You've done it. We've gotcha!'

One of my first steps was to ask that Lidari be swabbed then and there to check his cobalt level. I didn't want the stewards to come back the next day and do it. They could have said I'd given him something overnight to affect his cobalt reading one way or the other—either to try to push it up, to make it look like he had high levels normally, or to try to bring it down.

The stewards initially said no. I couldn't see why not. In the end, I had to insist on it being done, and had to pay for it myself. Clearly, I wasn't going to get one bit of help.

I then rang David Moodie to tell him about the positive swab. I respected his position. He was an RV board member, and our biggest client. I didn't want to create embarrassment or problems for him.

I also liked that he was in a position of power because he seemed to have positive views on racing.

However, I didn't feel support. I think David suspected I was cheating, which left me pretty disappointed, and stunned. Why would an RV board member keep his horses with a trainer he thinks is a cheat? I was a long time on the phone and I'm still not sure I convinced him I wasn't cheating. I didn't feel comfortable with some of the things he asked, or the way he questioned me.

When I got home, I made another call that ended in disappointment.

I feared when news broke that I had a drug incident, people would say that was why Black Caviar had been so good. I really didn't want that to happen, so I rang Robert Roulston and said: 'I'm not asking for any favours, but for the sake of Black Caviar, I believe you should go through her swabs ASAP, so the public can be told there was nothing untoward with her'.

Roulston told me he put this request to Bailey, but that Bailey and his integrity department weren't going to act on it. I was told their view was that it was in the past. There was nothing that could be done. I had thought it would be a no-brainer, and for the good of the industry. I couldn't understand why they weren't interested. By contrast, Racing NSW chief steward Ray Murrihy rang me to talk about the same subject. He then made a point of coming out publicly and announcing to the media Black Caviar's sample from her 2011 T.J. Smith Stakes win at Randwick had been recently re-tested (as part of a batch of retesting), and that all was clear. Her swab from her 2013 T.J. Smith victory was also retested soon after that, and was again given the all clear.

I believe Brisbane and Adelaide didn't have her frozen swabs. But I rang England because of her Ascot run, and spoke to Jamie Stier, the Australian who is the British Horseracing Authority's chief of race-day operations and regulations.

He said: 'I'm happy to do it, but are you sure this isn't gonna bite us on the arse?'

And I said: 'There's no worries at all'.

He rang back a week or two later and said unfortunately they throw their swabs out every two years or so, and her swab, from two and a half years earlier, had just been thrown out, so they didn't have the opportunity. But in Victoria, where she'd had nineteen of her 25 starts, the RV stewards weren't interested. I was left thinking that their attitude was that if people had their doubts about Black Caviar they could keep having them.

In refusing to put the issue behind us once and for all, I really don't think that Bailey acted in the best interests of the industry.

....

The morning after being told of Lidari's positive, something else pretty surprising came up. David Moodie rang and indicated I might not be the only trainer in trouble for cobalt.

I thought for a minute: 'Oh. Are there going to be a hundred others? Maybe there's a problem?'

I thought back to Queensland in the 1980s when all these trainers were getting pinged for caffeine in their horses. They later found the plastic sticks they used to stir the samples actually contained caffeine. I wondered if something similar could explain the cobalt swabs.

But that wasn't quite the scenario. David indicated there were two other trainers with cobalt problems: 'Your good mate at Flemington, and a mate of his'. By this I figured he meant Danny O'Brien and Mark Kavanagh.

It would emerge at their hearings much later that David was tipped off by Melbourne *Age* journalist Patrick Bartley, though who leaked to Bartley remains a mystery. In any case, I did think there was some irony in Danny getting implicated, since his owner Jeff Dimery had been attacking me on social media.

I rang Danny and said: 'Tell me to piss off if you want, we haven't spoken in a couple of years, but what's happened to me yesterday, do you have a similar problem?'

He said he didn't. He also said he felt sorry for me, which I felt was sincere.

I then rang Mark Kavanagh. 'Mark, have you got a problem with this?' He also said that he didn't. But seconds later, he said: 'I have to get off the phone. The stewards are at my door.'

He rang back an hour later and confirmed he had had a positive swab.

Then Danny rang me back after lunch and said: 'You were wrong. I haven't got one problem. I've got three.'

It was head-scratching time.

A few months later, Mark's son Sam Kavanagh was disqualified in New South Wales for cobalt and race-day treatments for nine years and three months, later reduced to three years on appeal. Two other trainers went down for cobalt in Queensland and Western Australia. It had come up in trots and greyhounds. It seemed widespread.

Mark, Danny, the Hopes and myself were dubbed 'the Cobalt Five'. Mark had one horse test positive in Magicool. Danny started with Bondeiger, De Little Engine and Caravan Rolls On, then had Bullpit added as a fourth two months later. The Hopes had three: Windy Citi Bear, Best Suggestion and Choose.

It was discovered that maybe Danny's, Mark's and Sam Kavanagh's cobalt had come through vitamin drips that Flemington vet Tom Brennan had supplied. That didn't help me. To this day, probably some people have got suspicions I was doing something similar with drips. I wasn't.

The stewards went through me like a dose of salts, interviewing everyone who had ever been associated with my stables to try to find a link between me, Kavanagh and O'Brien. They couldn't.

Other unsavoury things happened. Lee Freedman was unmerciful on social media with statements about cobalt, which I found pretty disappointing. And Lee wasn't Robinson Crusoe either.

But though these clouds were gathering in early 2015, I still just didn't take it that seriously. I knew we hadn't cheated. This had to be just a mistake, a fault in our regime.

There were still some bright spots in the midst of all this. I'd won the Orr Stakes with Dissident in February, then picked up another three Group 1s in the autumn in Sydney through Dissident, Plucky Belle and Pasadena Girl. Then came another when, in one of those quirks racing throws at you, David Moodie's Flamberge won the Goodwood in Adelaide under Vlad Duric. That gave his owner another reason to celebrate. Only the previous day he'd become RV chairman. Robert Roulston had resigned over an error in nominating a European horse for the Melbourne Cup in his other role as a bloodstock agent. It was a sudden resignation over a fairly minor infringement, with much noise made about the need for high standards of probity and integrity at RV.

....

Finally, on 10 July 2015, Terry Bailey called, wanting to see me at the stables. I started to feel relieved. I thought: 'This sounds positive. He's coming to see me, rather than demand I go to Racing Victoria.'

I thought they had finally concluded they didn't have enough evidence to have me disqualified, or even suspended.

For one thing, there was what you might call the entrapment period. There were two months between Lidari's positive swab and the stewards telling me about it (even though they were supposed to inform me earlier). They would have tested my horses then. Had

I been using cobalt and been oblivious to Lidari's positive, I would have kept using it. Yet they still came up with nothing else against me. I thought they might say: 'Hang on, he doesn't use this stuff. Let's try to find out how the anomaly with Lidari happened.'

The investigations of Kavanagh, O'Brien and Brennan had revealed evidence about these drips containing cobalt. Their investigations of me didn't turn up the use of any such things, or anything else unusual that might have caused Lidari's high reading.

However, Bailey sat down in my office and said: 'I've got some bad news for you. Here are your charges.' He handed me a piece of paper.

Still, as I started reading, I thought it would just say 'presentation', which you don't get suspended for. I was mistaken.

'You've charged me with administration?' I said.

I looked him in the eye and said: 'Do you think I cheat?' He'd known me for about 30 years. I asked him a second time, more forcefully, and maybe a third.

He finally said: 'Well, one of my old bosses once told me: "The horse didn't run down the chemist and get it himself"'.

I said: 'You've got all my history, all my records, you're still charging me with this. I can't fucken believe it.'

He said: 'I'm sorry', and left.

I was hit with three charges headed by one of deliberately administering cobalt to affect a horse's performance, which carried a minimum punishment of a three-year disqualification, enough to end your career. There was also a lesser 'non-intentional' administration charge, and one of presentation, for both of which there were no set penalties.

I just sat there, feeling numb.

Why bother coming to my place? I genuinely thought he was coming out to say: 'We've got no proof against you, but you will be charged with presentation'. But this? It hit me like a sledgehammer, I thought: 'Fuck—I didn't expect that'.

About the first thing I did was ring Brett Cavanough. He'd later have to recount that conversation when stewards went through my phone records and saw I'd called him just after Bailey left, as if I might have been telling him to quickly hide all the incriminating evidence or something. He was able to relay what I'd actually said: 'I'm fucked. Cobalt's got me. Some bastard's got at me. Here's twenty years of hard work down the gurgler.'

30

Fight of My Life

I was fighting an allegation that I'd cheated and, though innocent, it did feel a bit like the walls were squeezing in on me. And then I felt other people turn on me, such as some facets of the media.

Patrick Bartley from the Melbourne *Age*, who undoubtedly has very good access to RV, was unmerciful. This man who I worked closely with through the successful years I'd had—through which I'd had great media relationships—turned on me overnight. So did a lot of other media people, including Matthew Stewart at the *Herald Sun*. They were like rabid dogs chewing on my carcass.

I tried to have conversations with Bartley, but he wouldn't have it. I invited him, Shane Anderson of the racing radio station RSN and TV and internet outlet Racing.com, and Stewart to our stables to understand what we do. The latter two were open minded, but Bartley refused. It didn't happen.

RV remained staunch, 100 per cent fixed in their belief: Lidari had to have been purposefully administered cobalt. Their chief vet, Brian Stewart, had even been on the radio saying all these horses from the various stables most probably had to have been injected with this very dangerous substance.

We were painted as villains.

Before I'd been charged, I still hadn't taken this all that seriously. I hadn't even thought I'd get a lawyer, and would just represent myself. Now, of course, we had to get into gear.

My lawyer Matthew Stirling started looking into the science of cobalt. The only people fixed in their view of how Lidari could have had a high reading were at RV. All other experts we spoke to around the world were more open-minded.

We learnt cobalt not only naturally occurred in horses, it was present in nearly every dietary supplement we used. It's everywhere. And again, no one has shown this drug improves the performance of horses.

Kavanagh's Magicool won (at the same meeting where Lidari ran second) but was second and first at his previous two. Of O'Brien's, De Little Engine won, by four and three-quarter lengths, at Ballarat. Bullpit won at Moonee Valley after drifting in the betting, Bondeiger ran second in the Victoria Derby after drifting, and having won two of his previous three, but Caravan Rolls On ran eighth in the Lexus Stakes on Derby Day. All three Hope horses were unplaced.

Cobalt was being regarded like some modern-day elephant juice but it just can't be called a performance enhancer. The science around it was very cloudy, and there was certainly no clear pattern emerging from the swab results.

The threshold had been set at 200 micrograms per litre of urine. Looking at the higher of the two readings from the A and B samples tested from these horses, De Little Engine had 580 and won comfortably. Bullpit had only 320 but won by a length. Caravan Rolls On had 380 and ran eighth. Bondeiger had 370 and was beaten a long head. Lidari had 410 and was beaten a half-length. The Hopes' Windy Citi

Bear had 300 and ran fifth at Geelong, Choose had 450 and ran fifth at Caulfield, and Best Suggestion had 550 and ran eighth at Caulfield. Magicool had the highest reading, at 670, and won by a neck.

If you really did believe cobalt was a go-fast, surely you'd at least want to see some more consistent results before handing over your money for it. If I wanted to make a horse go faster I'd give it Bute, to take its pain away, or Lasix to make sure it didn't bleed, something like that. Why would anyone use cobalt?

Still, the stewards and the integrity department had created this massive hysteria around cobalt. Everyone was giggling about it. It was a bit like the 'Emperor's New Clothes', with the stewards playing the emperor.

Everyone was giggling, that is, except those of us unlucky enough to be charged. That was the galling thing: though this hysteria and this witch-hunt were just so short-sighted and stupid, the reality was we had very real cases hanging over us, threatening our livelihoods.

....

There was no evidence of me purposefully administering cobalt to Lidari. And that's because, on the lives of my children, I know I didn't do that.

But I also knew I wouldn't get off completely. The trainer is ultimately liable. What I thought would happen would be me getting a fine for presenting a horse at the races who returned a positive swab.

By now, I wanted it over with, so I requested, through Matthew Stirling, to meet the stewards. We hoped they would accept they couldn't prove administration, so let's get the presentation charge dealt with and get on with life.

The first worrying sign was Terry Bailey seemed to have no interest in attending. There was no point having the meeting without him. After some prodding though, he agreed to come. Matthew, myself, and my solicitor Tim Finemore met with RV's lawyer, Jeff Gleeson, at his Melbourne CBD office, along with their solicitors and Bailey.

While Matthew wouldn't let me talk, which pissed me off, we basically said: 'You've got everything, there's no evidence of administering, let's deal with the presentation charge and get it done'.

It was then, to our dismay, they said they actually wanted to push for a disqualification—for mere presentation. No one had ever been even suspended for presentation, let alone disqualified. There had just been fines. As you'd expect, the meeting wound up fairly quickly.

After months of being baffled by a minor irregularity, I knew now that these blokes were *really* coming after me. Everything we'd built up, everything Sarah and I had worked so hard for over twenty years, to become one of the biggest stables in Australia and I guess the world, was now in serious danger of being ripped away.

I was in for a massive fight.

....

After I was charged, we ramped up the investigations around the stables, and we finally found something. Our vet Peter Angus brought up the subject that this hoof supplement we used, Availa, contained large amounts of cobalt, more so than your average supplement. Lidari needed it because of his soft hoofs, but we'd been using it for years on lots of horses, as had lots of other stables.

We then called in one of our feed men, Rami Myala, to ask him about this, and he said he'd been feeding Lidari more Availa than recommended around the time in question. In fact, a lot more. How this came about, I don't know. But here was one possible explanation for Lidari's positive.

Of course I can see why some people might have thought Rami's late emergence into the picture might have seemed like a ruse, and an amateurish one at that. He hadn't been interviewed by stewards earlier, so it may have seemed a bit suspicious to some—including the stewards at my hearing—that we had suddenly produced this bloke who said it was his fault. I admit the timing was unfortunate. In fact, the revelation was delayed further when my legal team made us sit on the information for another month before we told anyone. It all also made our stable look pretty disorganised, but there was an explanation, backed by documentation.

When Lidari's swab was announced, he was in our main barn, where the feed man was Neil Alexander. When the stewards came, they asked: 'Who feeds the horse?' Neil answered their questions and said nothing was up.

Unfortunately, we had overlooked something until much later. At the time Lidari had contested that Turnbull Stakes and had his sample taken, he was actually stabled in our B barn, where Rami did the feeding. I had shown the stewards our worksheets from 2014, to show them Lidari was in the B barn. Unfortunately though, we'd all just still linked Neil with the horse. After I'd been charged, Rami came to me to point out it was actually he who had been feeding Lidari before the Turnbull. Had we been able to tell the stewards this earlier in their investigations, it might have helped our cause. Then again, maybe it wouldn't have. The focus early on, from stewards and us, was not really heavily centred on feeding anyway, but more about the cobalt having entered the horse's system by some other means.

Then on top of that cock-up over who had been feeding the horse, Rami also told us he had mistakenly been mixing too much Availa in with Lidari's feed. He had been adding three scoops a day instead of one—two every morning and one every afternoon—and believed that's what he'd been told to do. Rami had come from India about five years earlier. He worked hard, but only speaks broken English.

Worse still, what then emerged was that Rami had been using the wrong scoop. Instead of a 5-millilitre scoop, he had used a 30-millilitre scoop. That still wouldn't have seemed a big issue, in something the size of a horse. That's a teaspoon compared with a tablespoon. But when the manufacturer's recommended dose of Availa was a teaspoon and a half a day, it meant Lidari was getting twelve times the recommended daily dose of this hoof powder, which, it turned out, contained a lot of cobalt.

Rami also fed Brambles, and they were on the same treatment. But Brambles didn't return the same reading as Lidari. Who knows? Did Brambles not eat all his Availa? Did he absorb it differently?

We also considered, and told the stewards about, a multivitamin injection, which also contained cobalt. This was given to Lidari the day before the race instead of the usual two days before, for reasons I'm still unsure about. Maybe, since he's such a pig, someone had tried and failed the day before. It's a possibility I'd also authorised the vitamins because I had a thought Lidari wouldn't run in the Turnbull, but later changed my mind on studying the field.

So there were a couple of stuff-ups that maybe left us guilty of incompetence. But surely not deliberate administration? My history showed I didn't cheat.

I had no idea how you'd administer cobalt, but when people said— as the stewards and their experts would in our inquiry—that Lidari's cobalt must have come from an intravenous drip, they didn't know Lidari. These drips take fifteen to twenty minutes to administer. You just couldn't do that with this horse. He bites, strikes and kicks, and is near impossible to treat in that manner. His next trainer after me, Darren Weir, found this out too.

To me, the Availa, coupled with the multivitamin, was the only thing that could have possibly, *possibly*, caused Lidari's positive. At the same time, that meant the horse would've probably had to have licked every last skerrick of it off the bottom of the feed bin, which wasn't always the case with him.

So there's still a bit of doubt. To this day I truly don't know for sure why he had a raised level of cobalt. A supplement can cause it. Or was it caused by something untoward, something more sinister, that I can't explain, but that the stewards can't explain either?

By the time of Lidari's positive, there had been a set of my stable keys at RV for six months. There was never any logbook produced to say who had the keys ahead of that Turnbull Stakes. We had the situation where I didn't know who had the keys to my own stable, who could have let themselves in, or who could have done any number of things. Were the keys even logged in or out? Or are they just thrown into a box at Racing Victoria?

....

Other things had been mounting up, major distractions that began to take their toll on me and my business, making 2015 comfortably my worst year in the industry. Funny to think it still brought five Group 1s, 200 winners for the 2014–15 season, and the Australian Horse of the Year award with Dissident.

One Saturday morning in June, while on a war history holiday in Turkey, I was awoken by a phone call from the stable.

Our mare Noela's Choice was $2.50 favourite for a race that day at Moonee Valley. The stewards had been to the stable in the morning and convinced themselves they'd found 'a white substance' around her mouth. They believed she had had a treatment on race day, which is illegal.

My staff assured me they hadn't given her a treatment. I rang Terry Bailey and said we were happy to take her to the races. She went. The stewards scratched her at the track for an alleged race-day treatment.

Then came the headlines: Moody caught cheating again. Patrick Bartley and other media outlets went to town on me once more.

If we had been made to look a bit silly over who fed Lidari what when, here's where the stewards also made a mistake. We took photos of the horse, and showed previous photos of her racing. They showed she had a lot of white pigmentation around her mouth, naturally. What the stewards saw that morning was what she normally looked like. On legal advice, they dropped the case. So here was the favourite in an $80,000 race being scratched, my name dragged through the mud, and the owners, stable and jockey Regan Bayliss being penalised, for absolutely no reason.

While I was cleared, there was no publicity for that. The stewards made an error, but they were allowed to do that. I wasn't.

The House Of Hingis ibuprofen case was similar. In January, I had been charged by New South Wales stewards over that, days after the Lidari positive was announced. I was found guilty on two charges of presentation and fined $12,000. That's what normally happens with presentation charges—a fine rather than a suspension, much less a disqualification. New South Wales stewards also took into account my good record as a trainer over seventeen years.

Those charges also ended up being withdrawn, and I had my $12,000 refunded, in May 2016. The New South Wales stewards found House Of Hingis, and a couple of other trainers' horses who'd tested positive, had had their ibuprofen at a treatment farm, and that the trainers weren't cheating. This also didn't make the news.

In another of racing's quirks, House Of Hingis had been our two hundredth winner of that 2014–15 season with a July victory at Donald. I was very proud of our team to reach that mark for the third time, especially amid all the drama. That was starting to take its toll.

As the matter dragged on, you couldn't help but be affected. I don't think I was training that badly, but in hindsight there were probably some fifty-fifty calls where I made wrong decisions.

'Drained, wrecked, stressed, cranky and depressed' was how Sarah later described how I was then. She could probably see it better than me. I know I was smoking way too much. And going to work was less enjoyable than it had been.

There's no doubt where the nadir was.

A couple of weeks after I was charged, I was back at a place that held many fond memories for me—the Lewis family's Emerald Hotel in South Melbourne—at a dinner to publicise the Murtoa Cup. Half an hour before I was due to speak I got another phone call. This cobalt case had taken another twist.

Terry Bailey had now decided to call a 'show cause' hearing, before the actual inquiry. Normally, you would be charged and it would be sorted out at the hearing. But now, in what I felt was a bit of grandstanding from Bailey, I'd have to show cause why I shouldn't be suspended *before* the actual charges against me were heard.

So there I was, charged and preparing my defence, but with the stewards now wanting to stop me from training before my trial. I'd have thought there was a presumption of innocence until proven guilty, but they had to puff their chests out before the spring carnival. 'Let's spend more of the industry's and participants' money on lawyers and go through this bullshit show-cause hearing.'

It was another kick in the teeth, and it just absolutely gutted me.

I had to get up and be interviewed, along with some other trainers, at this function, which drew about a hundred people. I was visibly upset, so much so that I was shaking. I got asked about the cobalt thing, and it all came out. I said I'd just been told I'd have to show cause, and unfortunately that became the topic of the night. I felt bad that Murtoa's function got swamped, but one question led to another and on it went.

I got emotional, quite upset, and I broke down a bit about it during the interview. In the end I got through it, but driving home later it just all got on top of me. I pulled over on the side of Wellington Road and I just broke down and cried, sitting in the car by myself.

I just thought: 'Why? Why me? What the fuck is going on here? Why is this organisation so dead set on destroying me?'

I sat there for a while, in a moment on my own. I thought at least that was good, since there was no public display of being a sook, but everything had obviously just built up and boiled over.

I was just totally, utterly, bewildered.

....

What I felt was that I was the stewards' human headline. Danny O'Brien, Mark Kavanagh and the Hopes would have to show cause too, but with respect, no one outside racing knew them. Because of the deeds of Black Caviar, I was the public face of this stupid cobalt hysteria.

I was also the one who kept Bailey and his integrity unit in the news.

I thought: 'What have I done so wrong? Yes, I've questioned you but isn't this a bit over the top?'

I thought about how anyone in RV who didn't roll over and agree with this integrity department wholeheartedly was shown the door, from the chairman Robert Roulston to vets and other employees. And I was the same obviously.

And what I'd done in terms of training and promoting the industry within and externally meant absolutely nothing, because I didn't lie down and agree with everything they said or brought in.

I wasn't stupid or arrogant enough to think I would have a positive swab forgotten about because of Black Caviar. But I did think my work for the horseracing industry might have earned me an ounce of respect. It was very disappointing that I got none.

31

Trials and Errors

We went through the show-cause show trial, which cost a lot of money in legal fees again. The stewards had at first wanted it held in private. Who knows why? Maybe they were scared they'd be embarrassed.

They came out of it in early August saying, of course, that we five could continue to train pending our hearings, but then came another move. They wanted to hang on to our 10 per cent share of any prizemoney from big races that spring, pending our hearings. Not all races, just Group and Listed ones. Of all the idiotic ideas. So it'd be okay, if we were indeed crooked, to keep picking up money winning maidens at Pakenham, but not in a stakes race at Flemington?

Danny O'Brien and Mark Kavanagh challenged that idea in court and needless to say it was thrown out, but not until after the spring carnival (when I got a little money released to me). But it was more legal fees, more time, more stress. But once again, that was just a mistake, and an expensive one, from the stewards.

August also brought the Victorian Horse of the Year award for Dissident, which I didn't attend, saying RV had clearly decided I was prejudicial to the image of racing. (Likewise, I'd also skip his national award in October.)

But while the Murtoa Cup function had been my lowest ebb, September brought just about my last straw.

We had a horse entered at Pakenham on Wednesday, 16 September, called Lady Tatia. The stewards visited the stable in the morning and found she had a poultice on her legs. They charged me with race-day treatment.

It's a serious charge, with a potential six-month disqualification. But here's where there was just no common sense from stewards.

The treatment was called Kelato Swelldown. Its main ingredients are peppermint and eucalyptus oil. Unfortunately, it had been put on the wrong horse because a stable worker stuffed up, forgetting she was racing that day. But seriously, I'd have more chance of improving the horse's performance by pissing on its legs than using that mud.

Yes, we'd broken the rules. It was a treatment on race day. It was a law I was aware of, but it should've been: 'Oi, wash the mud off, don't be stupid, here's a fine, make sure it doesn't happen again'. Instead, we went to the races and the stewards scratched the horse, costing me and the owners, who'd spent good money on getting Lady Tatia ready for the races. The rules only said they *may* scratch the horse, so they did have room for discretion.

My staff had simply made a mistake. But we all know about the double standards that apply to making mistakes. So, when the stewards scratched the horse, that was it for me. After nine months of build-up, and some major issues in the couple of years before, I blew up.

I was absolutely spitting chips, and after a chat with Racing.com's Shane Anderson it was agreed that he'd interview me on TV.

David Hayes was around, my long-time friendly adversary. He knew what was going on, and advised caution: 'Think. Think. Think. Think, before you go on air.'

I appreciated his input but my attitude was: 'Fuck it. They've worn me down. I've had enough. I've fucken had enough.'

Between races, I went on air for the interview. I wasn't looking for sympathy, I didn't want to look like a sook, but it just all came out.

I said my treatment from the stewards was becoming personal, that I was sick of it and could walk away from racing very bloody easily. To do what, I didn't particularly mind. I said I could go and be a navvy on the railways for all I cared.

'I have got to the point where I don't care and that saddens me, it really saddens me,' I said.

I could also no longer see the need to keep quiet about the spy disgrace. I revealed how Bailey and Brown had offered a man—who I would name if asked—employment to spy from my stables.

'They obviously believe I'm a cheat,' I said. 'If that's the case surely they all need to hand in their briefs because they've been incompetent in not being able to catch me.'

I said former RV chairman Robert Roulston, his successor David Moodie and chief executive Bernard Saundry were aware of the spy attempt.

I said the stewards, after several months, had found no evidence of me or our stable administering cobalt to Lidari, nor any evidence of me sourcing anything to do with cobalt, but still saw fit to charge me with administering.

I said RV needed to grow some balls and look at some of the more stupid laws, and that laws should be drafted in consultation with participants like trainers. I said some trainers didn't feel as able to stand up and fight for their rights as I was. I said I was financially secure, debt-free, and thus, I could walk away from it all.

And I challenged officialdom to stop hounding me.

'Am I bad for the industry?' I said. 'Am I that bad for it? Maybe people out there think I am. Maybe they need to take my licence off me and push me away, and I've got no doubt what I'm saying now might make them think about that. But I've got to the point now where I don't care.'

I added this: 'Make a decision or let me get on with my job'.

....

The Lady Tatia hearing came in late October. I represented myself. It seemed a simple case, plus I'd get some relief from my mounting legal bills.

I pleaded guilty and got fined $1500 for a mistake my staff made because they are human.

....

My Pakenham purge made a big splash in the media. Was it wise? Probably not. But it felt good in a way. I don't think I did anything wrong. More importantly, I didn't lie, unlike some.

It was over to Bailey to respond on the spy issue, which he did in a ham-fisted way. In a Melbourne *Age* story by Patrick Bartley, Bailey said Michael Healy had suggested the spying idea, which was a complete fabrication.

Bailey said Michael, a former acquaintance of his from their early days in Rockhampton, had gone to him, down on his luck, looking for work.

Bailey said: 'We considered him as the sort of bloke who could go into a stable—not Moody's—but one that may have been causing us grave concerns'. Not Moody's? That was interesting.

The *Age* report said senior integrity officers had then put the idea of 'using Bailey's acquaintance in this role' to racing's integrity commissioner Sal Perna, that Perna had said the negatives outweighed the positives, and that was that. That was Bailey's story, anyway.

The *Herald Sun*'s report on the same day contrasted Bartley's appreciably. That paper's Matt Stewart reported Bailey had confirmed the meeting with Healy took place and that Healy had been offered a 'covert role'.

Stewart wrote that Bailey had at first rejected the claim secret payments would be made to Healy, but had then said: 'Look if he was going to go covert with us and work for Moody, then he would have copped two wages'.

Stewart got hold of Michael and reported him saying he'd rejected the approach.

Bailey made excuses for the plan: 'It wasn't just Moody. The cops do similar things. We were merely going to start at the top and work our way down. We wouldn't have considered such action had we not had significant integrity concerns (about some stable practices) at the time.'

Even if that was the case, where is the presumption of innocence until proven guilty? The cops need some pretty strong suspicions to tap people's phones, or go undercover. Just what was it about our stable's record that was so suspect in 2013—before Lidari, or even before House Of Hingis, Noela's Choice and Lady Tatia? Our horses were tested all the time and nothing was showing up.

I felt Robert Craddock, in the Brisbane *Courier Mail*, wrote the spy issue up very well the next day.

'It was a cockeyed idea delivered in a ham-fisted sort of way and lacked commonsense,' Craddock wrote.

Bailey initially confirmed the spy plan in a generic sense, telling *The Age* newspaper 'to say that we had Moody in mind is plainly and simply wrong'.

No it was not. Moody was the target all right.

Bailey later had to concede this after Healy confessed the full story.

It is never a good look when stewards are grappling with facts.

Someone should tell Bailey he is not Elliott Ness and Moody is not Al Capone. Stewards are supposed to be the bastions of integrity in racing.

Craddock made another good point: had Bailey considered what would happen to the vulnerable Michael Healy if he became a spy and was found out? He would have become unemployable.

Bailey said stewards would look at my comments from Pakenham to see if I deserved punishment. I wasn't surprised when they opted not to have my allegations aired at another hearing.

Two days after my interview, Lee Freedman said he had no problem with spies in stables, along the old 'if you've got nothing to hide' theme. In Sydney, Chris Waller voiced his support for me, which I appreciated a whole lot more.

Finally, in late September, the stewards offered a choice of two hearing dates. It could wait until 14 December or, if we agreed not to challenge the stewards' science on cobalt, including whether it was performance enhancing, we could get it started on 5 October and have it over in three days.

Was that 'early and quick' carrot really supposed to sound appealing? Of course I didn't trust it. I had zero trust in the stewards, and in the science on cobalt. We'd wait until December. Lee and Shannon Hope's inquiry would be first, in mid-October, with the Kavanagh–O'Brien–Brennan case starting two weeks before mine.

....

Another month, another black spot, and another apparent downturn in officialdom's regard for trainers.

In late October, at the height of the spring carnival, news broke that Bailey's front door had been shot at. Six bullets were fired at it on the Sunday night after the Cox Plate. It was huge and dramatic news. The aftermath, to me, was purely disgusting.

Bailey made a public statement to the media, with RV bigwigs Bernard Saundry and Dayle Brown at his side, indicating the shooting had happened due to his crackdown on drugs in racing.

'These things happen, but it's the job we're in,' he said. 'We've had similar incidents over the years and we're accustomed to it now.'

He added: 'Over the years when you're in these integrity roles obviously sometimes people don't like the way you go about your job'.

Brown vowed officials would 'keep investigating the racing industry without fear or favour'.

Those comments meant the finger was pointed at Moody, O'Brien, Kavanagh and the Hopes, we who'd suffered the most from this. It was almost libellous, really, despite them not naming names.

Later, a month before I was sentenced, Bailey was featured in the Fairfax newspapers' *Good Weekend* magazine under the headline of 'The lone ranger'. It was all about the shooting. There was a photo of one horse trainer in the article: me.

That was so wrong—disrespectful not only to me, but to every other participant in the industry. It again left that speculation out there that someone in the industry had some part in this shooting. And all this while a police investigation was ongoing.

If you talk to a few old coppers they'll tell you no one's ever had their door shot who doesn't know who's doing the shooting. For Bailey to put that speculation out there, and for RV to allow it to get out there, was I felt very wrong, and very disrespectful.

People might want to put two and two together and say: 'Oh come on—it just *had* to be racing people'. They could say that a thousand times. And a thousand times you could say back: 'Where's the proof?' As with any serious criminal matter, as this was, you can't just go running around saying: 'It was someone from this group of people'.

Surely there has to be evidence, and proof beyond doubt, before someone is found responsible. Who knows who might do something and what their motivations are?

From my perspective, two years earlier I was winning the premiership and training the world's best horse. Now, I was having it insinuated that I might have had shots fired at a house while a man and his family were inside. I'm a big boy, but as an affront to my character, that was very hard to take.

Months later, Sarah sent out a tweet poking fun at the chief steward and his supposed war on crime, joking about an upcoming telemovie called 'UnderBailey'. She got fined $1500 (as a licensed owner and stablehand), after Bailey told an inquiry he felt like he'd been painted as a crook. I'd have thought speculation about who might be responsible for a house shooting was a bit more serious.

Around the time of the shooting, Dayle Brown said he'd seen a threatening-looking bloke perched on a motorbike outside his house. For some reason, this person wasn't identified. I know if someone was parked outside my house looking threatening, I'd try to find out who he was by getting a number plate or a photo.

Instead, Brown and Bailey just left it open for people to speculate that racing people were responsible for these things, leaving a blight on the industry at the height of the spring carnival.

I also thought about David Moodie. The fact that he was RV chairman when these comments about the shooting were made, and yet nothing was done to clarify, correct or retract them was, I thought, incredibly weak of him and the organisation he headed.

I respected David's position. But I thought the fact he knew, for example, that Bailey had lied about the spy situation, might have made him wary about a few things.

I'd done a lot of business with him, trained a lot of winners for him. I'd have thought he would respect what I had done for the industry too. But it meant nothing. He knew people had been moved on if they hadn't agreed with RV's integrity department, or hadn't lain down and accepted everything it said. He was probably more worried about David Moodie than Peter Moody. Still, my sense that he didn't believe me when I told him, on the night of Lidari's positive, that I didn't cheat, left me pissed off from day one—not to mention hurt.

It was also clear that Bailey and the integrity department wielded unbelievable power over RV, and no one—from the chairman to the CEO—had the balls to even question that, which I found unbelievable.

At least I knew where I stood. I was going to get no support whatsoever.

32

The Hearing

Finally, in December, eleven months after being notified of Lidari's positive, it was time for the hearing. I was optimistic, rather than confident. There was no evidence against me, but I knew the integrity department had become manic about this nothing substance cobalt.

The Hopes had been banned a few weeks earlier, Lee for three years and son Shannon for five. Danny O'Brien and Mark Kavanagh's case had started, and it wasn't looking great for them either.

The pressure was on. I was fighting for my very livelihood—a business with a $15–$20 million annual turnover and more than fifty staff. There had already been a major casualty. In November, I had had to close our Sydney stable after three years of operation. Clare Cunningham had decided to do different things, perhaps because of the pressure I was under, and the logical step was to shut it down.

That really hurt. We'd built it up, and moved from Rosehill to the more prestigious Randwick, my first home track. But with my trial and tribulations, I didn't have enough time to concentrate on Caulfield, let alone Sydney.

At least, going into RV headquarters at Flemington on day one, I had greater faith in the Racing Appeals and Disciplinary (RAD) board than in a stewards' inquiry. The panel—Judge John Bowman, lawyers Chris Fox and Jeremy Rosenthal—seemed an erudite bunch, and had some knowledge of racing. I was hopeful they'd see that there was never any evidence against me.

Of course I pleaded not guilty to all three charges. The main charge was administering cobalt with the intention of affecting Lidari's performance. This carried a minimum three-year disqualification. There was a lesser administering charge, basically having a horse with cobalt in its system. Then there was the charge of presenting a horse at the races with the substance in its system. The second and third charges carried no set penalties.

The hearing would play out over not weeks but months—evidence, adjournments, delays, et cetera, stretching it from December into March. I'd only ever spent an hour or two in stewards' inquiries—so this would become a torrid, draining time.

As for the details, we asserted the most plausible explanation for Lidari's positive was that Rami Myala had given him too much Availa, and the horse had had that multivitamin injection, which also contained cobalt, the day before the race.

Of course we had to say this amended our original advice to the stewards that Neil Alexander had fed Lidari. Of course RV's lawyer Jeff Gleeson used this as an excuse to say I was lying.

Gleeson also highlighted that the details of my story, Rami's story and Neil Sullivan's story on how much Availa was fed to Lidari didn't all match up 100 per cent. Gleeson thought this was dodgy. I say it proved there was no collusion. If we were colluding, you'd think we'd get our heads together. If the three stories matched 100 per cent, you'd smell a rat.

We said we didn't really know why Lidari had got his multivitamins the day before the race. But our main point was it wasn't suspect. It was documented, like we documented everything. Had we been cheating, had that injection contained anything untoward, you just wouldn't document it in your veterinary paperwork. If someone gave me money to buy cocaine, I'm not going to write down '$10,000 payment from Joe Bloggs, cocaine deal'.

The stewards' side attacked our practices, particularly that our staff would make up our horses' vitamin injections and the vets would administer them. I used to inject my horses' vitamins myself, but when we got big, the staff would make them up and then the vets would inject them. The stewards alleged the vets didn't know what was in the vitamin injections, specifically that vet Amber Thiel, who worked with our main vet Peter Angus, had no direct knowledge of what she injected into Lidari the day before the Turnbull.

Again, all treatments were documented, and there was trust between our staff and the vets. The practice was about as worrisome as a bloke getting his secretary to make the coffee.

It was the same with Availa. You get these products from professionals you trust. I hadn't known it contained cobalt, or how much. In fact I had no understanding of cobalt whatsoever.

For the stewards to suggest cobalt was rampant was just rubbish. Well, it was rampant, because every trainer who feeds horses supplements has therefore got cobalt in his feed room. They mightn't know it, or they didn't until these cases.

(Six months after I quit, RV vet Brian Stewart admitted in the O'Brien and Kavanagh appeal hearing that RV should have issued warnings that standard doses of vitamin and mineral products containing cobalt could push horses' levels above the permitted threshold. I tweeted: 'Bit late for some'. That sounded flippant, but I was ropeable. RV was admitting it had stuffed up, yet I'd lose everything—my business, my occupation, and almost half a million dollars in legal fees.)

We also argued RV had, shambolically, ignored protocols under the Australian Rules of Racing in relation to Lidari's A and B urine samples. The samples had gone to the independent Racing Analytical Services Laboratory (RASL) in Melbourne. Since it didn't have the facilities to test for cobalt at the time, they had to send part of the A sample to Perth's ChemCentre for an initial, indicative, screening. That showed the presence of cobalt, and that should have triggered a full confirmatory analysis of the rest of that A sample, and of the B sample at a separate facility, which is supposed to be nominated by the first facility.

However, RASL then advised the RV stewards there wasn't enough urine left over from the A sample to conduct a full analysis. RASL then told the stewards that therefore, under the rules, the analysis of Lidari's urine could not and would not proceed. But the stewards ignored that. They intervened in what is supposed to be an independent testing process, and directed the B sample be split in two, with one bottle to be tested at ChemCentre and the other at the Hong Kong Jockey Club. Australian Rule of Racing 178D says the A sample should be tested in one lab and the B sample in another (to be nominated by the first testing centre, not by RV stewards). However, the stewards forgot about that part of the rule book. They were pretty determined.

My lawyer Matthew Stirling asked RV for emails relating to this matter, but RV refused. Judge Bowman eventually ordered RV to hand them over. This was a win for us, but only a little one.

We argued the stewards had also neglected protocols in that they should have informed me of my horse's positive swab when they were first advised of it from the A sample screen—on 20 November 2014. Instead, they told me almost two months later, after what I call that period of entrapment.

Still, the RAD Board found the breach of testing protocol wasn't serious enough to make the sample test results inadmissible and throw the case out. They also ruled that failing to notify me didn't affect the results of the testing. It makes you wonder what the testing protocols are for, really. (Mind you, the testing protocols would become pretty crucial in the cases of O'Brien and Kavanagh.)

All the same, to have the case thrown out on a protocol technicality wouldn't have achieved my main aim—to be unequivocally cleared of cheating. My history, and the fact no other horse of mine tested positive for cobalt during my entrapment period, should have strongly suggested it wasn't part of our regime. They would still have to have found some amazing as-yet-unseen evidence to prove we gave Lidari cobalt intentionally.

....

While the stewards' breaches of testing protocols was farcical, even more farcical was their prosecution of the charges, led by Gleeson.

The onus was on them to prove me guilty, the RAD Board said, to a state of 'comfortable satisfaction on the balance of probabilities'. I knew I couldn't avoid a guilty verdict on presentation, but to prove the more grave charge of deliberate administration, surely there had to be some hard evidence.

They had none.

Their entire case didn't consist of proving allegations. It was just based on calling us liars. It was like school-playground stuff, and might almost have been comical were it not done in the cause of ending someone's career.

They wanted to call Neil Alexander a liar, Rami Myala a liar, Peter Moody a liar, Peter Angus a liar. Everyone was a liar. That was the best form of evidence they had: 'You're all liars'.

I started my two days on the stand on the third day, and was duly called a liar by Gleeson. He said I was making up the evidence about Rami. He seemed to doubt me in other areas—that I hadn't read up on cobalt when the thresholds came in, or that I hadn't conducted reviews on Availa. (The question has also been asked whether I would have known Lidari was on Availa. I can definitely say that I did.)

In hindsight, I'll admit we could have tightened some practices, put more checks in place. At the same time, we'd had our regimes in place for years, and they were obviously working. Peter Angus had been my vet for ten years, and there was no more honourable vet in the business.

What was really aggravating was the stewards had had no interest in coming to really study our stable, to see how such a huge operation ran, what it's really like training and feeding 80 or more horses when it's 4.00 a.m. and freezing and pouring rain. With that many horses and more than 50 staff, many of whom aren't rocket scientists, mistakes will happen. That's human nature. Why wouldn't someone running an investigation go look at a stable? If they were studying how a doctor had stuffed up, they'd send someone to see how the hospital worked. Gleeson even doubted me when I told him I didn't personally feed every horse. It shows how much he knew about stable life.

Since telling the truth is something I've always held as very important, I felt for Gleeson to just sit there and call me a liar, when he doesn't know me, was particularly affronting. If you weren't in such a forum, you might reach across the table and snot the bastard.

But to me there was just one massive main point.

Outside Lidari having cobalt in his system and me being the trainer, there was just no evidence around along the necessary categories—of me procuring the drug, administering the drug, getting someone else to do it, or knowing it was being done and failing to stop it.

Matthew Stirling, in his closing arguments, highlighted a fundamental rule of law: he who makes an allegation must prove it. I liken it all to a murder investigation. There's the body. There's the knife. And there's a bloke in the house, and that's me. But the stewards just couldn't tie the three factors together. There's no fingerprints on the knife, no blood on me. I thought if I was found guilty of administration, I'd take it straight to VCAT (the Victorian Civil and Administrative Tribunal) or to court. Outside racing's jurisdiction and in the public legal system, the charge would get tossed out. It wouldn't have even gone to trial.

It would have been important for them to look at our stable, but they were happy to just sit there and call me a liar. The ex-coppers in the integrity unit must have been pretty ordinary policemen. Never once did they get off their arse and investigate properly. It was just 'Gotcha, gotcha, gotcha'.

The stewards even said from the outset they might appeal whatever happened. After taking this long to get their stuff together, were they still not confident they had enough to prove the case before the RAD Board? Again, had this been a court of law, they would have been told to go away and find some evidence.

The case became more involved, in scientific detail as well as time.

We were there at 10 p.m. one night when an RV witness gave evidence from Dubai. Dr Martin Wainscott, former head vet for Harness Racing New South Wales, had written a report for RV on the oral ingestion of cobalt, and doubted that Availa could have caused Lidari's high reading. But then Matthew Stirling cross-examined him, focusing on a trial RV had ordered on six mares who were given the same amount of Availa as Lidari. While those six mares showed lower readings than Lidari, Dr Wainscott admitted that every horse was different regarding how much Availa, and therefore cobalt, gets absorbed in its system.

We were there at midnight another night taking evidence via video link from another RV expert—Stuart Paine, associate professor of veterinary pharmacology at the University of Nottingham, England. He had done computer modelling based on Lidari's feed and supplement regime and said there was only a one-in-10,000 chance the Availa had led to his positive. But, again, under cross-examination from Matthew Stirling, he admitted his modelling stopped on the day before the race. He hadn't accounted for someone giving Lidari any Availa whatsoever on the morning of the race, which Rami Myala had done, and with much more than the recommended dose. That threw his modelling—and so two out of two of RV's expert witnesses—out the window.

We called Andrew Van Eps, associate professor of veterinary internal medicine at the University of Queensland. He said even giving a horse much less Availa than Lidari was on might cause a reading like the one the horse returned—there just weren't enough reliable studies on cobalt digestion out there. That could also explain why Brambles didn't test positive yet Lidari did, even though Gleeson would cling to that disparity in his closing argument.

....

After those initial six days in December, the hearing was adjourned until 16 February. After closing arguments were heard then, the RAD Board said they'd come back again a month later for the verdict.

The delays were crippling enough for me, regardless of the outcome.

I'd still have to go to the January yearling sales, but clients weren't exactly scrambling to give me horses with a potentially long ban over my head. Already, my 'cobalt year' had brought a downturn of about two-thirds of my normal business. I had been given only five horses to train, outside those I'd bought myself. And while I'd normally buy twenty or so yearlings at the Magic Millions sales, in 2016 I came home with ten.

I was still training, and winning races, but my enthusiasm was way down.

When we resumed in February, we at least had a win. Matthew Stirling told the RAD Board Dr Stuart Paine had found a bug in his software. When it was fixed, the 10,000/1 chance of Availa causing Lidari's high reading became 31/1. Then, if you said Lidari was given Availa on the morning of the race, which he was, it became an 87 per cent chance that this had caused his high reading.

As Matthew said in his closing arguments, with this star witness rendered irrelevant, it left the stewards having to cobble together their case on the run, and resorting to calling us liars.

In the end, the main thing they could allege was that I was incompetent. To a degree, I had to agree. But again, they'd never seen how human error can occur in a stable. I was thankful later for my mate and fellow Caulfield trainer Mick Price for appearing as my character witness, and for standing up to Gleeson when he asked if my regime was above board. Mick said it was probably the most professional and as good as any in Australia.

As their exchange got tense, at one point Gleeson said Mick had given him a stupid answer. Mick said: 'Well, they're stupid questions—you don't know, you've never had a look at a stable!'

When my clean record was mentioned, the stewards responded along the lines of: 'Just because a bloke hasn't robbed a bank before, doesn't mean he can't do it now'. But that bloke doesn't have 40 chances a week of an honest pay-off, like I did.

That disappointed me, because they knew I didn't cheat. They had got all my records; they'd interviewed everyone from my pre-school teacher to my great-aunt; they investigated for sixteen months, and they *still* had no evidence.

So I felt I should at least beat the administration charges. It had even got to the stage where we'd be outside during a break and joking with the media about how much time I'd get for presentation. Some of them had realised: 'Hang on, there *is* no evidence against Moody'.

Still, I feared the stewards would come up with some sort of curve ball, because I'd learnt their mentality towards me. I thought they'd try to tie me into the O'Brien–Kavanagh intravenous-drip issue.

Some disconcerting news had come in late January on those cases, with O'Brien and Kavanagh disqualified for four and three years respectively, and the vet Tom Brennan for five. The two trainers started their appeals at VCAT, which would play out into 2017, costing them millions in legal fees and affected business.

I was confident that, while I wouldn't walk free, I wouldn't lose my licence. I felt I'd be able to maintain my business and recover from this catastrophic financial loss. My legal bills from the ordeal ended up around the $400,000 mark. And again—all for what?

I thought I'd get a fine for presentation. These were usually around $1500 or $3000. I had no clue how big mine would be, but I hoped the RAD Board would see through the integrity department's cobalt hysteria.

At least I'd got one major point out when I told the hearing: 'Cobalt is a big balls-up and is going to play out for a lot of years'.

Meanwhile, I got some good news on the track—and it came once again through David Moodie's Flamberge. He was a great little horse, who did far more than I ever expected. This time, he just held on to win the Oakleigh Plate first up under Damian Lane at $31.

33

Decisions

On Wednesday, 16 March 2016, it was verdict time.

While I was still a little apprehensive, mostly I just wanted it over. I told my legal team unless something ridiculous happened, there would be no appeal. I'd just had enough, and I told Sarah that too. Appeals might have made it all drag on another year or two.

I had been ready to quit training a few times through those fourteen months. I'd question how it was affecting me, and whether they were just going to bleed us dry—of sanity, of money. I wondered if I shouldn't have just rolled over at the start. I could have just packed up and walked away and they could stick the racing industry up their arse. Why put myself through this?

But then I'd feel: 'Hang on—I deserve more than that'. If I had just walked, some would see an admission of guilt. It would have let down my staff and clients too.

With a full house in the hearing room, I listened, a little nervously, as Judge Bowman read the decision.

On the main charge of administration for the purpose of affecting Lidari's performance . . . not guilty.

That was a relief. I wouldn't get rubbed out for three years, minimum. Most importantly, I'd been cleared of cheating.

Unfortunately, though, they found me guilty on the charge of non-intentional administration. This wasn't a cheating charge, but basically meant the buck stops with the trainer, for one of his horses having an illegal level of cobalt in its system.

Though there were no set penalties for this charge, it seemed more serious than the third charge of mere presentation—which the Board now didn't need to find a verdict on, having found me guilty on the second charge. I still felt I should have only been pinged for presentation, but I think the Board went for the more serious of the two minor charges to strike some middle ground.

And while I was relieved at first to be cleared of cheating, things started to get a little worrying.

Though the Board didn't reach any conclusions on whether Availa had caused Lidari's high reading, they hammered me for the 'careless' way the supplement had been given to the horse, and for my limited knowledge about the product. As we left for the day I thought there was a chance they might want to make a bit of an example of me for the practices in my stable.

When penalty arguments were heard the next morning, RV showed they were still after blood. Gleeson urged I be disqualified for two years because my conduct had led to Lidari's positive swab.

After the way the hearing had gone, I did have to pinch myself. I thought: 'They're kidding. This isn't happening.'

After Matthew Stirling argued for a substantial fine and no ban, the Board retired to consider penalty and we waited outside.

To see RV keep going after me left me with a very bitter taste in my mouth, and a deep sense of betrayal. Yes, racing had been good to me, but I also couldn't help but think of all I'd done for the industry—not just Black Caviar, but full stop. Obviously she had been a massive part of it—and the hours, the hundreds of hours, I'd spent promoting the industry in a positive light.

You'd think it at least might have tempered the stewards' determination to get me disqualified on the lesser charge. Why were they so hell-bent on getting rid of me? I just keep coming back to the fact that I'd caught the integrity department lying over the spy issue, then publicly caught them lying, and that I questioned their decisions instead of rolling over and agreeing.

....

After just half an hour, we were called back in. Despite RV's wishes, I thought I'd be rubbed out for three or six months, but that was workable. At least I could save my business. I could save the jobs of my staff. I could work to get back the $400,000 I'd paid my lawyers.

But here came yet another sting in the tail, thanks to Bailey.

The Board announced I was suspended for 12 months, and would have to serve six of those months, with the other six suspended. Still, at least I wasn't disqualified, which would've stopped me going to the races or to yearling sales.

I felt it was still very harsh, but we could survive six months. We could bring in another trainer. I could take a six-month holiday, do some more war history.

So as everyone started leaving, I asked Bailey to stay behind for a chat. Everyone looked at me like, 'What's this?' but I gestured to them to leave us to it.

I was hoping for a reasoned one-on-one discussion on how we could work out a way forward. But in the otherwise empty room, the first thing Bailey said to me was: 'You're lucky'.

That was very cold.

I ploughed on: 'My idea is we get in a stand-in trainer, and I'll bugger off for six months'.

I indicated the stand-in would be my old mate, Mornington trainer David Brideoake, who had said he was prepared to do it.

There were a handful of precedents I knew off the top of my head. When Lee Freedman was outed for four months in 1995, his brother Richard stepped in. Bart Cummings was suspended for three months in 1979, and Mal Barnes had been his stand-in.

I didn't think it'd be a problem. Again, I'd be mistaken.

Bailey asked me to come back the next day to discuss details, and when I went in to meet with him and an RV solicitor, they put up the shutters.

They just kept talking about what the public perception would be. I said David Brideoake would simply be employed by Moody Racing as a trainer. I said the stewards had a hefty bit of security to ensure I'd have no interaction—the suspended six months of my suspension.

But they wouldn't accept that either.

They'd need us to sack all our staff—the redundancy payouts would be enormous—and then re-employed by David. He would have to do all the invoicing, all the HR, workers' compensation liabilities, insurances, the lot.

I'd already spoken to the Melbourne Racing Club at Caulfield and they were happy for David to take over my stables, and happy for Moody Racing to run the business and pay the bills. But RV wouldn't cop it. They were tightening the screws, or even hammering in the nails.

Again, I couldn't believe it.

'Lloyd Williams employs a trainer in Robert Hickmott,' I said. 'Darley employs one in John O'Shea. There are numerous organisations around Australia that employ a trainer. I'll resign as a director of

Moody Racing, Sarah Moody then owns Moody Racing, she employs David Brideoake to train the horses. What's wrong with that?'

Public perception. Public perception. Public perception.

That's all they were worried about. I found that pretty rich after the lies about the spying issue, and the speculation RV allowed to fester in the court of public opinion that racing people had shot Bailey's house. Who was bad for public perception—me, or the integrity department?

They weren't worried about me. As far as they were concerned, they'd got me.

The realisation sank in that changing everything over to David was going to be a nightmare. And my suspension was starting in six days—at midnight on Easter Thursday, 24 March. We had asked for an extra week but the RAD Board said the rules stipulated that the ban had to start seven days after sentencing. It could have been handy if the authorities had shown the same sort of flexibility on this rule as with the testing protocols, but each to their own I guess.

Other options popped into my head, such as Brett Cavanough, who trained at Albury, but David would be a better fit as he was just down the road at Mornington.

I thought Jeff O'Connor could get a trainer's licence, or Steph Little, who was my assistant trainer by then, or even Sarah.

But I hit the same conclusion: RV wouldn't accept any of them while Moody Racing was the employer.

I thought of appealing. I had seven days to do so. My legal team offered to do the appeal pro bono. Matthew Stirling had said he could go to VCAT to get a stay of proceedings to allow me to keep training, like Danny O'Brien and Mark Kavanagh.

But when I thought about it, it was just too much. I'd had enough. I was fucked. It had gone on for fourteen months and I was sick of the pressure.

I went home, talked to Sarah, but didn't really resolve anything.

I went to bed resigned to this latest setback, with options seemingly dwindling. But deep down, I still had the basic assumption: 'Well, it's going to be extremely difficult, but I've obviously got to keep this all going somehow'.

I would look into doing it Bailey's way.

....

The next morning, Saturday, 19 March, I got up at 3.05 a.m. and drove to Caulfield. I worked some horses, and we were getting ready to go to Bendigo, which had the metro meeting that day.

About 5.00 a.m., Sarah called me. She was worried about me mentally, as well as herself.

'Is it worth it?' she said. 'Do we need to put ourselves through this any longer?'

And then and there, in a two-minute phone conversation, we both knew.

We'd close down. We'd shut the doors on everything we'd built over twenty years.

Going on wasn't going to be fair on David Brideoake. It wasn't going to be fair on us.

I got off the phone and the realisation started sinking in: the following Thursday night at Moonee Valley, I would have my last runners and that would be the end of my career as a horse trainer.

It was a big thing to get my head around. Training was all I had ever done, the field I'd worked in since I was eleven, and I was now 46.

To be honest, I'd never thought I would be a 'lifer', training until the day I died like Bart Cummings or T.J. Smith. And more lately I had thought I would beat this charge, train for four or five more years, then Sarah and I could walk off into the sunset. But still, I'd wanted to go out on my terms. Now, I'd been hounded out of the game. And, without putting too fine a point on it, under a bullshit charge that felt like a personal vendetta. So that hurt.

At the same time, now the decision was made there was also a bit of relief, like when we retired Black Caviar.

There would be no going back.

....

On the drive to Bendigo I started ringing my owners who had horses in that day: 'Your horse races today, then it needs a new trainer tomorrow'.

That day I told the staff that, unfortunately, as of midnight the following Thursday, they wouldn't be employed. That was the hard part, unbelievably hard, telling people like Jeff O'Connor it was all over.

And from that Saturday, until the Thursday night, we dispersed the best part of 400 horses. It was full on: working the phones, lining up new trainers, moving horses all over the place.

It started on the Saturday. Some horses went to Bendigo and raced, then went to a different stable. Just to aggravate things, it was a frustrating day at the races too, with three second-placegetters, all in a row. The contentious Noela's Choice went round for me one last time, but came sixth.

On Sunday we worked the phones again. On Monday, back in office hours, we sent notifications to our 1200 or so clients, and there was a lot of toing and froing between Jeff and myself as we 'placed' our horses for the last time.

Come Easter Thursday we had six left, and they would be racing at the Valley that night. I had to call Bailey to ask one last thing.

'We can't be expected to deliver these horses to people at midnight on Thursday night. Do you mind if I have access to the stables on the Friday morning to get rid of them?'

At least he granted me that.

....

On the Thursday afternoon the Moody family drove across Melbourne to Moonee Valley. A week earlier I had been cleared of cheating. Yet somehow I was going to my last meeting as a trainer.

It was Melbourne's last Group 1 of the season—the William Reid Stakes. In another plot twist, I'd be saddling two runners—both of them owned by David Moodie. He owned Flamberge himself, and was managing owner of Kinglike, in a syndicate including some special connections for me: Typhoon Tracy's owners John and Fu-Mei Hutchins, and Stuart Ramsey.

And yes, it was an emotional night.

We started with a second placing for Better Land and the wonderful Linda Meech. Then we had nearly three hours to wait for the feature race. A lot of people came up to wish me the best, and I had a couple of catch-up beers with people.

I had continued to do business with David Moodie through that torrid fourteen months, but in a more guarded fashion. I didn't feel great animosity towards him as much as the organisation he was running. Still, things were a little cool between us that last night. (As a postscript, several months later he'd resign as RV chairman over the O'Brien–Kavanagh appeal, when O'Brien named him as the source of the tip-off to me about his cobalt positive. Perversely, David had been told by Patrick Bartley, as Bartley revealed in an article in the *Age*.)

One thing that definitely pissed me off about David, though, was he always had a dislike of Luke Nolen as a rider. Hence, Flamberge was ridden by Brad Rawiller, with Damian Lane on Kinglike, although Luke had ridden both.

Damian didn't ride Kinglike all that well, and he finished last. But wouldn't you know it, the one Moodie owned outright, Flamberge, sneaked up along the fence in the straight and edged out John O'Shea's Holler by a nose.

'Peter Moody, I think you might've done it!' said Greg Miles, one last time, as they hit the line.

Bingo. Group 1 No. 53. And out.

Now came one of the most surreal moments I've had on a racetrack. I was of course very happy. It was great to fire a parting shot by winning a Group 1. It felt great to have Sarah and the girls there with me too.

At the same time, the mounting yard was also full of our staff members in tears. Moodie was emotional. His wife Jenny more so. I think she felt the enormity of what had happened.

It wasn't quite my last race. I had my last three starters in the next, the Group 2 Sunline Stakes over 1600 metres. Luke Nolen and I ended our association with Dig A Pony, part-owned by Jeff O'Connor, who ran ninth. Metaphorical got third for Luke Currie. And you could say my very last horse was the mare Anfitriona, who came tenth under Daniel Stackhouse (though maybe we'll talk more about Flamberge's Group 1 than that one). In another twist, my last race was won by Miss Rose De Lago, trained by Danny O'Brien.

My girls and I decided to leave before the last, and walked across the track to the infield car park, rather than through the crowd and the tunnel. Unbeknownst to us, the TV cameras showed the five of us, with the commentator saying: 'There's Peter Moody, wandering off the course for the last time'.

And that was it. A torrid week. A fraught fourteen months. And an unbelievable 30-year ride.

34

Reflections

I bowed out with 2402 winners from 13,163 starters, a win rate of 18 per cent, plus 3308 placegetters. I had 53 Group 1s, four Melbourne premierships, a Victorian country premiership, three Victorian overall titles and one national title, with my horses winning $113 million in prizemoney, and with Luke Nolen and me going down as the most successful trainer–jockey combo in modern times. It's a little strange to think I didn't get one of the big four—the Caulfield and Melbourne cups, the Cox Plate or the Golden Slipper. I would have liked to have won all four, of course, but I did have the best horse in the world, so I'm not that bothered. We also built ourselves up without the backing of any mega-rich clients who sent me to the sales; I'd always buy horses myself and then find the owners. I guess that's slightly frustrating yet satisfying at the same time.

My ban didn't just affect me. It put a huge hole in several other people's businesses as well, like Brett Cavanough and Julian Welsh (another pre-trainer and breaker), David Brideoake for his pre-training and spelling business, numerous other spelling farms we used about the place, as well as Mick Bryant and Peter Angus. Of course it affected all our laid-off staff as well.

I still had a nervous three weeks after my last win, waiting for Flamberge's swab from the Reid to clear. After all, I'd not quite been killed off completely, just suspended for six months. I had it in the back of my mind: 'What if they're going to do something sneaky to me? Or what if someone in Racing Victoria got at Flamberge's sample, or if anyone got to the horse full stop, to try to make a mug out of me?'

I'd had hate mail through the cobalt thing. I'd had owners not wanting to pay their bills, clients writing in: 'You filthy cheating fuck. You don't deserve to get paid. Low scum of the earth.' It was hurtful, and incredible, the reactions of these people who didn't know the truth or wanted to believe the worst. Many months later I was still chasing clients' money, still owed the guts of a million dollars in training fees.

It's one of the things about being a horse trainer you don't hear. In fact, it's an unusual profession. It's probably similar to a football coach—people tugging at you from all sides, and you're in the middle. A footy coach has the players, their agents, the fans, the club's owners, the press. A trainer's got officialdom, owners, jockeys, staff, horses, and you're supposed to have a family too.

I was a horse trainer, but also a husband and a dad. I felt horrible that my family had to go through it. It seemed one day my kids would have their friends over to ride on Black Caviar, then a bit later I'd pick them up from school sport, not knowing if I should show my face. Their dad went from hero to villain, very publically.

I'm thankful they were in their late teens by then, and able to process it. I'm also thankful Sarah held so much together then, as she always has. I couldn't have done it without her, nor get through the cobalt mess without the support of my family, who have had to wear the downside of my success.

You end up reconciling: if you're going to have success, you've got to make sacrifices. Anyone who's had success knows it's hard to create that balance. And you don't get a second chance.

And here's something a lot of people wouldn't think of—it can be a very lonely life being a horse trainer. People see trainers saddling horses, getting trophies, winning premierships, but don't see the other side.

And the more successful you get, the lonelier it can become. It's a peculiar situation, and a bit hard to explain, but the bigger I got the more people tended to withdraw. It was like: 'We don't want to disturb Peter. He's got too much on his plate.' They'd want to give you space, or downtime. They'd have good intentions, but in the end you'd often feel lonely, short of a mate. You'd wish they wouldn't give you that space.

You don't see much of your family when you're going to bed at 8 p.m. On top of that, the plain obvious truth of getting up in the middle of the night, every night, is that you're always just knackered.

So if something did come up, like a fishing trip with some mates, you wouldn't want to do that either because you wanted to rest up, or spend time with your family.

Sometimes, even when I was really flying and Black Caviar was being a phenomenon, I'd look at mates in that lifestyle I left behind—shearing sheep, working on the railways, on farms—and I'd feel jealous, thinking I could have been as happy doing similar things. It'd be a nice lifestyle. And they got an annual holiday with their family. I don't think we've ever had two or three weeks away as a family together our whole life.

Despite its bugbears, I wouldn't really swap it. It's been an unbelievable ride, from when I was a kid getting up in the dark, with old Frank tooting his horn out front.

Would I ever go back to training? I'd never say never, but I doubt I'd go back as long as the Victorian regime was headed by Bailey. I'd struggle to work in a place where I didn't respect the people with ultimate authority over my career. I could look at different states, or overseas—Hong Kong, elsewhere in Asia, Europe or America. Or I'd be open to being a private trainer, where someone else pays the bills, including in Australia.

But being a big trainer in the public sphere? That will never happen again. Just picking up and starting again would also say that what was done to me—the sickening end to a distinguished career—was okay.

It certainly wasn't.

I had my business, my livelihood, taken away, but I beat the charge of being a cheat, which was the most important thing. Mind you, I might rather have the $400,000 and let people think I'm a cheat! But Sarah and I agreed the record we'd built deserved better.

I actually feel sorry for Terry Bailey, that he's got this mentality towards the participants in the industry. It must be a sad way to go through life. I don't go to the footy thinking everyone's cheating. I don't walk down the street thinking everyone's a murderer or a thief.

Why can't you walk out there and think: 'These trainers are having an even crack. If there's someone cheating, we'll try to catch them, but on the whole they're not a bad bunch of people.'

Why take the human element out of it? The overwhelming majority of trainers are decent people, working hard and doing the right thing.

....

A year on from my retirement came a stunning postscript. Two years after Danny O'Brien and Mark Kavanagh had been charged by the stewards, their appeals were upheld by VCAT and their suspensions thrown out. I was happy for them. The decision also had possible ramifications for my case, and that of the Hopes (which was still ongoing at VCAT).

In a ruling that reminded me of what we had argued about administration in our case, VCAT President Justice Greg Garde said he was not satisfied to the required standard that O'Brien and Kavanagh had caused cobalt to be administered to their horses (by their vet Tom Brennan).

More significantly for me, Justice Garde said the cases against O'Brien and Kavanagh had to be thrown out because the test results were inadmissible. This, he said, was because the way Racing Victoria handled testing for cobalt between April 2014 and August 2015 had 'substantially departed from the requirements set out in AR 178D of the Rules of Racing'. This of course covered the period of Lidari's positive (and the Hopes' three). We had argued that RV's departure from the rules should have made Lidari's test results inadmissible, but the RAD Board had decided to plough on.

More than mine, the O'Brien, Kavanagh and Hopes cases dwelt on the testing protocols, whether the labs had the accreditation to test for cobalt, and whether RV was in the wrong for not notifying the trainers immediately after their positive swabs. (Justice Garde said, by the way, the stewards were not under an obligation to notify trainers of a positive screening result, just a positive on a full confirmatory analysis. If you apply that to my case, that means they did not have to notify me on 20 November 2014, but on 29 December. They didn't tell me until 13 January 2015, the day after I returned from the Magic Millions sales, where I spent a good couple of million dollars. Had I known I had a positive swab hanging over me and my training future, there's a fair chance it would've had a pretty big impact on how much money I spent at those sales!)

If the Hopes are successful at VCAT too, or even maybe if they aren't, I would think the positions of Bailey, and the entire RV board who in my view, rubber-stamped this cobalt inquisition, would be totally untenable.

RV has wasted millions of dollars of industry money on this. I expect they would appeal and appeal if these cobalt decisions go against them, because, if they lose, some bigwigs surely have to walk away after the way the whole matter was handled.

And it seems so stupid that so much is riding on something like cobalt, such a nothing substance. It's not a go-fast, and it's nothing worse than everything else we do with horses. We nail pieces of steel to their feet, for Christ's sake. We do things a hundred times more detrimental to horses than give them cobalt, which occurs naturally in their system.

At the time of writing, my lawyers were going through Justice Garde's decision and we were thinking about our options. Trying to get my charge expunged from my records was a big consideration. Then there was the possibility of damages as well. I'd spent a lot of money on legal fees, to say nothing of having my $20 million–a-year business shut down. Terry Bailey was also quoted as calling me a 'drug cheat' in a *Herald Sun* newspaper report in July 2016, which we were thinking about taking a look at.

As for me and training though, my position wasn't changed by the VCAT ruling on O'Brien and Kavanagh, which RV sought leave to appeal. I'd still not want to go back to training while Terry Bailey was chief steward in Melbourne.

....

Aside from Bailey, the integrity department, and RV being a weak organisation, I can't see too much wrong with the racing industry, which remains an industry I love. The trainers' associations could get their act together. And the differences between states should be ironed out. It's ridiculous, for example, that the Australian Guineas at Flemington and the Randwick Guineas are on the same day. And then you've got to get your head around different rules when you go to different states.

Some rules are plain stupid, like the modern whip rule, saying jockeys can only use the whip five times in a race until the 100-metre mark, then it's open slather. Their brief is to win the race, but they're being restricted. It's yet another piece of nanny-state bullshit, in which the minority is appeased and the majority ignored. It's not about the jockeys being cruel to the horses. The whip is a control and encouragement tool—it's not just about whuppin' horses everywhere they've got hair.

Another example of dumb overreaction is in jumps racing. People screamed that it was cruel. They made the jumps lower. That makes it more dangerous because horses run faster at them, which increases the chance of mistakes.

Rules are forever changing. I guess that's progression, but we really have created a nanny-state for ourselves. We're over-policed, over-governed, over-ruled, not just in racing but in all forms of life. Common sense and discretion aren't allowed, in our industry with the stewards.

There's no doubt Australian racing would benefit from national, rather than state, management. We all know a national tote system would be great, to create huge pools for people to bet into, but because totes are independently owned it's probably not going to happen in our lifetime.

But if management could be done nationally, that'd be to the betterment of the industry, as long as it didn't just focus on the big centres and ignore country racing. We need that food chain, for horses who aren't good enough for metro racing. And it's no fluke that half the leading jockeys and trainers in the last hundred years had a rural upbringing.

....

In the months since I retired, I've been surprised by one thing. As much as I'm disappointed about the way my career ended, I don't really miss training. I know a lot of people, Luke Nolen being one, are tipping that I'll come back to training in some form because it's in my blood, but so far that's not on the radar. I thought I'd miss it more, especially around spring carnival time, but I can't say I have. I've got a bit more time on my hands, more time with my family, and yes, I'll admit it's nice to be able to get up for a pee at 5 a.m. and then hop straight back into bed.

I'm still heavily involved in racing though, and imagine I always will be. After retiring I became racing manager for Victoria's Rosemount Stud and an ambassador for bookmakers Ladbrokes, and I still buy yearlings for people as a consultant. I've also enjoyed some media work, which showcases my great eloquence and intellectual side!

I'll also have more time for my other great passion, war history. It's fascinated me since I was a kid, looking at the pictures in all these leather-bound Charles Bean books we had. There's been some terrific stuff written about the world wars lately, maybe because old diggers who didn't want to share their memories, letters and so forth have died, and their families have shared them.

I've been to several war sites, from Gallipoli to the Western Front and the beaches of Normandy, to Crete, Singapore and Vietnam.

After reading about it, it's very moving going to these places and imagining what the soldiers went through—surely the most extreme thing human beings can go through. Those blokes fought for the lifestyle we've become accustomed to, and that's what I think about when I'm in those places, and what Australia has become, and why it is like it is now.

I've been to the French village of Villers-Bretonneux, and seen the school with the big sign in English: 'Never forget Australia'.

These young blokes had no idea what they were facing. You think about the courage, the mateship. You stand in those trenches in Gallipoli and picture what they were looking at, and it's just horrendous. You wonder why. It's a shame so many young lives, or lives at all, were lost. It still happens now, unfortunately.

Whether or not you agree with why they came about, the wars are a big part of Australia's history.

I attend dawn services when I can, though Anzac Day's usually a busy race day. I've also appreciated being invited to the Simpson Barracks in Melbourne a few times, where I've done a couple of Melbourne Cup sweeps. It was also great getting emails and letters from our servicemen and women abroad during the Black Caviar years. I got a photo of some of our soldiers in Afghanistan, who'd set up a bar with her photo on the wall, with a TV for watching her races.

I've also started naming horses we own after Australian war people, like Nurse Kitchen, Sister Sylvia and Matron Wilson, all nurses at the Australian 'Gallipoli' hospital on Lemnos Island. (It was great to see Nurse Kitchen win her third start on Cox Plate day to get a Group 2 for her trainer, none other than David Brideoake.)

Our daughter Celine has now joined the army after finishing high school, and I'm proud of her for that.

I generally get more time to spend with my family now, though it's a bit of bad timing now the girls are grown and moving out. But there's been a bit of excitement in that department. Our daughter Breann has become the latest Moody to enter the sports pages, having been drafted to play for Carlton in the first season of the women's AFL, which was a great success. I was a proud dad cheering her on, as I was through her big sister Cara's high-jumping days earlier on, when she was state under-age champion for about six years running, came second in the nationals once and captained the Victorian team one year. And Sarah and I suddenly have more time to talk now, which is nice. She's also got more time to spend on her equestrian interests. It's great she has the chance to do that after so long managing our business and family.

35

From Royal Ascot to a Bundaberg Dunny

About an hour after Black Caviar's last race, I'd done the rounds of the media, Nelly had gone for a hose-down, and I was standing in the Randwick mounting yard with Luke Nolen. I looked up and noticed these two blokes over the fence, who'd been there a long time. I said to Luke: 'Let's go say "g'day".'

We walked towards them and as we got closer, you wouldn't believe it, I realised I knew one of them.

It was Neville Gorrie—the kid I'd gone to school with, who had been with me when we first went to work with old Frank in Charleville. Neville and his father Peter had driven from Queensland to see Black Caviar. I hadn't seen them for 25 years.

I got over, we shook hands and Neville, the bastard, started crying. It started me crying too.

We stood there having a blub, and it was an amazing, poignant moment. Just to see that amount of emotion in Neville, for me and for this great horse, was very moving. Here was someone I'd drifted apart from, but he'd obviously watched me from afar, never wanting to get in my way or ring up and bug me when things were going good. He'd appreciated from a distance. And no doubt had I not seen them that day, they would still have gone away happy.

It was one of those moments that made you appreciate what Black Caviar meant to people—like in Brisbane with Andrew Porter, the young man with terminal cancer.

It was also the sort of 'time machine' moment that I guess crystallised how far I'd come, and the success I'd achieved.

Someone said after I retired that I'd been associated with one of the top handful of horses in world history. I'd never really thought about it that way—I suppose it's the way I am—but I guess it is pretty amazing when you look at it like that.

If you look on Google for undefeated horses across the world over history, there's Black Caviar is, second on the list. Above her is only Kincsem, the Hungarian horse of the 1870s who won 54 on the trot, in a few countries, and must have been some sort of freak, regardless of the standard of racing in those days. Below Nelly are names like Eclipse, Ribot, Nearco and Frankel, with his fourteen.

If I'd trained out my career, won four premierships, got to the top, but didn't have Black Caviar, it would've been: 'Peter Moody's not a bad horse trainer'.

But to have trained her? Yeah, that's pretty special.

I'm on a plaque with her at the Australian Sports Hall of Fame, in there with people like Don Bradman, Rod Laver, Dawn Fraser, and other greats who've represented this country. To be in their midst is phenomenal, as was collecting the plaque at a glitzy presentation night in Melbourne.

That sort of thing wouldn't have happened without Nelly.

And then there's the other end of the spectrum, like the public toilet at Bundaberg racecourse.

I was a special guest at their cup meeting soon after I retired, and every time I'd go for a leak it happened to be at the same time as this little bloke of about sixty.

He might have been an old trainer by the look of him, I'm not sure. But about the third time it happened, he's just blurted out: 'Well fuck me dead, I can't believe it! Here I am, shaking hands, having a beer and having a piss, in company with Peter Moody. I can't bloody believe it!'

I had to laugh, but those sorts of things do make you think: 'Shit, maybe you *have* achieved something if you mean that much to someone'.

In 50 years will people still remember Black Caviar and her bushie trainer from Charleville, like we remember Phar Lap and his strapper, Tommy Woodcock? Perhaps they will. I guess I did play a pretty major role in one of the biggest stories in Australian turf, or in Australian history for that matter. Being remembered in 50 years won't mean much to me, but it might mean something to my family.

That'd be nice, and it'd be nice to be remembered as being not a bad horse trainer.

But more important than that, I'd hope I'm remembered for being a decent bloke.

Not a bad trainer, but not a bad bloke.

Acknowledgements

The ghostwriter wishes to thank Bart Sinclair, Ian Fuge, Jan Moody, Sarah Moody, Luke Nolen, Bill Mitchell, Alan "Alf" Moody, David "Crockett" Power, Brett Cavanough, Matthew Stirling, Alison Moody, Tony Haydon, Gary Wilkie, Neil Werrett, Stephen Silk, Michael Shea, Keiron Long, Darren Galley, Andrew Eddy, Peter Angus, Peter Clarke, Damien Oliver, Ray Murrihy, Terry Catip, Justine Garvey, Leo Sabatino, Michael and Ainsley Crutcher, Malcolm Knox, Martin Blake.

Thanks to Wotta Krakka, for leaping out of the ground one day and sparking a lifelong fascination.

And special thanks to Evie, Lani, Stef, Warwick and Val.